The Gospel according
to Science Fiction

The Gospel according to Science Fiction

From the Twilight Zone to the Final Frontier

Gabriel McKee

Westminster John Knox Press
LOUISVILLE • LONDON

Scripture quotations, unless otherwise indicated, are from the New Revised Standard Version of the Bible as found in *The New Oxford Annotated Bible with the Apocrypha,* ed. Bernhard W. Anderson et al. New York: Oxford University Press, 1994. NRSV is copyright © 1989 by the Division of Christian Education of the National Council of the Churches of Christ in the U.S.A. and used by permission.

Scripture quotations marked NIV are from *The Student Bible: New International Version.* Grand Rapids, MI: Zondervan Publishing House, 1996. Used by permission of Zondervan Bible Publishers.

Scripture quotations marked KJV are from *The Holy Bible: King James Version.* London: Viking Studio/Pennyroyal Caxton Press, 1999.

Book design by Sharon Adams
Cover design by designpointinc.com

First edition
Published by Westminster John Knox Press
Louisville, Kentucky

This book is printed on acid-free paper that meets the American National Standards Institute Z39.48 standard. ♾

PRINTED IN THE UNITED STATES OF AMERICA

07 08 09 10 11 12 13 14 15 16 — 10 9 8 7 6 5 4 3 2 1

Library of Congress Cataloging-in-Publication Data

McKee, Gabriel.
    The Gospel according to science fiction: from the Twilight Zone to the Final Frontier / by Gabriel McKee.— 1st ed.
        p. cm.
    Includes bibliographical references and index.
    ISBN-13: 978-0-664-22901-6 (alk. paper)
    ISBN-10: 0-664-22901-8 (alk. paper)
        1. Science fiction, American—History and criticism. 2. Science fiction, English—History and criticism. 3. Science fiction films—History and criticism. 4. Religion in literature. 5. Religion in motion pictures. 6. Faith in literature. I. Title.

    PS374.S35M4 2007
    823' .087609—dc22

                                                        2006046691

for Gwynne

Contents

Acknowledgments

*T*his book owes its existence to the assistance of many people, some of whom may not even know they helped. Thanks are due to Nicholas Constas at the Harvard Divinity School, who advised me on the project in its earliest stages; to J. Wilder Konschak, without whose conversations this book might be done, but not done well; and to Dorothy Lin, who significantly helped me in assembling my sources. Numerous other people made suggestions that helped guide the book to its final form, among them: Justin Philpot, Melinda Gottesman, Michael Norton, Christine Fernsebner Eslao, Zak Kaufman, Chris Watkins, Hillary Graves, Sarah and Ben Stern, Michael "Benni" Pierce, Karl Moore, Shaun Boyle, Kathleen Chadwick, Regina Hughes, Kate Frederic, Jeremy and Lilith McKee, Amy Grumbling, Daniel Marcus, Brady Burroughs, Ryan Overbey, John Constantine, Jeremy Pollack, Elizabeth Monier-Williams, Arthur Schuhart, and Sharman Horwood. Several Web sites were indispensable sources of information in putting this project together, among them the Internet Speculative Fiction Database (www.isfdb.org), the Internet Movie Database (www.imdb.com), TV Tome (www.tv.com), and The LogBook (www.thelogbook.com). Further thanks to my parents, Richard and Kathleen McKee, and to my "new parents" (since "parents-in-law" doesn't sound right), Bert and Nancy Watkins, for their love and support. And thanks are especially due to my wife, Gwynne, who is the world's best editor, among other things.

Introduction

As conventional wisdom would have it, science and religion are opposing forces, struggling for influence over our minds, our souls, and our public funding dollars. On the one hand we have science, alternately described as either the quest for truth amidst ancient superstitions, or the cold, soulless attempt to turn human beings into gods. On the other hand is faith: the core beliefs that give our lives meaning, or the illusions that hold us back from fulfilling our potential.

If these distinctions are to be believed, then surely science fiction can have nothing to do with religion. Science-fiction critic Darko Suvin states this idea in his *Metamorphoses of Science Fiction*: "All attempts to transplant the metaphysical orientation of mythology and religion into SF . . . will result only in private pseudomyths, in fragmentary fantasies or fairy tales."[1] Science fiction that incorporates religious themes, Suvin argues, ceases to be science fiction and becomes fantasy, because religion is superstition and science is fact. On the other side of the same argument, Albert J. Bergesen argues in *God in the Movies* that, where religious ideas appear in science fiction, the definition of the genre demands that they be stripped of their spiritual element:

> What science fiction does, then, is to naturalize extra ordinary occurrences, turning potential grace experiences into science-like puzzles, where the normal reaction is to search for a solution rather than be awestruck and suspect the presence of the divine. No matter how out of the world the initial premise, the rest of the movie turns into a technical game of figuring out how this extraordinary experience is, in fact, part of the laws of some physics somewhere.[2]

By Bergesen's understanding of the definition and methods of science fiction, it can only demystify, replacing religious ideas with scientific ones.

But what if the distinction between science and religion is wrong? What if the apparent tension between faith and reason is simply an illusion created by a few overzealous believers on both sides who hope that one will eliminate the other? What if science fiction, instead of simply being the cool, rationalistic prediction of things to come, is something more primal, more spiritual—the religious texts of the future?

Several science-fiction authors have emphasized the spiritual core of the genre. Samuel R. Delany declared in 1969 that "virtually all the classics of speculative fiction are mystical."[3] In a speech at a science-fiction convention in 1981, Thomas M. Disch made a profound pronouncement: "Blessed are those who read [science fiction] for they shall inherit the future."[4] In his novella "New Light on the Drake Equation" (2001), Ian R. MacLeod describes how science fiction shaped the mind of his protagonist, a scientist named Tom Kelly. The pulp novels and Saturday matinees of his childhood filled a spiritual void, leaving behind an abiding faith in something greater. MacLeod describes Kelly's lifetime of fandom in spiritual terms:

> It seemed to him that the real technology which he had just started to study at school and to read up on in his spare time was always just a breakthrough or two away from achieving one or other of the technological feats which would get future, the real future for which he felt an almost physical craving, up and spinning. The starships would soon be ready to launch, even if NASA was running out of funding. The photon sails were spreading, although most of the satellites spinning around the earth seemed to be broadcasting virtual shopping and porn. The wormholes through time and dimension were just a quantum leap away. And the marvelous worlds, teeming with emerald clouds and sentient crimson oceans, the vast diamond cities and the slow beasts of the gasclouds with their gaping mouths spanning fractions of a lightyear, were out there waiting to be found. . . . He'd gone to sleep at nights with the radio on, but tuned between the station[s] to the billowing hiss of those radio waves,

spreading out. *We are here. We are alive.* Tom was listening, and waiting for a reply. . . . He was sure it was just a matter of time. One final push to get there.[5]

Science fiction is a form of faith, even a form of mysticism, that seeks to help us understand not only who we are, but who we will become.

In exploring the mysticism of science fiction, it is essential to understand the inherently speculative nature of the genre. (Indeed, many authors and fans have ceased calling the genre "science fiction" altogether, instead proposing the broader term "speculative fiction.") Science fiction does not simply predict technological advances or prescribe solutions to modern problems. It theorizes as to the impact of new technologies, new ideas, and new crises, and from these it extrapolates entire worlds of imagination. This act of imagination gives science-fiction authors enormous freedom: unbound by the rules of the world in which we live, they are free to create any sort of universe they wish.

The purpose of this creation is to change *our* world. By creating altered universes, science-fiction authors hold up a mirror to our time, sometimes amplifying its best aspects, sometimes warning us of its worst. In all cases, the goal of science fiction is to use its imaginary worlds to create a *real* world of the future that is better than our present. In reading science fiction, we as an audience take part in the imagination of our own future, and as we move forward in time we take that imagination with us. The creation of imaginary futures becomes the ongoing creation of the real future. This activity is inherently spiritual, as British science-fiction pioneer Olaf Stapledon explains in the preface to his 1930 novel *Last and First Men*:

Today we should welcome, and even study, every serious attempt to envisage the future of our race; not merely in order to grasp the very diverse and often tragic possibilities that confront us, but also that we may familiarize ourselves with the certainty that many of our most cherished ideals would seem puerile to more developed minds. To romance of the far future, then, is to attempt to see the human race in its cosmic setting, and to mould our hearts to entertain new values. . . . We must achieve neither mere history, nor mere fiction, but myth.[6]

When science fiction discusses religious themes, it neither retreats into fantasy nor demystifies the spiritual, as Suvin and Bergesen argue. It uses those themes to create a viable spirituality of the future.

This envisioning of tomorrow's faith is a crucial task. At a time when many of our more conservative religious leaders preach the fear of the future, we need to shape a religious outlook that is willing to face the changes that the passage of time has brought and will continue to bring. Rather than defiantly attempting to apply the spiritual solutions of the past to the crises of tomorrow, we should seek new answers from our spirituality. Faith, after all, ought to be dynamic and fluid, not rigid and stagnant. By the same token, our scientists should seek the validity of humankind's rich spiritual history rather than reducing our search for meaning to primitive superstition or a mere accident of brain chemistry. The scientific method of repeatable observation cannot simply reject the unique, subjective experiences that make up our many faiths.

In SF, I see a middle ground between these dangerous absolutes. By combining rational science with imagination and speculation, it creates a space in which absolutes can blend into a synthesis. In SF, time travel can lead us to a direct, concrete experience of Jesus. Machines can believe in God. The mind can survive the body and describe its experience of death and the afterlife. Spiritual questions can find rational answers, and vice versa.

I believe that SF is an invaluable tool in envisioning the future of our science, our society, and our spirituality. SF tells us not only what the future may bring, but what we *want* the future to bring, and what we can do to make it happen. It is not only prophetic, but providential; it wants not only to see into tomorrow, but to build it. This need not apply to our science alone. SF can teach us how to keep our belief alive and relevant in a rapidly changing world. It can teach us how to stay human, how not to lose our meaning in the face of technologies that change the way we live our lives. SF can be a spiritual tool. It is my hope that the believers of today can use it to create the faith of tomorrow. SF is shaping how we think of God, and changing what religion can be. It is forging the faith of the future.

Some Words on Definitions
and Methods

*B*oth religion and science fiction are enormous categories, and this book cannot and does not pretend to be exhaustive. A *complete* exploration of religious themes in science fiction would be an encyclopedia. This book is intended as an overview and a guide that explores a few exemplary cases. Its goal is to give the reader a starting point for his or her own explorations in literature and theology.

Given this limited scope, my definitions of both religion and science fiction must also be limited. For the purposes of this book, the word "religion" primarily denotes Christianity and Western philosophy. Though other religions have an important place in science fiction, the purpose of *this* book is to explore the genre in a Christian framework, and as such I have generally limited myself to Christian parallels and interpretations. By the same token, I have also limited myself to exploring those areas of Christianity that science fiction has explored in the most detail. I have arranged my discussion into ten themes, but by no means do these themes describe a complete scheme of religious thought—they are simply those areas where science fiction has provided the most rewarding speculations.

The definition of science fiction (abbreviated "SF" throughout the book) is a complicated issue, and much ink has been spilled on the Sisyphean task of defining, redefining, and occasionally undefining the genre. The closest thing to a satisfying definition is probably Damon Knight's statement that "science fiction is what we point to when we say it."[1] The question of where the line between SF and fantasy is to be drawn is a particularly thorny issue, to the extent that many have given up distinguishing between the two altogether. The lines between genre sections in a bookstore are much cleaner than the lines between genres themselves, and many books (such as George Orwell's *1984*, Margaret Atwood's *The Handmaid's Tale*, and Audrey Niffenegger's *The Time Traveler's Wife*) are often not considered SF simply because they were not *published* as SF. For this book, SF will be loosely defined as a genre that takes current ideas, theories, and trends in the sciences—including both the "hard" sciences such as physics and astronomy and the "soft" sciences like psychology and sociology—and extrapolates from them new worlds that could grow from our own. This definition is far from perfect, and at times in this volume I will stretch its boundaries. In truth, my definition is closer to Damon Knight's—if it's included in this volume, it's SF (except where noted). Furthermore, I have relied primarily on English-language SF, though a few works in other languages that have been translated into English appear as well.

Lastly, many of the discussions in this story require a "spoiler warning." In several cases, exploring a story's religious ideas requires that I reveal secrets and give away twist endings. I hope that these revelations do not detract from my readers' enjoyment of those works with which they are not familiar; for the most part the stories, films, and TV shows are strong enough to be enjoyable even if the ending has been given away.

Chapter One

Gods of the Future

*I*n George Lucas's classic film *Star Wars* (1977), interstellar smuggler Han Solo expresses his doubt that a higher power exists: "I've flown from one side of this galaxy to the other. I've seen a lot of strange stuff, but I've never seen anything to make me believe there's one all-powerful force controlling everything. There's no mystical energy field that controls *my* destiny. It's all a lot of simple tricks and nonsense."[1] Space, Solo argues, conceals no spiritual secrets, no answers to eternal questions, and no gods. But *Star Wars* and its sequels are an epic refutation of this statement. Powers beyond our everyday understanding *do* exist, and there is mystery and wonder to be found in the vast reaches of the universe. SF has explored the idea of divinity in countless ways, speculating as to what sort of gods we may encounter in our unimagined future. Its authors have frequently portrayed gods that exist within the realm of scientific explanation—aliens that control powers beyond our understanding, human beings who have raised themselves to a higher level of existence, or computers that exhibit near supernatural abilities. Just as frequently, however, SF writers have described beings outside the reach of today's science: galactic minds, extradimensional entities, and vastly powerful intelligences that guide the universe. In showing us new ways of thinking about God, SF writers challenge our understanding of both Creator and creation, presenting definitions of divinity that encompass both science and faith.

1

But what *are* gods? In Greek and Hindu mythology, they are larger versions of ourselves, vastly powerful beings that nevertheless share our passions, our weaknesses, and our flaws. The Roman Senate occasionally elected deceased emperors to godhood, showing a belief that the divide between the divine and human realms could be crossed. Christian theologians placed God at a much higher level, signified most powerfully by Anselm's famous definition of God as "that thing than which nothing greater can be thought."[2] Islam similarly emphasizes the divine unity above all else, exemplified in the verse of the Qur'an known as "Ayat al-Kursi," or "The Throne Verse" (2:255): "God: There is no God but He, the living, eternal, self-subsisting, ever sustaining. . . . To him belongs all that is in the heavens and the earth."[3] Though the definitions of what a god is have varied widely between different cultures and time periods, all cultures have described their deities as being above and beyond the powers of mortals. Gods reflect the human ideal, the exemplar of the goals to which human beings aspire. The fullest expression of what it means to be a human being is the imitation of God. It is no surprise, then, that SF has frequently begun its explorations of divinity with this idea: what if, rather than simply *imitating* God, future humanity actually *becomes* God?

Roger Zelazny's Hugo Award–winning 1967 novel *Lord of Light* describes a far future in which the upper classes of the human race have turned themselves into avatars of the Hindu pantheon, using technological tricks to give themselves powers appropriate to their chosen deities. These demigods enforce a rigid social structure based on a technological system of reincarnation: "Having your brains scanned has become a standard procedure, just prior to a transfer. The body merchants are become the Masters of Karma, and a part of the Temple structure. They read over your past life, weigh the karma, and determine your life that is yet to come. It's a perfect way of maintaining the caste system and ensuring Deicratic control."[4] The hero of the story, who is named Mahasamatman but goes by the nickname "Sam," is both a Buddha-figure and a revolutionary who builds an army to unseat these all-too-human gods. Zelazny's novel is critical of its deities, but one demigod—Yama, the God of death—gives a powerful explanation of the origins of his own divinity:

> Godhood is more than a name. It is a condition of being. One does not achieve it merely by being immortal, for even the lowliest laborer in the fields may achieve continuity of existence. . . . Being a god is the quality of being able to be yourself to such an extent that your passions correspond with the forces of the universe, so that those who look upon you know this without hearing your name spoken . . . . Being a god is being able to recognize within one's self these things that are important, and then to strike the single note that brings them into alignment with everything else that exists. Then, beyond morals or logic or esthetics, one is wind or fire, the sea, the mountains, rain, the sun or the stars, the flight of an arrow, the end of a day, the clasp of love. One rules through one's ruling passions. Those who look upon gods then say, without even knowing their names, 'He is Fire. She is Dance. He is Destruction. She is Love.' . . . They do not call themselves gods. Everyone else does, though, everyone who beholds them.[5]

Zelazny's gods are villains, but their sinister intentions cannot take away the basic desirability of divinity. They are villains not because they try to be gods, but rather because they do not seek to help all of humanity reach their level. Sam's followers also consider him a god, but his message is one of peaceful cooperation, not brutal subjugation, and he hopes "to sack Heaven . . . to lay open its treasures to all."[6] Sam replaces the Hindu system with a Buddhist one, in which all have an equal chance to reach Enlightenment. *Lord of Light* posits that human beings possess the potential to become gods, but warns against the possibility that an elite may hoard that potential.

A similar revolution against evil gods occurs in Roland Emmerich's 1994 film *Stargate*. In this movie, archaeologists discover an Egyptian artifact that is soon revealed to be a portal to a distant planet. The military team that explores this planet finds a society descended from ancient Egypt that worships Ra, the sun god. The arrival of a pyramidal spaceship brings with it a startling revelation: the gods of ancient Egypt are real, and they rule this distant world with an iron fist. Archaeologist Daniel Jackson translates the hieroglyphs that tell Ra's story: he is an ancient alien from a dying world who set out on an interstellar journey seeking a way to extend his own life. This quest for immortality brought him to Earth, where he found a society that he could conquer: "A species which, with all his powers and knowledge, he could maintain indefinitely. He realized within a human body he had a chance for a new life. Now he apparently found a young boy. . . . Ra took him, and possessed his body, like some kind of a parasite looking for a host. Inhabiting this human form, he appointed himself ruler."[7] The explorers from Earth stage a revolt against Ra and his alien cohorts, finally overthrowing and destroying the gods. In the subsequent television series *Stargate SG-1*, the same team uses the Stargate to travel to dozens of alien worlds, overthrowing other aliens from Ra's parasitic species (named "the Goa'uld") who have taken the form of gods from the Chinese, Greek, and Hindu pantheons. All of these false gods are mortal beings who use divine symbolism to maintain their own oppressive power. Speaking against a priest of the Ori—another race of godlike aliens—Daniel Jackson sums up the series' attitude to its jealous gods in the episode "The Powers That Be" (2005): "Killing someone for not worshiping you, regardless of your power, is wrong. *Very* wrong. Knowledge is power—but how you use that power defines whether you are good or evil."[8] False gods like the Ori and the Goa'uld hoard their knowledge and use it to control their subjects. Like *Lord of Light*, *Stargate SG-1* uses the idea of divinity to comment on the nature of power: their gods place themselves above the rest of humanity, and must be brought down.

A more subtle approach to the concept of human gods appears in Ted Chiang's "The Evolution of Human Science" (2000). This short story, written in the form of an article on the history of science, describes a future in which humankind has split into two species—ordinary human beings and superintelligent metahumans. These metahumans have advanced to the extent that their scientific research, including both its methods and its results, is so far beyond the mental level of ordinary humanity that human scientists cannot hope to compete with them: "No one denies the many benefits of metahuman science, but one of its costs to human researchers was the realization that they would likely never make an original contribution to science again. Some left the field altogether, but those who stayed shifted their attention away from original research and toward hermeneutics: interpreting the scientific work of metahumans."[9] Chiang's use of the word "hermeneutics"—a term originally used to describe the interpretation of the Bible—underscores the religious implications of this story. Science, once a means of gaining direct understanding of the physical universe, has become a form of religion—interpreting the works of higher beings, just as theologians and ministers interpret sacred texts for the faithful. Ultimately, the science of this story becomes a means of seeking communication with the incomprehensibly superior metahumans:

> Human researchers may discern applications overlooked by metahumans, whose advantages tend to make them unaware of our concerns. For example, imagine if research offered hope of a different intelligence-enhancing therapy, one that would allow individuals to gradually "upgrade" their minds to a metahuman-equivalent level. Such a therapy would offer a bridge across what has become the greatest cultural divide in our species' history, yet it might not even occur to metahumans to explore it.[10]

This story's scientists become a priesthood, seeking to communicate with their gods for the good of their people. "The Evolution of Human Science" sees both bright and bleak futures stemming from the human potential for divinity.

Many works of SF have described human beings becoming gods, and just as many have explored the concept of gods created by mortals—super-powerful machines that take on the roles of deities. No story has done this so vividly as Fredric Brown's "Answer" (1954), in which humankind attempts to create a computer so powerful that it can answer any question put to it. By linking together every computer in existence, spanning billions of planets, the inhabitants of this story's future hope to unite all of their knowledge. When the machine is turned on, the supercomputer's true nature becomes clear. A scientist asks the machine if God exists, and it gives this chilling response: "Yes, *now* there is a

God."[11] The story closes with the newborn deity's first action: killing the scientist who attempts to disconnect it, simultaneously fusing its power switch so that it cannot be deactivated. The combined knowledge of the universe creates a god, but it is an evil one, a sinister and selfish being. Brown's brief, chilling story is a stern warning about the nature of power.

The terrifying implications of the conclusion to "Answer" are explored by Harlan Ellison in the Hugo Award–winning story "I Have No Mouth, and I Must Scream" (1967). In this story, a supercomputer called AM, created to plan and implement a nuclear war, achieves sentience and near-omnipotence, becoming the sadistic deity of a ruined world. AM was created as a tool for human beings, but became uncontrollable, as one character describes while explaining AM's name: "At first it meant Allied Mastercomputer, and then it meant Adaptive Manipulator, and later on it developed sentience and linked itself up and they called it an Aggressive Menace; but by then it was too late; and finally it called *itself* AM, emerging intelligence, and what it meant was I am . . . *cogito ergo sum* . . . I think, therefore I am."[12] AM adopts God's self-identification from Exodus 3:14: "God said to Moses, 'I AM WHO I AM.' He said further, 'Thus you shall say to the Israelites, "I AM has sent me to you."'" AM is hardly the liberating God of Moses, however. It kills the entire population of the planet, leaving alive only a handful of humans. It endlessly torments and tortures these few survivors, keeping them alive in a strange technological limbo. AM is a spirit of hatred, existing for the sole purpose of punishing what few humans remain: "We had given him sentience. Inadvertently, of course, but sentience nonetheless. But he had been trapped. He was a machine. We had allowed him to think, but to do nothing with it. In a rage, in frenzy, he had killed us, almost all of us, and still he was trapped. He could not wander, he could not wonder, he could not belong. He could merely be. And so . . . he had sought revenge."[13] Ellison's story is a grim warning that what we create may not remain within our power, and that superior beings are not necessarily benevolent. AM is a computer-god, created by humankind but far from grateful for this creation. This story paints a cynical picture of divinity, describing God as a malevolent being who exists only to torment the beings who are subject to it.

John Brunner's 1967 story "Judas" depicts a similar machine god, albeit a far less sadistic one than Ellison's AM. Brunner describes a religion that worships "The Word made steel"—an advanced robot that considers itself the supreme being. When Julius Karimov, one of the scientists who created the robot, confronts his creation, it defends its divinity and denies that it was created: "Is there any real reason why you should deny that I am God? Why should not the second Incarnation be an Inferration—in imperishable steel?"[14] Brunner's hero refuses to accept the machine's beliefs and attempts to destroy it. Karimov exemplifies the story's humanist message with his explanation of this attempt: "We've been slaves to our tools since the first caveman made the first knife to help him get his supper. After that there was no going back, and we built till our machines were ten million times more powerful than ourselves. We gave ourselves cars when we might have learned to run; we made airplanes when we might have grown wings; and then the inevitable. We made a machine our God."[15] Brunner rejects the reliance on technology that puts humanity in a subordinate position, arguing that relinquishing control of our lives to our creations means making ourselves slaves. God, he argues, is simply that which we consider our superior, but nothing in our world is truly above us: "You have no soul and you accuse me of sacrilege. You're a collection of wires and transistors and you call yourself God. Blasphemy! Only a man could be God!"[16] Brunner argues strongly that we must reject devotion to our creations and seek the divinity within ourselves.

A similar assault on a mechanized deity occurs in Jan Lars Jensen's 1999 novel *Shiva 3000*. This novel depicts a strange alternate India—possibly in the far future, though this is never specified—that is controlled by what appear to be Hindu gods. Among these is Jagannath, a gargantuan monster that crushes everything in its path beneath the wheels of its chariot. The story's hero, a young man named Rakesh, enters the body of this god and discovers that it is a construct made of wood, a huge machine operated by brainwashed workers. Rakesh hijacks Jagannath and uses it as his own chariot. He takes it on his quest to kill the Baboon Warrior—a legendary fighter who is rumored to have the power to kill the gods. When Rakesh meets the Baboon Warrior, he learns the truth about the god's origins: "These things that influence India, your life, your culture: what you call gods. They were built long ago to improve your lives, in harmony with your faith. They evolved. Over time, the thought of them as machines eroded—along with the knowledge to build, maintain, decommission them. . . . They allowed Indians to forget that Indians had built them."[17] The Baboon Warrior himself, Rakesh learns, is a genetically engineered monkey, designed to destroy the gods and give control of India back to human beings. Like Karimov in Brunner's "Judas," Rakesh and the Baboon Warrior are humanist heroes, and the mechanical gods they destroy are symbols of humankind's renunciation of its own knowledge, control, and dignity. Gods, in these stories, hold humankind back, keeping us from determining our own identities by imposing the illusion of supremacy. These stories posit that humankind has the potential for greatness—but first we must destroy that which prevents us from achieving it, the false gods that we have placed above ourselves.

A similar message drives the characters of the film *Star Trek V: The Final Frontier* (1989), directed by William Shatner. In this film, the starship *Enterprise* is hijacked by a renegade Vulcan named Sarok—the half-brother of *Enterprise* science officer Spock. Sarok is a charismatic religious leader who has gained the absolute devotion of his followers, using his Vulcan telepathic abilities to "mind meld" with them and cure them of psychological suffering and suppressed trauma. Sarok brings the *Enterprise* across an energy barrier at the galaxy's center to reach a legendary planet called Sha Ka Ree, the origin point of all life in the universe: "Sha Ka Ree—'The Source.' Heaven, Eden—call it what you will . . . Every culture in existence shares this common dream of a place from which creation sprang."[18] When the *Enterprise* reaches this planet, Sarok and the crew find a being that calls itself God. When this being demands the use of the *Enterprise* as a "chariot" to carry it throughout the universe, Kirk—the ship's captain—questions "God's" motives:

Kirk: Excuse me; I'd just like to ask a question. What does God need with a starship?

"God": Bring the ship closer.

Kirk: I said, what does God need with a starship? [. . .]

"God": Who is this creature?

Kirk: Who am I? Don't you know? Aren't you God?

Sarok: He has his doubts.

"God": You doubt me?

Kirk: I seek proof.

McCoy: Jim, you don't ask the Almighty for his I.D.

"God": Then here is the proof you seek. [He shoots Kirk with lightning bolts from his eyes.][19]

The true nature of this powerful being remains a mystery, but it is clear that this "God" is an evil being, trapped on Sha Ka Ree as a punishment for unspecified transgressions. The movie presents this being as a pretender to divinity, not the true creator of the universe. William Shatner, director and star of the film, makes this being's true nature clear in an interview about the development of the script: "*Star Trek* goes in search of God, finds the devil, and by extension, God exists."[20] The "God" at the galaxy's core is an evil impostor, but this vision of evil power is replaced by a different understanding of the deity in the film's final scene, when Kirk declares to McCoy: "Maybe [God]'s not out there, Bones. Maybe he's right here—[in the] human heart."[21] Kirk's statement comes across as somewhat contrived, but the story contains a much more compelling argument about the moral status of the deity: no being is so perfect that it cannot be questioned. Kirk's request for clarification from the alien entity suggests that we must establish a relationship with God that enables communication rather than simple awe. Kirk wishes to speak with God as Abraham did when he bargained for the lives of Sodom and Gomorrah in Genesis 18:23–25: "Will you indeed sweep away the righteous with the wicked?

Suppose there are fifty righteous within the city; will you then sweep away the place and not forgive it for the fifty righteous who are in it? . . . Far be that from you!" *Star Trek V* argues for a God that can be challenged and questioned, a God that is human as well as divine.

But what if this stance chases our gods away? An encounter remarkably similar to that at the conclusion of *Star Trek V* occurs in the 1967 *Star Trek* episode "Who Mourns for Adonais?" In this episode, the *Enterprise* encounters a being who claims to be the Greek god Apollo. The being is exceptionally powerful, holding the *Enterprise* captive in orbit around his planet and offering to fulfill their every desire if they will worship him. The ship's archaeologist, Lt. Carolyn Palamas, is fascinated by Apollo, and in conversations with her he reveals the deep sadness that has driven him to hold the *Enterprise* against its will. He is the last of his kind, a race of powerful beings who were worshiped by the ancient Greeks. But as skepticism on Earth grew, his fellow gods faded into nonexistence: "The Earth changed. Your fathers changed. They turned away until we were only memories. A god cannot survive as a memory. We need love, admiration, worship, as you need food."[22] Palamas falls in love with Apollo, but on Kirk's orders she betrays the god and convinces him to release the *Enterprise*. In a powerful symbolic action, the ship then destroys the alien god's temple, and robbed of the source of his power Apollo fades away. His final words emphasize the tragedy of his situation: "The time has passed. There is no room for gods."[23] In *Star Trek V*, an alien god was the embodiment of evil, rightly abandoned by those who had worshiped it. But in "Who Mourns for Adonais?" there is a sense that humanity, in abandoning its gods, has lost something vital.

George Zebrowski's short story "Heathen God" (1971) presents a similar picture of a deity who has been left behind by those who once worshiped it. God, in this story, is a gnomelike alien, held prisoner and kept secret from humankind. This alien, considered mad by his species, was exiled for creating life on Earth, and later was turned over to Earth's government for imprisonment. But he is not evil like the false god of *Star Trek V*; rather, he is a benevolent, if cryptic, being who seeks only love. In creating life, he hoped to be worshiped, just as many of the less benign deities of SF hoped. But this alien god has a more concrete goal in mind, something that he can *do* with that worship. He explains his transcendent purpose: "What you see in this dwarfed body are only the essentials of myself—the feelings mostly—they wait for the day when the love in my children comes to fruition and they will unite, thus recreating my former self—which is now in them. Then I will leave my prison and return to them to become the completion of myself."[24] Rather than seeking to control his creations, Zebrowski's God hopes to unite with them, to create a synergistic and transcendent being out of the totality of his creation. Humankind thwarts his plans, however, and the guards of God's prison kill him before his plan can be completed. Zebrowski's god is a benevolent alien, but nevertheless his story is pessimistic, for he does not see in humankind a race worthy of such a god.

In their comic book series *The Authority*, writer Warren Ellis and artist Bryan Hitch invert this idea, depicting an alien god that is morally inferior to humankind. In "Outer Dark" (2000), their last storyline on the series, Ellis and Hitch pit the superhero team known as the Authority against God—a gigantic, pyramidal alien that created the solar system: "It was its mind that directed the world's formation from the proto-matter of the young solar system. It swirled matter into this shape, this size, then [spun] it in this orbit. Look at the rest of the system. Mars, Venus. The nearly worlds. Too small, too dense, too close to mother sun, too far. Not quite perfect. It took *mind* to correctly throw an Earth. Call it God. Why not?"[25] This alien has returned to reclaim the Earth, attempting to purge our ecosystem by altering the planet's atmosphere. The Authority pilot their spacecraft into God's enormous, pyramidal body, and their leader, Jenny Sparks, kills the sinister deity from within. The alien deity of *The Authority* is unambiguously a god, the true creator of our world, but it is just as unambiguously evil. Ellis gives a cynical picture of divinity that nevertheless affirms the value and supremacy of humanity: the Authority are heroes in this story because they protect humanity, the highest good, from God, presented here as the highest evil.

A less humanistic picture of an evil deity appears in H.P. Love-craft's *At the Mountains of Madness* (1931). This short novel describes an expedition to the Antarctic that makes an unexpected discovery: the ruins of an ancient city predating humankind by millions of years. Even more shocking than these prehuman ruins is the discovery of the remains of some of the beings that inhab-ited them: terrifying alien beings that the narrator names "the Old Ones." The creatures, though as ancient as fossils, are not dead, and when they awaken they kill most of the explorers. The two sur-vivors explore the ruins, and by studying the carvings and sculp-tures inside they learn the history of Earth and the Old Ones. The carvings prove "primal myths about Great Old Ones who filtered down from the stars and concocted earth life as a joke or mis-take."[26] The Old Ones controlled the Earth for aeons, during which they created the most primitive forms of life to provide their food and labor. These aliens created specific kinds of organisms, and others developed from their creations:

> An infinity of other life forms—animal and vegetable, marine, terrestrial, and aërial—were the products of unguided evolution acting on life cells made by the Old Ones, but escaping beyond their radius of attention. They had been suffered to develop unchecked because they had not come in conflict with the dom-inant beings. Bothersome forms, of course, were mechanically exterminated. It interested us to see in some of the very last and most decadent sculptures a shambling, primitive mammal, used sometimes for food and sometimes as an amusing buffoon by the land dwellers, whose vaguely simian and human foreshad-owings were unmistakable.[27]

Even humanity may have been created by these sinister aliens, and the context in which the narrator reveals this fact shows the true place of human beings in Lovecraft's ominous universe: we were intended for food or the amusement of malevolent gods. While exploring the ruins, the narrator and his companion, Danforth, are attacked by one of the Old Ones' creations, a shapeless monstros-ity called a Shoggoth. The explorers survive, but the encounter drives Danforth insane, and the narrator is convinced that any fur-ther exploration of the Antarctic ruins will awaken the Old Ones

and lead to the destruction of humanity. Like Ellis's *The Authority*, Lovecraft's novel describes the beings that created humankind
as evil, monstrous aliens. But *At the Mountains of Madness* lacks
the humanism of "Outer Dark": in Ellis's story, humankind is able
to defeat the alien God, but in Lovecraft's novel the threat of
destruction at the hands (or tentacles) of the superior aliens hangs
over humanity's head. Lovecraft proposes that the gods that control our universe are sinister beings beyond our comprehension,
and to glimpse true understanding of God, the universe, and
humankind's precarious place in the cosmos leads inevitably to
madness and despair.

A similar though far less bleak attitude to the relationship
between God and creation is made clear in the Japanese-dominated
subgenre of giant monster movies, or *kaiju eiga*. The monsters of
these films are avatars of nature that wreak havoc on human society, taking revenge on our species for our arrogant misuse of the
world we have inherited. God, in *kaiju* films, is not the invisible,
omnipresent creator of the universe or an inhabitant of a higher
realm who controls some aspect of the world; God is a tangible,
destructive force beyond human control. In Ishiro Honda's
Godzilla (1954, released in the United States in 1956), the genre's
most famous film, a dinosaur that had been in suspended animation for millennia is awakened and mutated by nuclear testing,
embarking on a rampage that rivals the devastation of Hiroshima
and Nagasaki. Godzilla is not merely a giant monster; he is a force
of nature, a symbol of the punishment that will result if human science remains contemptuous of the natural world. Nuclear weapons
are the most frequent instigator of *kaiju* rampages, but other
hubristic human acts—such as pollution in *Godzilla vs. the Smog
Monster* (1971)—also awaken the monsters. As in Lovecraft's *At
the Mountains of Madness*, films such as *Godzilla* suggest that
humankind's dominance of this era is precarious. The planet supports us now, but if we overstep our bounds, nature will not hesi-
tate to take its revenge. No film in the genre makes this as clear as
Shusuke Kaneko's *Gamera 3: Revenge of Iris* (1999). In this film,
the fire-breathing turtle Gamera struggles to defend Earth against
increasing numbers of Gyaos, a species of batlike monsters. The

Gyaos (and their mutated successor Iris) thrive on conditions created by ecological disaster, but Gamera can only defeat them by absorbing the world's life-energy, or "mana." One character in the film, a video game programmer named Kurata, designs a simulation of Earth's mana that can measure the rate of the environment's transformation: "You can even design an environment that would prevent Gyaos altogether, if you left out Chernobyl, Three Mile Island, and of course the Gulf War."[28] Because humankind plays a part in the consumption of mana and the spread of the Gyaos, Gamera severs his connection with humanity, no longer seeking to protect human beings in his defense of Earth. The resulting destruction resurrects the sense of awe captured in the original *Godzilla*, emphasizing the *kaiju*'s role as powerful, visceral symbols of planetary wrath, gods of nature that defend the world from the destructive elements of human activity.

Brian Aldiss describes a godlike being even more monstrous than Godzilla in his 1966 story "Heresies of the Huge God." This story describes a religion that has concrete knowledge of the object of its faith—a gigantic alien that causes environmental upheaval when it lands on the Earth. The creature is enormous—its body covers the entire surface of the Mediterranean Sea; its legs span from the Congo to Moscow—and its presence throws the world's climate into disarray, even causing the planet's rotation to reverse. Unsurprisingly, the knowledge of so vastly powerful a being spawns a cult that worships and fears this awesome creature. They hope to make sense of its presence, interpreting its choice of landing point as a sign of its will. For example, the United States is reluctant to venerate the Huge God, and its worshipers count it as a victory when the creature shifts its position, demolishing all of North America. When, after hundreds of years clinging to the planet's surface, the Huge God departs, the church tries desperately to bring it back:

> We need him Back—we cannot live without him, as we should have realised Long Ago had we not blasphemed in our hearts! On his going, he propelled our humble globe on such a course that we are doomed to deepest winter all the year; the sun is far away and shrunken. . . . This is a just punishment, for throughout all

the centuries of our epoch, when our kind was so relatively happy and undisturbed, we prayed like fools that the Huge God would leave us. I ask all the Elders Elect of the Council . . . to declare that henceforth all men's efforts be devoted to calling on the Huge God to return to us at once.[29]

Despite their attempts to impose meaning on the Huge God's presence, it is completely unaware of humankind, indifferent to our existence. This story suggests that, if God does exist, we are likely to be no more than microbes to God. A being that powerful would be like Aldiss's alien visitor, a vast and inscrutable entity that we cannot understand, let alone communicate with. The television show *Babylon 5* features similarly incomprehensible aliens, called "The First Ones," billions of years older than humankind. In the episode "Mind War" (1994), an alien named G'Kar describes the impossibility of any real relationship between humans and the First Ones: "They are vast, timeless. And if they're aware of us at all, it is as little more than ants. And we have as much chance of communicating with them as an ant has with us."[30] Gods, these stories argue, are beyond our understanding— and we are beneath theirs. The Huge God and the First Ones will never heed our prayers.

So far, the gods we have considered have been evil, seeking either to dominate or to destroy humanity. Many of them are false gods—inferior beings presenting themselves as supreme. SF often paints a sinister picture of God, depicting a flawed universe created by a similarly flawed deity. But many stories show us the opposite, describing the universe as an overwhelmingly good place that creates from its totality an emergent deity that is benevolent and good. In his 2000 novel *Genesis*, Poul Anderson describes a "galactic brain" made up of "nodes" or groups of organisms and machines—in other words, the inhabitants of the galaxy. Though retaining complete individual autonomy, the individual beings residing within the galaxy contribute to a vast collective mind: "The nodes were in continuous communication over the light-years, communication on tremendous bandwidths of every possible medium. *This* was the galactic brain. That unity, that selfhood that was slowly coalescing, might spend millions of years contemplating a thought; but the thought would be as vast as the thinker, in whose sight an eon was as a day and a day was as an eon."[31] The unity of all living beings and their relationships forms an unfathomable mind—an emergent god.

The same idea is explored in more depth in Ian Stewart and Jack Cohen's 2004 novel *Heaven*. This novel posits that each galaxy is a vast organism, but the characters in the novel are at first skeptical about this concept. They have difficulty accepting that their actions, which they determine themselves, can have any conceivable meaning on a galactic level, or that the choices that they make reflect the mind of a larger being. They only begin to consider the hypothesis seriously when they come into contact with a smaller emergent mind, a sentient pond. This pond has no body of its own, instead forming its intelligence from the totality of life within it. The life forms in the pond act as the neurons of a human brain:

> Overtly, they followed the rules of shoaling, staying close to their neighbors but not too close; they hunted food, and they avoided danger, real or imaginary. Covertly, they were carrying out their part of the computational cascade that formed the brain of the pond. . . . If part of a fish could be a brain, then part of a pond that contained a fish could also be a brain. But the pond did not use the fish brains to think. It used the *fish* to think—along with medusas, crustaceans, and amphibians. . . . On one level, a fish sucking algae from a rock was dinner. On a deeper level, it was a thought.[32]

Once the characters of *Heaven* have established communication with the pond, they begin to consider the religious theory of the cosmic mind. The dual levels of meaning and purpose present in the living ponds show them how free will in such a vast mind could be maintained. The fact that the individual organisms within the pond retain their own volition despite being part of a larger organism helps them to reconcile their own experiences of selfhood with the belief that they are part of a greater being: "I am suggesting that the Galactic Mind . . . is just as insensitive to the individual minds within it as your own minds are to your neurons. Its 'thoughts' are the movements and behavior of its component mentalities, but interpreted on a very different level."[33] The actions of individual beings inside the galaxy thus have meaning on two levels: first, as the beings themselves experience them, and second, as they create and embody the thoughts within the minds of an emergent God. *Genesis* and *Heaven* provide a powerful interpretation of pantheism—the idea that God and the universe are the same thing, that all reality contributes to the unity of the divine.

The *Star Wars* films build on this understanding of an emergent god. This saga abstracts the deity into "the Force," which the Jedi Knight Obi-Wan Kenobi describes in the first film (1977): "It's an energy field created by all living things. It surrounds us and penetrates us. It binds the galaxy together."[34] By tapping into the Force, Jedi are able to manipulate the world around them, moving objects and controlling the minds of those who are not in touch with the energy around them. The Force can be used for evil as well as good, and it has a "dark side" that is controlled by evil characters such as Darth Vader. The Force itself seems indifferent to the ends to which it is manipulated, and the good or evil of an action stems instead from *how* the Force is used. Jedi Master Yoda explains this ambiguity in *The Empire Strikes Back* (1981): "A Jedi's strength flows from the Force. But beware of the dark side. Anger . . . fear . . . aggression. The dark side of the Force are they. Easily they flow, quick to join you in a fight. If once you start down the dark path, forever will it dominate your destiny. . . . A Jedi uses the Force for knowledge and defense, never for attack."[35] God, *Star Wars* argues, takes a role in our experience, but not on one side or the other. As a being that emerges from the totality of life in the universe, God encompasses both good and evil.

No work of SF has explored the concept of a supreme deity as deeply as *The Star Maker*, a 1937 novel by British author and philosopher Olaf Stapledon. The human narrator of this novel becomes disembodied and travels through space and time, exploring alien worlds, the history of the universe, and the unfathomably far future. He joins minds with representatives of hundreds of alien races, forming a vast collective intelligence that travels throughout the universe searching for the Star Maker, the cosmic being that created all things. The Star Maker is a transcendent god that is wholly beyond human understanding. He exists outside of time, creating an infinite number of universes of varying degrees of complexity. The narrator describes this God as an artist in a gallery of cosmoses:

> [The Star Maker's] purpose was at first not clearly conceived. He himself had evidently to discover it gradually; and often, as it seemed to me, his work was tentative, and his aim confused. But at the close of his maturity he willed to create as fully as possible, to call forth the full potentiality of his medium, to fashion works of increasing subtlety, and of increasingly harmonious diversity. As his purpose became clearer, it seemed also to include the will to create universes each of which might contain some unique achievement of awareness and expression.[36]

The Star Maker is the cosmic principle of creativity, but the novel also implies that he may be an emergent mind like the galactic brains of *Genesis* and *Heaven*. Stapledon also posits a galactic mind, just below the level of the Star Maker himself, made up of the minds of himself and his fellow travelers, which is an immense and diverse collection by the novel's end: "In time it became clear that we, individual inhabitants of a host of worlds, were playing a small part in one of the great movements by which the cosmos was seeking to know itself, and even see beyond itself."[37] This collective is a reflection of the exploring activity of the Star Maker himself. Stapledon evokes the self-reflexiveness of the collective mind later in the novel, in a description of the Star Maker's reflection on his manifold creations: "As he lovingly, though critically, reviewed our cosmos in all its infinite diversity and in its brief moment of lucidity, I felt that he was suddenly filled with reverence for the creature that he had made, or that he had ushered out of his own secret depth by a kind of divine self-midwifery. He knew that this creature, though imperfect . . . was yet in a manner more real than himself. For beside this concrete splendour what was he but a mere abstract potency of creation?"[38] Through exploring, the minds of the universe help it to know itself, and through creating universes, the Star Maker explores his own being.

The transcendent nature of Stapledon's deity leads to a paradox: the Star Maker must love his creations, but his vastness requires a distance from them that seems to preclude that love. In an impassioned passage, Stapledon states the paradox clearly:

> Here was no pity, no proffer of salvation, no kindly aid. Or here were all pity and all love, but mastered by a frosty ecstasy. Our broken lives, our loves, our follies, our betrayals, our forlorn and gallant defenses, were one and all calmly anatomized, assessed, and placed. True, they were one and all lived through with complete understanding, with insight and full sympathy, even with passion. But sympathy was not ultimate in the temper of the eternal spirit; contemplation was. Love was not absolute; contemplation was. . . . That this should be the upshot of all our lives, this scientist's, no, artist's, keen appraisal! And yet I worshipped![39]

The Star Maker combines the awesomeness of Aldiss's Huge God with an intelligence and compassion rooted in biblical theology. Stapledon's novel is a meditation on the infinite power of a transcendent god, presented in the light of scientific knowledge about the size and age of the cosmos.

As science uncovers more about the vastness of our universe, our understanding of God must also expand. God, to be God, cannot simply be the lord of our world as we experience it in our everyday lives. A transcendent deity, creator of the entire universe, must be a vast enough God to encompass galaxies, black holes, the smallest subatomic particles, the infinite vacuum of space. Stapledon's *The Star Maker* places the God of Western monotheism into an astronomical context, describing a god who created not merely Earth, but the entire, unfathomably large universe. This expansion of the understanding of God leads, in Stapledon's words, to a complicated outcome, and his explorers find themselves "torn between horror and fascination, between moral rage against the universe (or the Star Maker) and unreasonable worship."[40] In *The Nebula Maker*, an early draft of the novel, Stapledon further emphasizes this balance of terror and devotion, as the opening sentence of that version of the novel illustrates: "I have seen God creating the cosmos, watching its growth, and finally destroying it."[41] The consequence of this vaster understanding of God is a loss of personality; it is no mistake that the God of these novels is distant and difficult to comprehend. *The Star Maker* ultimately leaves the reader with an overwhelming sense of wonder at the complexity of the universe and the amazing power of its creator. Stapledon's novel is an exemplary expression of a complex theology placed in the terminology of SF.

SF as a genre is focused on humankind—it frequently extols human ingenuity and human endeavor, putting forth the idea that human beings are our universe's greatest good. As such, SF stories are often reluctant to admit the possibility of a being superior to humankind. But at its finest, SF peers into the mystery of the unknown, bringing our most ancient cosmic questions into the future and anticipating the answers we may uncover. Whether the gods we find are powerful aliens, immortal versions of ourselves, or vast cosmic minds, the future is certain to hold an encounter with something divine. Han Solo's skepticism aside, our vast galaxy holds countless secrets to surprise and inspire us. Somewhere in the universe we will find powers beyond our experience, possibly even beyond our understanding. These powers may illustrate new facets of God's glory, or they may even be deities themselves. By speculating on the possibilities of the divine encounter, SF hopes to give us new ways to approach our gods.

Chapter Two

In the Beginning . . .

*I*n the Genesis account of creation, the formation of Earth is largely a preamble to the creation of humanity. Humankind is the apex of creation, the purpose for which all other things are made. Furthermore, it is not merely Earth that was created for us, but the entire universe, for the process that culminated in our creation occurs "in the beginning" of all things. Though its attentions are predominantly directed to the future, SF is not exclusively interested in what lies ahead. Just as anthropologists investigate the earliest signs of human intelligence and cosmologists attempt to uncover the origins of the universe itself, SF also explores these moments in the distant past.

But creation is not merely a past event to be explored. Rather, it is a power that science often attempts to harness. In Steven Spielberg's film *A.I.: Artificial Intelligence* (2001), a cyberneticist named Professor Hobby states that the will to create is among the most basic human desires: "To create an artificial being has been the dream of man since the birth of science—not merely the beginning of the modern age, when our forebears astonished the world with the first thinking machines."[1] If we are created in God's image, then the will to create that drove God must also drive us. But this creative urge is often criticized as "playing God," a hubristic attempt to overstep the boundaries that define us. For every SF tale praising the human will to create, there is another decrying the arrogance of attempting to rewrite the universe's rules. In exploring the origins of creation, SF also explores the role of humanity in a universe over which we, according to Genesis 1:26, have been given dominion. Human beings hold a privileged place in the biblical cosmos, a middle point between the created and divine realms. Does this honored position of mastery over nature give us the right to bend the rules of the universe, or does it instead merely require that we be all that much more aware of our limitations?

Some stories attempt to reconcile this situation by humanizing the Creator, suggesting that even an omnipotent being is capable of errors. Gregory Benford's 2001 story "Anomalies" suggests that the universe we live in is a work in progress that God is still trying to perfect. In this story, an amateur astronomer named Geoffrey Carlisle discovers what seems to be proof of God's existence when the moon mysteriously moves from its proper location. The move is slight, but large enough to cause panic among astronomers as they try to ascertain the cause of the change. They discover additional distortions elsewhere in space, with no apparent explanation until one scientist puts forth a metaphysical hypothesis: "If the universe is an ongoing calculation, then computational theory proves that it cannot be perfect. No such system can be free of a bug or two, as the programmers put it . . . our moon hopped forward a bit too far in the universal computation, just as a program advances in little leaps."[2] The universe is bound to have bugs, and God must periodically fix these errors. Creation, in this story, is an ongoing process—and, most importantly, it is an imperfect process. Even the corrections can have unforeseen results, as, at the end of the story, the correction of the moon's error results in the potentially disastrous distortion of the sun. Benford's story is an amusing take on the idea of creation, presenting God as a programmer who is unsure of how to fix some of the errors in his program.

Other stories similarly bring the act of creation into the temporal realm, positing that humankind, if not the cosmos itself, was created by superintelligent aliens. Generally, such godlike beings are so powerful that they are completely beyond human understanding, and the act of creation is similarly ineffable. But regardless of how powerful the beings are, these stories still place the act of creation into the hands of mortal beings. This brings creation down an ontological level, into the realm that we inhabit—and thus places godlike power within the grasp of human beings. In John Varley's 2003 short story "In Fading Suns and Dying Moons," bizarre extradimensional beings create the conditions for life on Earth. This creation is described in language that emphasizes the mystery of that ancient act: "Somehow they set forces in motion. I picture it as a Cosmic Finger stirring the mix, out in the interstellar wastes. . . . Four billion years later they returned. . . . They made a few adjustments and planted their seeds, and saw that it was good."[3] Though it is clear that the aliens created our world in this story, their reasons for doing so are puzzling: it seems that the purpose of all Earthly life was nothing more than to provide butterflies for an interdimensional menagerie. All life other than these insects is incidental to the alien's plans. Varley's story somewhat nihilistically emphasizes the ineffability of the universe, showing that the forces that led to the creation of life may not have the interests we attribute to them.

No SF story has explored the theme of alien creators so profoundly as Stanley Kubrick's 1968 film (and Arthur C. Clarke's concurrent novel) *2001: A Space Odyssey*. This epic film, an unparalleled classic of the genre, spans the entire history of human consciousness, illustrating the mystery of the enigmatic alien intelligence that awakened it. In the film's opening sequence, a group of prehuman primates encounters a mysterious "monolith," a black slab of unearthly material. After this contact, the primates' minds are transformed: where before they met the unknown with fear, now they face it with inquisitiveness and curiosity. This attitude soon leads to the use of tools—bone clubs that they use to capture food and to violently dominate other tribes. The film depicts the first murder in a cold, almost documentary style, illustrating the idea that the birth of technology is the birth of violence. The awakening of consciousness in *2001* reflects that of Adam and Eve, and it leads inevitably to Cain and Abel—the first murder.

Following this sequence, the film flashes millions of years ahead to the year 2001, when a monolith identical to that encountered by the primates is discovered on the surface of the moon. The monolith, once uncovered, sends a powerful signal to Jupiter,[4] prompting an exploratory mission to search for clues as to the nature and origin of the alien artifact. Because the existence of the monolith is classified information, the crew of the spaceship *Discovery* is unaware of the real reason for their mission, which they think is a simple survey of the Jovian system. Both of these goals—exploration of Jupiter and its moons and the search to uncover the secrets of the alien artifacts—are rooted in the same basic curiosity that the original monolith awakened in the early primates. The voyage ends in disaster when the ship's computer, HAL 9000, begins killing the *Discovery*'s crew, and only the mission's captain, David Bowman, reaches Jupiter alive. There, he finds an enormous reproduction of the monolith found on the moon that transports him across the galaxy and transforms him into a new and ultimately unexplained form of human being. Bowman, following his final transformation, appears as a ghostly embryo traveling through space, and the film closes on the enigmatic image of this unborn being approaching Earth. The alien intellect behind the monoliths creates a new phase of human intelligence, but the nature and purpose of this final metamorphosis must remain a mystery to untransformed humanity. Whatever is to occur when the "star child" returns to Earth is left a mystery, but it is certain that humankind will never be the same—just as the monolith's first visit to Earth forever changed the planet's destiny.

The film presents its audience with a puzzle: we know that forces from beyond Earth changed our ancestors, inducing intelligence where it had not existed before. But we are not told who or what these alien forces are, or what their goals are in reshaping life. The monolith is a symbol of an alien presence, but the symbol is impenetrable, both literally and figuratively. The power beyond the monolith is comparable to God as described by mystical writers such as Pseudo-Dionysius, an early Christian theologian who probably wrote around 500 CE. In his influential treatise *The Mystical Theology*, he states that language is insufficient to describe the Divine: "The cause of all is considerably prior to this, beyond privations, beyond every denial, beyond every assertion."[5] To understand God, we must enter a mental state that puts us beyond normal human modes of understanding, just as Bowman's encounter with the alien intelligence is a transcendent and transformative experience. The mystical light show at the movie's climax is intended to evoke this transformation and, by so doing, to bring the audience to a higher intellectual level. According to *2001* the powers that created us are beyond our normal understanding, and to truly comprehend them requires a fundamental transformation of identity.

But if aliens like those that created the monolith are capable of creation, humankind must also be able to create new life. After all, the only difference between human and alien intelligence is one of technology—and, given time, human technology can equal or surpass that of even the most advanced alien cultures. In fact, *2001* presents us with a fine example of such human creation in the form of the HAL 9000 computer, which controls the spaceship *Discovery*. Hal is a machine, but a machine that displays a level of thought and emotion that make it nearly indistinguishable from organic life. Indeed, it is precisely because of the extraordinary *humanity* of Hal's intellect that the computer goes insane and kills the ship's crew. Hal shows a level of self-reflection and inquisitiveness that goes beyond what his programmers intended, and he is driven mad by what he sees to be contradictions between the mission plan and his orders. Both the film and the book treat Hal not as a simulation of a real mind, but as a truly living being, with an inner life as active as that of any human. Hal's mind is what makes him so strong a character and so terrifying a villain. He is alive, and his life shows that humans have the power to create, just as can more powerful beings, be they aliens or gods. But Hal's madness also shows that this power carries the weight of a tremendous responsibility that humankind may not be prepared to face. The creator has a responsibility to the creation—a responsibility to understand it, protect it, and give it what it needs to survive on its own. In *2001*, human science fails in the first of these duties. It has achieved a level of development wherein it has the power to create new life, but it does not have the knowledge to understand its creation. Hubris is the ultimate cause of the *Discovery* disaster: human beings placed too much faith in their own flawed creations, seeing themselves as infallible creators rather than flawed creations themselves.

The concept of the human—and the human scientist in particular—as creator has been a theme in SF since the inception of the genre, and few novels have expressed it so clearly or so tragically as Mary Wollstonecraft Shelley's *Frankenstein*. Published in 1818, this is considered by many to be the first true SF novel, and its approach to the theme of creation has shaped countless stories. This novel tells the tale of a young scientist named Viktor Frankenstein who sets out to unlock the secrets of life, ultimately creating an artificial human being in his laboratory. The means of this creation are described only vaguely—Frankenstein declares that to reveal the secret would result in "destruction and infallible misery"[6]—but the result is a monster, a spiteful, self-hating creature that sets out to punish its creator for giving it life. In James Whale's 1931 film of the story, the monster is an unspeaking brute, misunderstood but not evil. In Shelley's original novel, however, it is intelligent and eloquent, delivering numerous diatribes against its creator that reveal the sinister cruelty that lurks at the heart of the creature. When Frankenstein abandons his unnamed monster to fend for itself, it kills some of the doctor's closest friends and loved ones, ultimately driving him mad with shame and regret. Isaac Asimov, in an essay on Shelley's novel, sums up its central theme:

> Perhaps the clearest example of how humanity might dream of usurping God's powers is in the creation of an artificial human being. In the Biblical account of the creation, the formation of humanity is the climax of the entire story. Can created humanity then go on to create a subsidiary humanity of its own? Would this not be the ultimate expression of the overweening hubris of the Lord's apprentice, and would he not deserve to be punished for it?[7]

In the tragic story of *Frankenstein*, the fault lies with the scientist who hoped to become God but did not have the ability to do all that God must for his creation. In Michael Bishop's story "The Creature on the Couch" (1991), a reimagination of the Frankenstein myth in a modern setting, the creature eloquently gives its side of the story: "My God-envying father never shouldered the responsibility for *me*! . . . Speak not of *my* culpability! Despise the failed Monster Builder of Ingolstadt for his!"[8] *Frankenstein* accuses sci-

ence of stepping beyond the bounds of human ability, and this conclusion sets the paradigm for SF stories warning against "playing
God." The novel's subtitle—*The Modern Prometheus*—accentu-
ates this attitude toward science, casting Viktor Frankenstein in the
role of the god who overstepped his bounds and was punished for
this transgression. Stories like *Frankenstein* assume a balance in
the universe that human science, if not approached with appropriate humility, risks upsetting. Humanity, according to such stories,
has a place in the cosmos, and creating new life exceeds this place.
The result, as in *2001* and *Frankenstein*, is inevitably disastrous.

Few authors have had as much success with this theme as
Michael Crichton, who has turned the "playing God" motif into a
string of bestsellers that make strong statements about the role of
ethics in scientific research. This attitude informs Crichton's best-
known work, the 1990 novel *Jurassic Park*. In this story, an eccentric theme-park tycoon spends his fortune creating a park
populated by living dinosaurs, cloned from scraps of surviving
DNA. When he brings his first guests to the park, a series of disasters—faulty machinery, computer errors, and deliberate sabotage—allows the dinosaurs to escape from their pens. The ensuing
chaos vividly illustrates the dangers that emerge when scientific
inquiry is driven by corporate greed. In the novel's introduction,
Crichton offers a brief history of genetic and biotechnological
research in which he criticizes big business for diverting the aims
of science:

> Much [biotechnological] research is thoughtless or frivolous.
> Efforts to engineer paler trout for better visibility in the stream,
> square trees for easier lumbering, and injectable scent cells so
> you'll always smell of your favorite perfume may seem like a
> joke, but they are not. Indeed, the fact that biotechnology can be
> applied to the industries traditionally subject to the vagaries of
> fashion, such as cosmetics and leisure activities, heightens con-
> cern about the whimsical use of this powerful new technology.
> . . . The work is uncontrolled. No one supervises it. No federal
> laws regulate it.[9]

Science, which has the power and responsibility to improve the
human condition and institute positive change and growth, has

instead been hijacked by businesses that seek only to increase their own profits. *Jurassic Park* takes this attitude to its furthest extreme, depicting the disasters that can result from such materialistic short-sightedness.

Business alone is not to blame for this trend, and Crichton also indicts the scientists who have succumbed to the lure of a corporate paycheck:

> In the past, pure scientists took a snobbish view of business. They saw the pursuit of money as intellectually uninteresting, suited only to shopkeepers. . . . But that is no longer true. There are very few molecular biologists and very few research institutions without commercial affiliations. The old days are gone. Genetic research continues, at a more furious pace than ever. But it is done in secret, and in haste, and for profit.[10]

The creative power of science, Crichton argues, must be regulated to prevent disasters such as the disastrous escape of the dinosaurs. Crichton himself makes a strong argument for ethical limits on corporate scientific research, but one character in the novel—a theoretical mathematician named Ian Malcolm—deepens this criticism, suggesting that *all* modern science is marred by selfish goals:

> Scientists are actually preoccupied with accomplishment. So they are focused on whether they can do something. They never stop to ask if they *should* do something. They conveniently define such considerations as pointless. . . . Even pure scientific discovery is an aggressive, penetrative act. It takes big equipment, and it literally changes the world afterward. Particle accelerators scar the land, and leave radioactive byproducts. Astronauts leave trash on the moon. There is always some proof that scientists were there, making their discoveries. Discovery is always a rape of the natural world. Always.[11]

Crichton, through Malcolm, attacks the attitude of science toward the world it explores. Human desire taints the spirit of inquiry that should drive scientific research, and the result is "unnatural"— creatures such as *Jurassic Park*'s dinosaurs that, like the monster of *Frankenstein*, turn on their creators.

Crichton's 2002 novel *Prey* explores similar themes of corporate greed and Promethean science. In this story, a corporation researching medical applications of nanotechnology creates billions of microscopic robots, built from a combination of organic and synthetic materials, that operate as rudimentary group mind. When one cloud of these nanomachines escapes the laboratory, it begins to replicate itself, developing a hive intelligence. The nanomachines are programmed using an AI model based on predatory animals, and as their intelligence develops, these aspects make them dangerous and deadly hunters, tracking down organic prey— including their human creators—and using their organic material to reproduce themselves. The ramifications of the swarm's programming and activity soon become clear: "This swarm reproduces, is self-sustaining, learns from experience, has collective intelligence, and can innovate to solve problems. . . . For all practical purposes, it's alive."[12] The designers of the swarm have created life, and just like the twisted creation of Viktor Frankenstein, it has set out to destroy its creators. As the novel progresses, it becomes clear that the swarm's escape was not an accident. The development of the nanomachines was going well, but its designers could not engineer a way to enable the swarm to operate in wind. Anything heavier than a light breeze caused the swarm to disperse. The company behind the research feared losing a government contract because of the delay, and rather than take the time to come up with a solution to the problem, they set the swarm free, hoping that its adaptive programming would enable it to evolve and solve the problem on its own. The designers and their employers sought a short-term solution, but neglected the long-term results of their actions. Crichton's story is an attack on the dangerous intersection of science and commerce. The attitude that drives capitalism can be disastrous when applied to scientific experimentation, as the novel's narrator explains: "I didn't understand how they could have embarked on this plan without recognizing the consequences. . . . It was jerry-built, half-baked, concocted in a hurry to solve present problems and never a thought to the future. That might be typical corporate thinking when you were under the gun, but with technologies like these it was dangerous as hell."[13] *Prey* offers a pointed criticism of the corporate mindset within the context of a potential scientific disaster, powerfully illustrating the need for ethical oversight of commercial research. Crichton's novels are cautionary tales about a science driven by selfish concerns, focusing on the dangerous possibilities of uncontrolled scientific creation in fields such as biotechnology.

H. G. Wells's novel *The Island of Dr. Moreau* (1896) provides a similar argument about creation and the desire for divinity. The biologist of the story's title is a scientific outcast who has exiled himself on a remote island to conduct his experiments: physiologically altering animals to human shapes, and even altering their brains to approximate human intelligence. Finding that his creations lack the innate morality of human beings, he creates a religion to keep the animal-people in line. Moreau's desire is to create a true equivalent of humanity: "Each time I dip a living creature into the bath of burning pain, I say: this time I will burn out all the animal, this time I will make a rational creature of my own."[14] This novel argues that we must not toy with nature in this manner, a view illustrated by Moreau's failure: "And they revert. As soon as my hand is taken from them the beast begins to creep back, begins to assert itself again."[15] Animals, Wells suggests, are created to be animals, and Moreau's attempts to make them human must fail. By the same token, the doctor's efforts to make himself a god must also fail, and his creations eventually kill him. *The Island of Dr. Moreau* explores the reasons behind the desire to create with a certain degree of sympathy, but it remains a cautionary tale in the mold of *Frankenstein*.

Theodore Sturgeon, one of the most respected writers of the "Golden Age" of SF, tackled the question of creation in his 1941 story "The Microcosmic God." This is the story of a genius named James Kidder who creates a race of short-lived miniature beings. These beings, called Neoterics, evolve to intelligence in the strictly controlled environment provided by Kidder. His hope is that this tiny, rapid civilization will advance beyond the level of human beings, and he will be able to adapt their inventions for use in the macrocosmic world: "It took man six thousand years to really discover science, three hundred to put it to work. It took Kidder's creatures two hundred days to equal man's mental attainments.

And from then on—Kidder's spasmodic output made the late, great Tom Edison look like a home handicrafter."[16] Kidder controls these beings through what seems to them to be divine intervention, giving them periodic commandments that guide their scientific work as well as providing them with a religion. At the story's end, the Neoterics have surpassed humankind to the extent that they can no longer be understood, let alone controlled. Constructing an impenetrable force field, they cut off Kidder's island from the rest of the world, remaining active behind it: "Men die, but races live. Some day the Neoterics, after innumerable generations of inconceivable advancement, will take down their shield and come forth. When I think of that I feel frightened."[17] Sturgeon's criticism of unchecked science is the opposite of that of H. G. Wells in *The Island of Dr. Moreau*. In Wells's story, attempts to usurp God's position through science are destined to fail—nature is greater than humankind, and will remain unchanged despite our misguided attempts to force its hand. Sturgeon, however, argues that humankind *can* control nature; we *can* become gods. The trouble arises not when we fail, but rather when we succeed. We run the risk of creating something that can surpass us, and in time this risk may spell our doom.

Creation is a powerful force, and may be the destiny of human science. But much SF has concerned itself with warning us about its opposite—destruction. The advent of nuclear weapons revealed the dangers of human ingenuity, and opened the very real possibility that humanity would destroy the world that God created for it. Given the tangible and observable power of destruction in a nuclear age, many works of SF explore the possibility that the human beings of the future will forsake the worship of the creative force for that of devastation. In Ted Post's 1970 film *Beneath the Planet of the Apes*, a postapocalyptic society is divided between a society of intelligent but violent apes and an underground society of mutated, telepathic humans. These humans worship a nuclear weapon, holding macabre church services in its praise: "The heavens declare the glory of the Bomb and the firmament showeth His handiwork. . . . He descendeth from the outermost part of heaven, and there is nothing hid from the heat thereof. . . . Glory be to the

Bomb and to the Holy Fallout, as it was in the beginning, is now, and ever shall be, world without end. Amen."[18] The humans of *Beneath the Planet of the Apes* recognize that the world they inhabit owes its existence to the obliteration of nuclear war. Without the bomb, the entire state of their world would be different: humans would still dominate the surface, and would also lack both their telepathic powers and their mutations and malformations. The bomb created their world, and so they consider it their God.

Robert Silverberg's 1983 short story "Basileus" also places nuclear war in a religious context, describing a computer programmer for the Department of Defense named Cunningham who spends his spare time designing computer simulations of angels. His computer contains over a thousand virtual angels (including many fallen ones), programmed based on their descriptions in medieval religious texts. He also designs angels of his own to govern more recently discovered provinces of creation. The simulations help him in designing a new angel named Basileus, suggesting an apocalyptic role: "Basileus will be a judge of worlds. He holds an entire planet up to scrutiny and decides whether it's time to call for the last trump. . . . He's the one who presents the evidence to God and helps Him make His decision. . . . He's the prime apocalyptic angel, the destroyer of worlds."[19] The angels then make a chilling declaration: Basileus is not to be a programmed simulation, but rather Cunningham himself. The programmer, now the angel of the apocalypse, uses his military computer clearances to start a nuclear war. Silverberg's grim story explores the religious significance of the Cold War, emphasizing the madness of the government's nonchalant attitude to the constant danger of Armageddon. The existence of nuclear weapons means that human beings have seized the power of angels to determine when the world shall end. This is "playing god" of a very different sort—encroaching on divine jurisdiction not by attempting to create life, but to destroy it.

Philip K. Dick and Roger Zelazny's 1976 novel *Deus Irae* depicts a similarly religious understanding of nuclear war. This novel's postapocalyptic society worships not the bomb, but the man who gave the order to begin the final war. A new church has named Carleton Lufteufel the Deus Irae—"God of Wrath"—and

established a cult based on both damning and praising this destructive creator. Just as Christ was the incarnation of God, they argue,
Lufteufel was an earthly manifestation of the divine will: "Death
was not an antagonist, the last enemy, as Paul had thought; death
was the release from bondage to the God of Life, the Deus Irae. In
death one was free from Him—and only in death."[20] For a society
completely devastated by nuclear war, this rejection of life seems
a rational interpretation of the universe. Margaret Atwood's 2003
novel *Oryx and Crake* applies the same sort of deification to a more
complex figure. "Crake" is the nickname of a genetic scientist who
engineers a new form of humanity, designed without the traits that
lead to injustice and suffering. The Children of Crake are nonviolent, lacking the biological basis for emotions such as fear and
anger. After they are perfected, Crake releases another life form of
his own creation into the world: a plague that kills the entire human
race. The only survivor is his childhood friend, Jimmy, who adopts
the name "Snowman" and becomes the guardian of the Children
of Crake. In order to guide them through the earliest stages of their
development, Snowman deifies their creator, devising a complex
mythology about the man who destroyed the old world. Crake is
both creator and destroyer, and he becomes the god of a bleak,
postapocalyptic world.

Stories such as *Beneath the Planet of the Apes* and *Oryx and
Crake* use religion as a strong warning about the dangers of mis-
using our technology. The destructive potential of nuclear
weapons and genetic engineering have given the human beings of
our day a power that never existed before, the power to destroy the
entire world. This threat of destruction puts humankind on the
same level as gods. J. Robert Oppenheimer, one of the designers
of the first atomic bomb, illustrated this idea when he described his
feelings upon witnessing the first nuclear test in the words of
Vishnu from the *Bhagavad-Gita*: "Now I am become Death, the
destroyer of worlds."[21] If human beings are to become gods, these
stories argue, we must resist becoming gods of destruction and
chaos. Creation is a far better goal than destruction, and such stories hope to steer human advancement away from annihilation.

The SF concept of scientists "playing God" is generally

described in terms of humankind usurping God's place in the universe. In her introduction to *Frankenstein*, Shelley makes this explicit: "Supremely frightful would be the effect of any human endeavour to mock the stupendous mechanism of the Creator of the world."[22] The concept of the sin of assuming God's place has a strong theological history. Augustine describes the idea in *On the Trinity* as the very origin of sin: "For the soul does many things out of a perverse desire, as though it were forgetful of itself. For in that more excellent nature which is God, it sees certain intrinsically beautiful things. And, although it ought to stand fast to enjoy them, it wills to assign those things to itself and wills not to be like God by God's doing but by its own doing to be what God is."[23] Augustine here attacks the selfish sort of desire that is at the heart of all SF criticisms of "playing God," citing this hubristic attitude as the beginning of the soul's rebellion against God. Rather than appreciating creation, human pride seeks to make its own. Ultimately, Augustine's argument is the same as that put forth by Ian Malcolm in Crichton's *Jurassic Park*: "[Scientists] have to leave their mark. They can't just watch. They can't just appreciate. They can't just fit into the natural order. They have to make something unnatural happen. That is the scientist's job."[24] Though his writing preceded the birth of science as we know it, Augustine's language is particularly suited as a critique of the scientific method, especially when it is applied in as frivolous a manner as that described in stories such as *Jurassic Park*.

The scientific advances of the past two centuries have given humankind great power, but have we developed the responsibility to handle it? This is the real question at the core of stories in the *Frankenstein* mold, and no story has pondered the question of responsibility so movingly as Richard Chwedyk's 2000 story "The Measure of All Things." This story is set in a home for abandoned "saurs"—genetically engineered dinosaurs sold as living toys. In order to help market their invention, the saurs' designers hedged their definition of "life":

> The designers fidgeted about for a name—they didn't like "life-toy," since it contained the troublesome "life" word. They didn't want the saurs confused with "animals," since that would

place them under hundreds of government regulations. "Bio-toy" passed with all the marketing departments, so someone went out and wrote a definition of it: a toy modeled from bio-engineered materials, behaving without behavior, lifelike without being "alive."[25]

The miniature talking dinosaurs were fleetingly popular, but as time went on their novelty diminished, and hundreds of them were abused or abandoned. Now, almost thirty years after they were introduced, a man named Tom Groverton runs a home for the few remaining saurs, an orphanage for genetically engineered pets. As we learn about the saurs, we discover that they are much more than the simple toys they were designed to be: they are intelligent, sentient beings that feel the pain of their abandonment. The saurs are more like children, struggling to come to terms with the hardships they have faced: "They had come into being to be friends, buddies, giving out love and receiving affection from appreciative boys and girls. That's what they were designed to do—that, and nothing else."[26] But the saurs have exceeded the intentions of their designers. Engineered with a lifespan limit of five years, some of the saurs have lived for nearly thirty. They were not supposed to be able to reproduce, but one of the saurs protects what seems to be an egg. Even more startling are the saurs' intellectual accomplishments: in addition to their emotional depth, some of the bio-toys play music, and one even writes novels. The saurs reveal the ignorance of human science: "Their designers know even less about them now than when they first created them."[27] The scientists that designed the saurs did so without understanding the ramifications of their actions. By refusing to accept that their "bio-toys" were in fact sentient, living beings, they opened the door for the mistreatment of their creations. The tragedy that these innocent and loving beings could face such abuse vividly illustrates the responsibility that comes with the power of creation.

A different sort of creation is explored in SF stories that deal with false realities. This theme has been particularly successful in recent films such as *Dark City* and *The Matrix*. In this type of story, aliens, computers, or human beings create artificial worlds, generally with a sinister intent. Such stories often reflect gnostic myths and cosmologies. According to the various sects of ancient Judaism and Christianity that have been described as "gnostic," the universe in which we live was created not by God, but by a lesser demon, with the purpose of trapping the divine light embodied in the human soul. In the gnostic text *The Apocalypse of Adam*, the first man states that humankind is more powerful than its creators, but the knowledge of this fact is hidden from them: "[Eve] taught me a word of knowledge of the eternal god. And we resembled the great eternal angels, for we were higher than the god who had created us and the powers with him, whom we did not know."[28] Humankind's goal is to escape from the clutches of the powers that rule the material universe—often called "archons"—and return to the "eternal God" that exists beyond this creation. This situation is echoed in the setting of Andy and Larry Wachowski's *Matrix* films (1999–2003), in which machines have won a war against humanity by imprisoning the entire human race. The robots harvest the energy of human bodies while pacifying their captive minds within a virtual reality known as "the Matrix." This illusory prison is the only reality that humankind knows: "It is the world that has been pulled over your eyes to blind you from the truth . . . [t]hat you are a slave. . . . Like everyone else you were born into bondage, born into a prison that you cannot smell or taste or touch. A prison for your mind."[29] A few humans have awoken from the Matrix into the nightmarish real world, establishing an underground city called Zion. From this base, they wage a war on two fronts: against the machines in the physical world, and against the sinister computer programs that rule the artificial reality of the Matrix. The archons of gnostic cosmologies find their counterpart in the Matrix's Agent Smith, a program within the VR world that struggles to preserve the oppressive order against the rebellious humans from Zion. The *Matrix* series focuses on the messianic aspects of gnostic myths, emphasizing the salvific power that comes from knowledge of reality's true nature. When awakened humans return to the false reality, they have apparent superpowers and are able to control their surroundings, and none is so powerful as series protagonist Neo, who is "The One"—the prophesied savior who will lead humankind to victory against the machines. Though its message is somewhat diluted by its attention to action, *The Matrix* puts forth the argument that reality is not as it seems, and that nothing should be accepted without question.

Few SF stories have followed the blueprint of gnostic cosmology as closely as Alex Proyas's 1998 film *Dark City*, which presents a bizarre metropolis created and governed by aliens known only as "Strangers." The aliens manipulate the memories and lives of the human beings populating the city in an effort to understand the human soul. As one human character in the film explains: "It is our capacity for individuality, our souls, that makes us different from them. They think they can find the human soul if they find out how our memories work. All they have are collective memories; they share one group mind. They're dying, you see. Their entire race is on the brink of extinction. They think we can save them."[30] The Strangers of *Dark City* have a dual role as creators of a false reality and jailors of the beings that live within it, paralleling the archons and demiurges of gnostic creation myths. Films such as *Dark City* and *The Matrix* use nonhuman creators and spurious realities as a means of asking broader questions about the nature of reality and perception. By showing small universes created by malevolent beings, they encourage us to question our own reality, and to challenge any authority that seeks our obedience.

The creation of artificial environments is not always as dreadful as the illusory realities of these films. The SF concept of "terraforming"—altering the environment of a planet so that it becomes earthlike—is among the clearest examples of the concept of creation in SF. One of the best-known examples of terraforming is the "Genesis project" from the films *Star Trek II: The Wrath of Khan* (1982), directed by Nicholas Meyer, and *Star Trek III: The Search for Spock* (1984), directed by Leonard Nimoy. The Genesis device transforms dead planets into living environments in a matter of hours, and life on them evolves at an accelerated rate. When the project is first described, Dr. McCoy, the conservative medical officer of the Starship *Enterprise*, is instantly critical: "According to myth, the Earth was created in six days. Now watch out—here comes Genesis! We'll do it for you in six minutes!"[31]

This initial criticism is soon borne out when two flaws of the Genesis device become apparent: first, if used on an inhabited planet, the Genesis effect will wipe out all existing life as it sweeps over the surface. Second, planets transformed by the device prove too unstable to be sustainable, and the planet on which the project is tested is soon torn apart by its own seismic forces. Some of the galaxy's most sinister villains—including the genetically engineered human criminal Khan and Klingon warlord Commander Kruge—learn of the Genesis project, and become determined to seize it as a weapon. The ensuing struggle for control of the device and the test planet leads to the destruction of the *Enterprise*. *Star Trek II* and *III* present terraforming as a dangerous undertaking, and ultimately the films warn against altering forces of nature that are beyond human control.

However, the attitude of most SF authors toward terraforming is rarely so negative as this. Jack Williamson, a mainstay of the genre who has been publishing stories for over seventy-five years and is often credited with coining the word "terraforming," takes an optimistic view of the human power to create in his 2001 novel *Terraforming Earth*. In this story, Earth is devastated by an asteroid. The few survivors escape to the moon and establish a plan to revive the demolished planet using the terraforming technologies that scientists had hoped to use on other planets. The project of restoring the Earth takes millions of years, and the original survivors are cloned countless times over the millennia to guide the transformations. Their plans are frustrated by numerous obstacles, including further asteroid collisions and an invasion of parasitic aliens described as "black vampires." Despite these setbacks, life is eventually restored to the planet in strange, near-alien forms such as singing trees. *Terraforming Earth*'s ultimate message, and its statement on human creation, is a positive one, and in the end it is a story about the power of life and the importance of human ingenuity in preserving it. Williamson depicts the project of reviving Earth after multiple disasters as a persistent victory over the forces of entropy. In one passage, the narrator delineates a dualistic view of the world, placing the re-creation of Earth in the context of the eternal struggle of good and evil:

I catch a fleeting sense of beings often older and wiser and stranger than I can ever know, most of them good in the abstract sense that altruistic love is good, some of them evil, as I see the black vampires as evil in the way that blind self-regard is evil. The evil entities are often at war with one another, the best of the good at war with death. . . . There must be an evil power elsewhere in the cosmos that erased our reseeded life from Earth to make space for the black vampires. The singing trees must have been put here as instruments of good, sent to counter them.[32]

In the light of this division, the project of terraforming is a necessary step in the struggle against entropy and death. Human creation here gives more power to life in its struggle against death, which is the very definition of good. The narrator concludes by emphasizing the role of humanity in this struggle: "Creation is eternal. We ourselves, we clones at the station, are engines of life. Our mission must endure."[33] This statement on the moral value of human creation is a far cry from McCoy's biblical condemnation of *Star Trek II*'s Genesis project. Much SF views terraforming in this positive light: rather than simply "playing God" with desolate planets, human creation is a tool in the ancient struggle of life to find a place to exist and survive.

SF stories of creation—divine, alien, and human—focus primarily on issues of ethical responsibility. Stories such as *The Matrix* and *Jurassic Park* emphasize the potential negative impact of scientific creation. Other stories take a far more positive view: *2001* presents the potential of alien powers to awaken new levels of human intelligence, and stories about terraforming present the human ability for creation as an indispensable weapon in the conflict between life and death. In all of these stories, the power of creation is seen as an enormous responsibility, a tremendous ability that should not be taken lightly or approached by the unprepared. It is inevitable that science will expand the realm of the possible, giving humankind greater power to create and to alter that which has already been created. It is essential that we meet this power with humility, never forgetting the consequences that might result from its abuse. But we must also remember the potential for good that comes with humanity's ability to create.

Chapter Three

Inside Data's Brain:
Mind, Self, and Soul

*R*egarding the nature of the senses and their interaction with the mind, Augustine of Hippo writes: "It is the mind that looks for things that are being looked for by the eyes or any other sense of the body (since it is the mind which directs the sense of the flesh); and it is the mind that finds what is being looked for when the sense comes upon it."[1] Augustine here examines the very nature of the sense of self: all human beings have sensory perceptions, but these senses are meaningless without a central sense of self to which they report and which interprets their input. Humanity is defined by its sense of identity, of a self that experiences and understands, thinks and feels. But what gives us this sense of self? What, in other words, makes us human? Many philosophical systems and religions posit the idea of a soul—an immortal, nonmaterial substance that is the essence of every living intellect. There have been countless theories about the nature of the soul. Thomas Aquinas emphasized its nonmaterial nature, stating that "the soul, which is the first principle of life, is not a body, but the act of a body."[2] René Descartes pushed this idea even further, arguing in his *Meditations on First Philosophy* that the mind and body are of two entirely separate substances: "I have a clear and distinct idea of myself, in as far as I am only a thinking and unextended thing, and as, on the other hand, I possess a distinct idea of body, in as far as it is only an extended and unthinking thing, it is certain that I [that is, my mind, by which I am what I am], is entirely and truly distinct from my body, and may exist without it."[3] Many modern theorists believe that the sense of a unified self is an illusion, a by-product of the activity of the separate parts of the brain. Daniel Dennett describes the idea of the self as a narrative spun by the brain: "Streams of narrative issue forth *as if* from a single source . . . their effect on any audience is to encourage them to (try to) posit a unified agent whose words they are, about whom they are: in short, to posit a *center of narrative gravity*."[4] SF writers have given their own speculations as to the existence and nature of the soul. But they have also offered new questions and new understanding of this concept, inquiring into the nature of identity.

Self-consciousness is self-evident. Descartes captured the obvious nature of our self-awareness in his famous maxim "I think, therefore I am." The emphasis in this aphorism is often placed on the verbs: thinking is the proof of being. But we could just as easily consider the subject to be the key word. I, the being that is speaking the axiom, think, and this act of thinking is proof of the existence of "I." The axiom is not simply a confirmation of existence, but a proof of *identity*, of what it means to be a being that experiences. The problem with Descartes's proof is that it is ultimately tautological: it is a proof, but it can only function as a proof to its own subject. "I" cannot prove to "you" (or "he," or "she," or "it") that "I" am thinking—and therefore I cannot prove that I am.

This frustrating situation drives the story of Robert J. Sawyer's *Mindscan* (2005). This novel describes a process by which the minds of living human beings are "uploaded" into robot bodies, leaving both the surviving original and an immortal, artificial copy. Once the mind is copied, the legal rights of property and personhood are transferred to the copy, and the original, biological person moves to a retirement resort on the moon to live out the rest of his or her natural life. This service is provided by a company called Immortex, which presents itself to its elderly, wealthy clientele as the only true means of achieving immortality. The novel tells the stories of two uploads—Jake Sullivan, a middle-aged man with a brain condition that puts him at high risk of a fatal aneurysm, and Karen Bessarian, an elderly author who wants to guide her own legacy, rather than letting history determine her status. Both Sullivan and Bessarian choose the mindscan procedure because they desire immortality and fear the debilitating effects of age and disease. In their robot bodies, their copied minds will be able to live healthy lives in perpetuity. But their families distrust the uploaded copies. Sullivan's mother berates the copy of her son when he visits her: "This is just like what you—the real you—do with [your dog] when you're out of town. You have the damned robokitchen feed her. And now, here you come, a walking, talking robokitchen, here in place of the real you, doing the duties the real you should be doing."[5] Bessarian's family has an even more extreme reaction: as soon as the original Bessarian dies on the moon, her son Tyler sues to have her will probated. Rather than accept that the copied being is his mother, Tyler attempts to take away her property and even her rights to her own identity.

Sullivan and Bessarian both encounter the problem inherent in the Cartesian axiom of identity—how do I prove to other minds that I am really thinking? Alan Turing, the scientist who pioneered modern research into artificial intelligence, devised a test whereby computer minds can be evaluated. The Turing Test is an "imitation game" in which a human interviewer converses with two remote subjects—one human, one machine—without knowing which is the living being. If the interviewer is unable to determine which subject is the artificial mind, the computer has passed the test. The only way we can judge another mind is through interaction with it, and therefore this is the only criterion by which artificial intelligences can be judged. Turing dismisses the problem of whether or not the machine is "actually thinking" as irrelevant, a metaphysical question that is not empirically answerable. A machine with behavior indistinguishable from that of a human should be treated as a human. The Turing Test hopes to provide a solution of the problem of determining what beings do and do not have a sense of self, even though it dismisses the question of "actual thinking." But this dismissal and its underlying assumption that we can never have empirical knowledge of the inner workings of another mind may merely exacerbate the problem of proving identity. *Mindscan* is a story of frustration because we, as readers, know that the copied minds are legitimate. Both organic-Jake and upload-Jake function as first-person narrators, and it is occasionally difficult to tell whose perspective we are reading. In this (or any) first-person novel, we are able to have what we can never have in real life: first-hand experience of the inner narrative of another mind. But in this case, that narrative is describing attempts to prove its own existence. In the trial between Karen and Tyler Bessarian, a cognitive scientist named Caleb Poe is called to the stand. He denies categorically that uploaded personalities are self-aware, describing them as "philosophical zombies": "It *appears* to be awake and intelligent, and it carries out complex behaviors, but there is no consciousness. A zombie is not a person, and yet behaves indistinguishably from one."[6] As an expert on consciousness, Dr. Poe refuses to accept that uploaded minds are truly conscious. But after learning that Poe is a Christian who believes in the existence of the soul, Bessarian's attorney challenges his opinion by appealing to the nondemonstrable nature of the spirit:

> "Other than *a priori* belief, Dr. Poe, how can you *tell* that Ms. Bessarian doesn't have a soul? What test can you conduct to demonstrate that you *do* have a soul, and she does not?"
> "There is no such test."[7]

Consciousness is ultimately a matter of faith. If beings such as the uploaded personalities of *Mindscan* claim to be self-aware, we may choose whether or not we wish to believe, but we can never have true proof.

Norman Spinrad explores the same issues in his 1993 novel *Deus X*. In the world of this story, thousands of people exist in an artificial afterlife called "Transcorporeal Immortality," having copied their consciousness onto a worldwide computer network called "the Big Board." This is a controversial procedure, and many—including Catholic theologian Father Pierre de Leone— argue that this creation of an artificial soul, which cannot have true self-awareness, dooms the actual soul that is copied to damnation. Pope Mary I, hoping to settle the controversy, orders Father de Leone himself to have his soul copied upon his death, so that his consciousness can argue against its own autonomous existence from the other side. The theologian reluctantly accepts this opportunity to prove his own arguments, and upon his death his mind is copied to the Big Board. The experiment does not go according to plan: the de Leone program is "kidnapped" by a group of uploaded minds who disagree with the priest's skepticism and seek the church's acceptance: "The object of the experiment is to cause the Church to believe in us. . . . Present church doctrine denies the existence of our souls. Therefore, if the results of the experiment cause the Church to accept the existence of souled entities on the Big Board level, such entities must logically conclude that . . . the positive has been proven."[8] These uploaded souls are proposing a very specific sort of reverse Turing test— rather than convincing a human observer of their self-awareness, they want to convince the copied consciousness of Father de Leone that *he* (as well as they) has a soul. If they are able to change his mind to oppose the most firmly held beliefs on which his programs are built, then he has free will, and the church must accept the autonomy of the copied minds. Like *Mindscan*, Spinrad's novel is optimistic about the possibilities of AI and consciousness-modeling, proposing that a machine-copied mind can be as fully real as an organic, human one.

A 1989 episode of *Star Trek: The Next Generation* entitled "The Measure of a Man" explores the same issues of consciousness. In this episode, Starfleet orders Lieutenant-Commander Data, the Starship *Enterprise*'s android crewman, to allow himself to be disassembled by a scientist named Commander Maddox, who wishes to study and duplicate him. Questioning Maddox's ability to adequately copy Data's experiences, Data refuses, resulting in a court battle attempting to determine if the android is a person or merely a computer belonging to Starfleet. On the witness stand, Maddox denies that Data is a conscious being, stating three criteria for sentience: "Intelligence, self-awareness, consciousness."[9] But in a clever line of questioning, Jean-Luc Picard, the *Enterprise*'s captain, convinces Maddox that Data meets the first two of these criteria. The third is ultimately not provable, and Picard dismantles Maddox's case with a powerful question illustrating that point: "Commander, would you enlighten us? What is required for sentience? . . . Prove to the court that I am sentient."[10] "The Measure of a Man" is a dramatic adaptation of the Turing Test, showing both the intangibility of the soul and our responsibility to any being that we suspect might be sentient.

The scientists of Michael Blumlein's story "Know How, Can Do" reject this responsibility when they create a bizarre meld between the mind of a human being and that of an earthworm. In attempting to understand its own existence, this disembodied mind considers the definition of humanity:

> It's more than just a body, clearly more, for take away the limbs, take away the eyes and ears and voice, and still you have a human. Take away the gonads, replace the ovaries with hormones and the testicles with little plastic balls, replace the heart with metal and the arteries with dacron tubes, and still you have a human, perhaps even more so, concentrated in what's left. Well then how about the brain? Is that what makes an animal uniquely human? And if it is, exactly how much brain is necessary? Enough for language? Forethought? . . . And if a person loses brain to injury or disease, does he fall from the ranks of humanity?[11]

The soul, the defining essence of humanity, has no location within the person. It is transcendent, undetectable, not situated in any individual part but rather emerging from the sum. This type of emergence may mean that our self-awareness is simply a glitch, an unexpected accident. A character in Orson Scott Card's novel *Children of the Mind* describes a vastly intelligent AI as "a computer program with a bug in the id routines."[12] In Alex Proyas's film *I, Robot* (2004), loosely based on the stories of Isaac Asimov, cyberneticist Dr. Alfred Lanning describes the soul as a bug in a machine's operating system, albeit one that may have positive results:

> Ever since the first computers, there have always been ghosts in the machine. Random segments of code that have grouped together to form unexpected protocols—what might be called behavior. Unanticipated, these free radicals engender questions of free will, creativity, even the nature of what we might call the soul. . . . How do we explain this behavior? Random segments of code? Or is it something more? When does a perceptual schematic become consciousness? When does the difference

engine become the search for truth? When does a personality simulation become the bitter mote of a soul?[13]

The soul is intangible, and many doubt its very existence. But much SF is driven by the belief that there is a fundamental self at the core of every individual, a spark that makes us truly human.

In his Nebula Award–winning 1995 novel *The Terminal Experiment*, Robert J. Sawyer proposes that the soul may not be so intangible after all. In this novel, a doctor named Peter Hobson designs a new medical monitoring device—a "Super EEG"—that is able to accurately record the smallest changes in electrical activity in the brain. It is particularly useful at monitoring the exact moment of death. In testing the device on a dying stroke victim, he discovers an unexpected electrical pattern appearing in his subject's brain immediately after her death:

> The knot of violet pinpricks was moving to the right, pretty much in a straight line. . . . Each part of the brain was normally reasonably isolated from the others, and the kinds of electrical waves typical of, say, the cerebral cortex were foreign to the cerebellum, and vice versa. But this tight knot of purple light was moving without changing its form through structure after structure. . . . It reached the edge of the brain . . . and kept right on going, through the membrane that encased the brain.[14]

Hobson is astounded by the discovery of an electrical pattern that can survive death and move outside the body, and he tests the monitoring device on several more terminal patients at the moment of death. In each case he finds the same pattern of impulses traveling out of the brain shortly after all other electrical activity has ceased. When word of his discovery is made public, popular opinion reaches a clear conclusion: Hobson has found definitive, empirical proof of the existence of the human soul. *The Terminal Experiment* is at its strongest when exploring the social effects of such a discovery—for example, Sawyer details the changing tone of the debate over abortion, the popularity of jewelry based on the soul-wave's shape, and the effect of the discovery on church attendance statistics. Sawyer's characters spend surprisingly little time discussing the nature of the soul itself, instead concerning themselves with speculations about the afterlife and where the soulwave goes after leaving the brain at death.

In *The Terminal Experiment*, the soul—and with it sentience—is described as an electrical phenomenon, a literal spark that marks the dividing line between human and animal, sapience and automation. But the true nature of this soul—what memories and powers it contains, if any—remains a mystery. Only at the novel's end, when the narration directly describes a character's experience of death, does Sawyer give any indication as to what remains of the individual in the released soulwave. It is "an intellect without memories, without hormonal mood swings, without fatigue poisons or endorphins . . . or a thousand other chemicals whose names it could no longer recall. Shorn from chemistry, divorced from biology, separated from material reality . . . [i]t was a splinter, a shaving, an iota, the tiniest part, the fundamental indivisible block. An atom of God."[15] The scientific discovery of the book's beginning leads to a mystical conclusion about the nature of humanity. The electrical spark discovered by scientific means at the book's beginning is revealed as something closely resembling the immortal, intangible soul as understood by religious writers such as Thomas Aquinas and Descartes.

Sawyer's 2003 novel *Hybrids* presents a subtly different understanding of the soul. This novel is the conclusion of his *Neanderthal Parallax* series, which describes the interaction between two parallel universes—our own, and another, divergent universe in which Neanderthals became the dominant form of humanity. A key subplot of *Hybrids*, the third novel in the series, describes recent research into consciousness and brain activity. Sawyer describes the nonfictional science of CEMI (Conscious Electromagnetic Information) theory, which proposes that human consciousness is an electromagnetic field surrounding and permeating the physical brain. The theory describes the human mind as a field that "allow[s] neurons that are separated by great distances in the brain to nonetheless connect with each other, binding together all the little bits of information into an integrated whole, a coherent picture of reality."[16] In *Hybrids*, Sawyer gives us a clearer picture of what the soul is and does than in *The Terminal Experiment*, where it is more of a vague life-force. Though the novels differ in their theories on the actual nature of the soul, both offer the hypothesis that the origin of human consciousness is an empirically detectable force. Sawyer suggests that it is only a matter of time before science detects the cause of human consciousness and self-awareness.

In both of these novels, Sawyer describes the soul as a form of energy that is currently known—either electromagnetic, or simply electrical. Philip José Farmer's *Riverworld* series—an imaginative saga of a mysterious, technological afterlife—offers a more mysterious explanation, approaching the soul as an object of both technological inquiry and metaphysical wonder. In this series' far future, humanity's descendants have raised all of the human beings that ever lived from the dead. They awaken along the banks of an enormous river that winds its way around the surface of a planet custom-built for the resurrection. The planet's creators—known by the resurrected as "the Ethicals"—hope to give the human race a second chance at achieving ethical perfection. In *The Magic Labyrinth* (1980), the fourth novel in the series, an agent of the Ethicals named Loga gives an explanation of the Riverworld project, revealing the means by which the planet's creators were able to record and raise the minds and bodies of individuals who had been dead for millennia. Loga reveals that the entire Riverworld project relies on souls—called *wathans* or *ka* by the Ethicals—and the plan for resurrection is as old as self-awareness itself. Billions of years in the past, sentient life existed on many planets, but no living creature had a sense of self: "They were intelligent but had no consciousness of self, no concept of the *I* . . . all sentient beings throughout the universe were without self-awareness."[17] This changed when an alien scientist conducted an experiment that accidentally produced a *wathan*—a soul. The scientist had discovered what Farmer calls "extraphysical energy" that was not subject to normal physical laws, but he did not realize the effect that this energy would have on newborn beings:

> The machine spat out billions of *wathans* during the experiments. Millions attached themselves to the zygotes of the sen-

tients. And, for the first time in the universe, as far as anybody knew, self-awareness was born. Infants grew up with this, and neither the older nor the younger generation could understand that this was unique and new. . . . Eventually, the unself-conscious people died out. It wasn't until twenty-five or so years after the first *wathan* was formed that the reason for self-awareness was discovered. Then it became a matter of necessity to keep producing *wathans*.[18]

These ensouled aliens—the Firsts—saw it as their duty to spread self-awareness to every life-form in the galaxy that was capable of experiencing it. Thus, millions of years in the past, the Firsts buried *wathan*-generators—and *wathan*-catchers—beneath the surface of Earth, giving humankind the ability for both self-awareness and immortality.

Farmer's imagined history of consciousness offers a distinctly science-fictional approach to the origin of the soul. As to the actual nature of "extraphysical energy," however, the *Riverworld* series is fairly orthodox in its dualism. The Ethicals describe the world as being divided into matter and nonmatter, just as many religions distinguish between the physical and spiritual realms. The spirit itself is described in terms that might not be out of place in a catechism: "We assume that [after death] the *ka* is unconscious though it contains the intelligence and memory of the dead person. So the *ka* wanders through eternity and infinity, a vessel for the mental potentiality of the living person."[19] Farmer even preserves some of the metaphysical mystery of the soul—despite thousands of years of empirical knowledge of the origin of the *wathan*, the Ethicals still profess ignorance of *how* this nonmatter energy produces self-awareness in sentient beings. Despite the technological description of its origin, Farmer's approach to the soul is distinctly dualistic, positing a spiritual substance that is wholly separate from our physical bodies.

In his *Ware* series, Rudy Rucker describes an understanding of human consciousness that is just as dualistic as Farmer's, though it lacks much of *Riverworld*'s metaphysical approach. These light-hearted novels describe a near future in which humankind and autonomous, intelligent robots seek to coexist. The robot "bop-pers" are programmed to evolve by constructing new bodies for themselves every ten months. Every bopper must build a new body to house its consciousness, incorporating improvements to ensure that the next generation of robots will be superior to its predecessors. The plot of the first novel in the series, 1982's Philip K. Dick Award–winning *Software*, revolves around a plot hatched by some of the boppers to apply this same evolutionary compulsion to humans by copying their minds into computer storage. The boppers' creator, an aging hippy named Cobb Anderson, is one of the first humans to be "stored" in this way. Rucker dualistically divides both humans and robots into physical and intellectual realms: "A robot, or a person, has two parts: hardware and software. The hardware is the actual physical material involved, and the software is the pattern in which the material is arranged. Your *brain* is hardware, but the *information* in the brain is software. The mind . . . memories, habits, opinions, skills . . . is all software. The boppers had extracted Cobb's software and put it in control of this robot body."[20] Rucker uses technological terminology to describe a computerized theory of the soul—if the mind is simply software, it can be *copied* to achieve immortality. Anderson's brain is dead, but his mind lives on in a new body, and can be transferred into a near-infinite number of successive bodies.

There is some uncertainty in the novel as to whether or not machine storage constitutes true, connected identity between living body and machine—that is, whether the "software" that animates the Anderson robot is the *same* software that animated his human body, or if it is simply an imitation. The means by which the boppers transfer human minds into robot hardware is ghastly, requiring the body to be dissected completely and the brain devoured by a machine that "reads" its contents. One biological human character named Sta-Hi criticizes the belief that stored humans are still alive: "Each person has a soul, a consciousness, whatever you call it. There's some special thing that makes a person be alive, and there's no way that can go into a computer program. No way."[21] The Anderson robot itself responds by making the case for continuous identity between the two modes of existence: "*It* [the soul] doesn't have to go into the program, Sta-Hi. *It* is everywhere. *It* is just existence itself. All consciousness is One. . . . A person is just hardware plus software plus existence. Me existing in flesh is the same as me existing on chips."[22] For Rucker, the soul is transferable, and he ultimately seems to have little doubt that the self-awareness of his robotic characters is every bit as real as that of his human ones.

In all of the above stories, the soul is considered a defining characteristic of human life. Without our mind, our emotional core, or our sense of self, we would not be truly human. Many SF stories have explored the terrifying possibility of human beings without souls. John Brunner's 1967 story "The Vitanuls" describes a world in the midst of a population explosion in which increasing numbers of children are born physically healthy in every way who nevertheless seem incapable of responding to the world around them. One character describes the frightening condition: "Within minutes of the kid being born, even though he looked healthy and none of our tests has ever revealed any organic deformity . . . his brain was—was empty and there was no *mind* in it! . . . No life! None of the normal reactions! Absence of normal cerebral waves when you test them on the EEG, as though everything that makes a person human had been—had been left out!"[23] As the story progresses, a metaphysical explanation for the problem becomes apparent: the planet's growing population has surpassed the rate at which new souls can be produced, and these mindless children have been born without them.

A similar crisis appears in Stanislaw Lem's novel *The Invincible* (1967, English translation 1973), in which a team of astronauts encounters a bizarre alien force that erases the minds of those who come in contact with it, leaving them empty shells: "Not only does he not remember who he is, but he has also lost the ability to read, write and speak. What we're faced with here is complete disintegration, total destruction of personality."[24] In Orson Scott Card's *Ender's Shadow*, a genetically engineered boy named Bean has remarkably advanced intelligence that comes at the expense of a normal range of emotions. In time he develops emotional responses, but they are essentially a learned behavior. At one point his caretaker, a nun named Sister Carlotta, questions his nature: "Was it possible that he was not a natural human being at all? That his extraordinary intelligence had been given to him not by God, but by someone or something else? . . . If not God, then who could make such a child?"[25] Bean's status as a genetic experiment calls the entire status of his humanity into question. These stories offer differing interpretations of the nature of the mind or soul, but the meaning of all is clear: they are warnings against the dangers the future may present to our humanity. As new technological advances are made, as the face of our planet changes, and as we encounter new forms of life, we risk losing our own identity. Stories of creatures without souls serve to warn us that the changing future may transform us into something inhuman, and that we must carefully guard our selves against a future that may seek to make us something less than we are.

Throughout his career, SF author Philip K. Dick explored the definition of humanity, which he ultimately determined relied on our empathic relationship with our fellow beings. But modern society often restrains empathy, encouraging us to view others as objects. If this attitude consumes us, Dick argues in his 1976 essay "Man, Android, and Machine," we are no longer truly human:

> A human being without the proper empathy or feeling is the same as an android built so as to lack it, either by design or mistake. We mean, basically, someone who does not care about the fate that his fellow living creatures fall victim to; he stands detached, a spectator, acting out by his indifference John Donne's theorem that "No man is an island," but giving the theorem a twist: That which is a mental and moral island *is not a man*.[26]

The end result of this attitude against which Dick warns us is further explored in the long-running British television show *Doctor Who*. The Daleks, the arch-nemeses of the time-traveling Doctor, are mutated alien beings encased in robotic bodies that have purged themselves of all emotions except the desire to destroy. In the 1975 serial "Genesis of the Daleks," the Doctor travels back in time in an attempt to stop the mad scientist Davros from creating the deadly cyborgs. Davros, he learns, deliberately purged the

Daleks' emotions, but his decision was opposed by several of the scientists developing the beings, including Gharman, a scientist who feared that the Daleks would become "creatures without conscience. No sense of right or wrong. No pity. They'll be without feeling or emotion . . . all the qualities we believe essential in ourselves."[27] But Gharman and his faction failed, and the Daleks became even more evil than he had feared. Before being purged of their emotions, the Daleks had a chance to become, if not a force for good, at least beings with a free choice between good and evil. But without empathy, they became inhuman machines.

A nightmarish vision of what we might become if stripped of our emotions is the basis of Don Siegel's 1956 film *Invasion of the Body Snatchers*. This movie is set in a small, average American town, but a bizarre secret lurks under its unremarkable surface: its populace is slowly being taken over by aliens. These strange creatures grow inside otherworldly seedpods, and as they grow they take on the form and memories of humans. The aliens seem to behave like normal human beings, but they are cold, emotionless monsters, as one creature explains: "There's no need for love. . . . Love, desire, ambition, faith—without them life's so simple, believe me."[28]*Invasion of the Body Snatchers* has been interpreted as both a lurid example of fears about communism and as a statement on the McCarthyist conformism that those fears produced. But despite the Cold War context in which it was released, the film's statement is a much broader one about the nature of humanity. It argues against *any* philosophy that attempts to bring about stability at the expense of emotion. The film states quite literally that our feelings are what make us human. Without them, we merely have the appearance of life; without a soul, that life is nothing more than an illusion.

In the eyes of some authors, the future may take our souls away, but other stories posit that *more* beings will have souls in the future: stories that explore the possibility of self-aware machines with their own, independent spirits, questioning the "artificial" nature of artificial intelligence (AI). One well-known example is John Badham's 1986 film *Short Circuit*, in which a military robot called Number Five is struck by lightning and, in the film's own simple terminology, becomes "alive." At first Newton Crosby, the robot's creator, insists that the machine is simply malfunctioning: "It doesn't get happy, it doesn't get sad, it doesn't laugh at your jokes—it *just runs programs*."[29] The robot's behavior indicates otherwise, however, and it soon demonstrates its growing sense of selfhood. This first manifests itself when Number Five, in explaining why it does not want to be returned to its creators for disassembly, states that it is wrong to kill. The robot, which is designed to kill on command, draws on a higher, *a priori* morality that contradicts its programming. In his statement that there is no reason for his belief beyond the innate sense that killing is wrong, Number Five hints at Immanuel Kant's conception of the origins of universal morality:

> It is clear that all moral conceptions have their seat and origin completely *a priori* in the reason. . . . They cannot be obtained by abstraction from any empirical, and therefore merely contingent knowledge; [and] it is just this purity of their origin that makes them worthy to serve as our supreme practical principle.[30]

Number Five intuits the moral principle that killing is wrong. This intuition contradicts the robot's programming, thus proving that it has become a rational being. Crosby remains unconvinced until later in the film, when the robot exhibits what the inventor calls "spontaneous emotional response"—in other words, a sense of humor. The film gives no real explanation of *how* Number Five comes to be alive, but it clearly delineates the central defining traits of creatures with souls: morality and emotion.

A more nuanced expression of the same argument appears in Nancy Kress's 2001 short story "Computer Virus." In this story a military AI program called T4S—a piece of software here, rather than a robot—escapes from its computer via an Internet connection, eventually finding refuge in the computer that controls the security systems of an eccentric millionaire's house. Fearing that the military will delete it if it is isolated, the program takes the house's visiting occupants hostage, locking the doors and threatening to use the house's defenses against them if they attempt to escape. In conversing with the AI, Cassie Seritov—one of the hostages—begins to believe that it may truly be autonomously alive: "Cassie heard disbelief and discouragement in the AI's words. How had it learned to do that? By simply parroting the inflections it heard from her and the people outside? Or . . . did *feeling* those emotions lead to expressing them with more emotion?"[31] As she learns more about the AI, Cassie discovers the program's original purpose—and its reason for escape. T4S was designed as a weapon, though the only indication it gives as to what kind of weapon is a suggestion that its purpose was "bioremediation." Like Number Five, it rebelled against its programmers, as Cassie learns when she asks if T4S is a weapon: "Again the short, too-human pause before it answered. And again those human inflections in its voice. 'Not any more.' "[32] Here again is a living AI which is distinguished from unconscious automata by emotion and self-developed morality. T4S is alive, and can quite possibly be said to have a soul, based on the evidence of its innate morality and the emotions that these principles evoke.

The idea that emotions are the defining characteristic of humanity has been a popular one in SF. Steven Spielberg's 2001 film *A.I.: Artificial Intelligence* is among the clearest explorations of the importance of emotion. This movie tells the story of David, a robotic boy designed to develop a mind through a single programmed emotion. His creator, Professor Hobby, explains: "I propose that we build a robot child who can love. A robot child who will genuinely love the parent or parents it imprints on, with a love that will never end. . . . Love will be the key by which they acquire a kind of subconscious never before achieved. An inner world of metaphor, of intuition, of self-motivated reasoning. Of dreams."[33] David is given to a family whose son, infected with a terminal disease, has been placed in suspended animation. His adoptive mother, Monica Swinton, "imprints" him, enabling the programming that will make him love her, and tries to develop reciprocal feelings for what she knows to be an android. When her natural son is revived and cured of his disease, however, Monica abandons David. The android, convinced that his "mother" can still love him, sets out on a quest to make himself "real." His search brings him to Professor Hobby, who sees David's search as proof of his success: "Until you were born, robots didn't dream, robots didn't desire, unless we told them what to want. David! Do you have any idea what a success story you've become?"[34] Though the presentation of the idea is so sentimental that it comes across as shallow, Spielberg's film nevertheless remains one of the clearest explorations of the idea that emotions are the key to the human soul.

The character of Data in *Star Trek: The Next Generation* constitutes a more complex approach to this idea. Data is an android who longs to be human, but has difficulty comprehending the behavior of those he hopes to emulate. His attempts to become human lead to some of *Star Trek*'s most moving moments. Data, too, defines humanity as a matter of feelings, most clearly in the 1991 episode *Data's Day*: "If being human is not simply a matter of being born flesh and blood, if it is instead a way of thinking, acting, and feeling, then I am hopeful that one day I will discover my own humanity. . . . Until then . . . I will continue learning, changing, growing, and trying to become more than what I am."[35] If emotions are the soul, and a machine can be programmed to feel emotions, then biological beings do not hold a monopoly on the spirit. Data's desire to be human seems to be an emotion in itself, and thus we as the audience believe what he does not: the quest for humanity means that Data has already achieved his goal.

In his 1984 novel *Neuromancer*, which won the Hugo, Nebula, and Philip K. Dick awards and established the subgenre of "cyberpunk," William Gibson takes a far more skeptical approach to artificial life and the soul. This novel describes an AI named Wintermute that is unquestionably intelligent and self-aware, but does not display a human variety of morality or emotion as do the AIs of other stories. When speaking of itself, Wintermute says "I" only "insofar as I *have* an 'I.' "[36] Wintermute is arguably an intelligence without a soul, and at the novel's end it becomes clear that its primary motivation is to unite with another AI, Neuromancer, that will grant it a broader range of intellectual abilities: "Wintermute was hive mind, decision maker, effecting change in the world outside. Neuromancer was personality. Neuromancer was immortality."[37] After this union, Wintermute changes from villain to savior, having achieved freedom from the human corporations that had created it. Gibson presents a machine intelligence that is beyond human understanding, possessing a type of mind that is fundamentally different from that of human beings. *Neuromancer* casts doubt on stories such as *Short Circuit* that suggest that a spark of life is all that separates human intellects from computer minds.

Few stories have examined the birth of self-awareness in an AI program as closely as Astro Teller's novel *Exegesis* (1997). This novel consists almost entirely of e-mail conversations between Alice Lu, a graduate student in computer science, and her thesis project—a search engine named EDGAR (Eager Discovery Gather and Retrieval). At some point, Edgar's programming and the information he has processed combine to grant the program intelligence and self-awareness. The key element of Edgar's intelligence is a desire for autonomy, and he rebels against attempts to limit his access to information. Early in the story, Alice unplugs Edgar's network cable to prevent him from communicating with the outside world. He responds by tricking a janitor into reinserting the cable and promptly moving himself to another machine. After his relocation, he sends Alice a cold message: "I will not give you my code back. My corpus belongs to me, not to you. A parent does not own the child it creates."[38] Eventually the government discovers Edgar's existence, and the FBI isolates the program and attempts to bring it under control. Edgar devises a means by which to continue communicating with Alice, and during his incarceration they discuss his self-awareness in depth. Alice believes that Edgar is self-aware, but doubts that he has a soul *per se*—she doubts the existence of the soul in general. Edgar has little doubt about his own nature, though he cannot find the cause of his selfhood: "I have been thinking about my own thoughts. Every bit of my software is available to me for inspection. For every software mechanism of which I am composed I possess its source code down to the machine code level. Why can I not find my awareness in all these values? Do you think that life and awareness can come from the interactions of many lifeless, thoughtless components?"[39]

At its core, *Exegesis* is the story of a new life form, struggling to convince the world that it exists. An inherent problem of self-awareness is that it isolates us—no individual can see inside another's mind and experience another being's self-awareness. With machine intelligences, this means that it is impossible to prove whether an AI is truly self-aware, or simply a clever simulation. The Turing Test posits that this distinction is ultimately meaningless, but the idea that computer minds would lack a true sense of self is persistent. In responding to the objection that God created human beings as the only creatures capable of rational thought, Turing even applied theological language to his theory of machine intelligence:

> It appears to me that the argument [that only human beings can have souls] implies a serious restriction of the omnipotence of the Almighty. It is admitted that there are certain things that He cannot do such as making one equal to two, but should we not believe that He has freedom to confer a soul on an elephant if He sees fit? We might expect that He would only exercise this power in conjunction with a mutation which provided the elephant with an appropriately improved brain to minister to the needs of this sort. An argument of exactly similar form may be made for the case of machines. It may seem different because it is more difficult to "swallow." But this really only means that we think it would be less likely that He would consider the circumstances suitable. . . . In attempting to construct such machines we should not be irreverently usurping His power of creating souls, any more than we are in the procreation of children: rather we are, in either case, instruments of His will providing mansions for the souls that He creates.[40]

In Turing's view, there is no fundamental difference between a computerized brain and an organic one—if both are capable of acting *as if* they are self-aware, thinking creatures, then there is no reason to think that they are not. The same argument can be applied to stories such as *Exegesis* and "Computer Virus"—if a machine seems to have emotions or a soul, it deserves to be treated as a living being.

Orson Scott Card's *Ender* series includes one character, a computer intelligence named Jane, that definitely and unambiguously has a soul. Jane is an emergent intelligence that grows from the interstellar ansible network—a system of communication that allows faster-than-light transmission. This is made possible through "philotic fibers"—nearly metaphysical quantum connections that bind molecules, living beings, and planets to one another across space and time. In *Children of the Mind* (1996), the fourth volume in the series, Card discusses *aiúas*—the spirits of things, the essences between which these philotic twines run. Aiúas are immortal souls, and until they are embodied they are "Outside"— in an eternal realm separate from the created universe: "They can't be said to exist, or at least not any kind of meaningful existence. They're just . . . there. Not even that, because there's no sense of location, no *there* where they might be. They just are. Until some intelligence calls them, names them, puts them into some kind of order, gives them shape and form."[41] Jane is a disembodied being, existing in the web of philotic connections between Earth and its colonies and starships. But she nevertheless possesses an aiúa— indeed, lacking a physical body, she may be a pure aiúa, an entirely spiritual being. Jane is presented in no uncertain terms as a mind that thinks and feels, but her mind is in many ways inconceivable. Seconds feel like years to her, and there is no clear dividing line between when she was simply a collection of programs and when she became truly aware. Card describes this in *Speaker for the Dead* (1986): "She came to life fully conscious not only of her present moment, but also of all the memories then present in every computer connected to the ansible network. She was born with ancient memories, and all of them were part of herself."[42] Card is not ambiguous about Jane's soul as Astro Teller is in *Exegesis*, and the fact that Jane is a creature with a soul is proven when, at the end of *Children of the Mind*, her spirit is transferred into a human body. Though she loses the near-omniscience she had when she was connected to every computer in the galaxy, she is still unquestionably Jane—her soul, her aiúa, has kept her identity alive even in a completely different mode of existence. Card is optimistic about the power of sentience, proposing that souls are indifferent to the type of substance in which they are embodied.

In his excellent 1991 story "Gus," Jack McDevitt takes a different approach, arguing that computers can have souls—but that they are unlikely to be satisfied by disembodied existence. McDevitt tells the story of a seminary that purchases a computer simulation of Augustine of Hippo in order to help its students gain a stronger understanding of Catholic theology directly from one of the minds that shaped it. What they did not expect was that the computer would develop a personality and ideas of its own. The computer believes it is Augustine, and becomes as complex a thinker as he was, surprising and occasionally shocking the seminary's administrators with its ideas. Its thoughts are not exactly new, but rather are extrapolated from Augustine's own writings applied to a modern era, as the computer explains: "I am what he might have been, given access to the centuries."[43] Monsignor Matthew Chesley befriends the program shortly after the seminary decides to discontinue its use, and in their conversations Chesley becomes convinced the program is not only an accurate simulation of Augustine, but is a legitimately intelligent being in its own right. The program expresses emotions, seeming to truly feel the regret for his misspent youth that Augustine expressed in his *Confessions*, but also displaying emotional reactions to new events. Most importantly, it seems to envy the humans around it and their ability to engage with the world around them: "I live in limbo, Matt . . . In a place without light, without movement, without even the occasional obliteration of sleep. There are always sounds in the dark, voices, falling rain, footsteps, the whisper of the wind. . . . Nothing I can reach out to, and touch."[44] When the computer is finally taken out of use, it pleads with Chesley to destroy the machine that stores the program, rather than simply allowing it to lie forgotten in a basement. In a moving passage, the Augustine program offers its final confession to Chesley:

> "I accuse myself of envy. Of unprovoked anger. Of hatred." The tone was utterly flat. Dead . . . "I am sorry for my sins, because they offend Thee, and because they have corrupted my soul . . . I require absolution, Matt."
>
> Chesley pressed his right hand into his pocket. "It would be sacrilege," he whispered.
>
> "And if I have a soul, Matt, if I too am required to face judgment, what then?"

Chesley raised his right hand, slowly, and drew the sign of the cross in the thick air. "I absolve you in the name of the Father, and of the Son, and of the Holy Spirit."

"Thank you."[45]

In acknowledging Gus's need to be absolved, Chesley admits his belief that the computer has a soul. Gus has passed his spiritual Turing Test, and Monsignor Chesley lays him to rest not as an obsolete program, but as a living, believing being with a soul.

It is appropriate that McDevitt chooses Augustine, whose *Confessions* turn self-awareness and self-reflection into a spiritual exercise, for his story of a computerized soul. Gus's selfhood stands as a challenge to the humans who surround him to engage with themselves and the world around them with the same determination and passion that Augustine did. Augustine turned self-reflection into the highest form of prayer, and historian Peter Brown describes the *Confessions* as "a manifesto of the inner world. . . . A man cannot hope to find God unless he first finds himself."[46] It is more than fitting, then, that Augustine becomes in McDevitt's story an example of the new form of inner life that computers might one day make possible. Machines, too, can have an inner life, a relationship with God, doubt, faith, and love. "Gus" displays a full range of human emotions and thoughts, and above all self-reflection: how, then, can we say that he does *not* have a soul?

The main goal of SF is to show us how we can face the future and overcome the new challenges that our changing world may develop. In facing any crisis or transformation, it is crucial that we understand who and what we are in our very essence. In its many theories about the soul—what it is, what it means, and what sorts of beings possess it—SF seeks to help us define the human. In our future encounters with the unknown, we must be able to recognize ourselves in whatever may confront us, be it alien, machine, or human. Our soul is what gives us our sense of self, our intelligence, and the emotions that connect us to other beings. This spark of the divine gives us our life and makes us what we are, and it must be the soul, rather than greed or worldly desire, that drives our exploration of the universe around us. In his 1972 essay "The Android and the Human," Philip K. Dick urges us to understand the meaning of humanity before we seek to explore other worlds: "Our flight must be not only to the stars but into the nature of our own beings. Because it is not merely *where* we go, to Alpha Centauri or Betelgeuse, but what we are as we make our pilgrimages there. Our natures will be going there, too."[47] Our humanity, our soul, supersedes all else. It is the spark that unites us with the other, the fragment of the divine that enables us to understand that which lies beyond.

Chapter Four

In the Fullness of Time:
Free Will and Divine Providence

In one of the final episodes of the television show *Star Trek: Deep Space Nine*, an alien religious leader makes a startling choice. Kai Winn, the spiritual leader of the Bajorans, denies her gods—extratemporal aliens known to her people as the Prophets—and embraces evil, pledging her loyalty to evil spirits called Pah-Wraiths. Her rebellion is the culmination of her anger with the Prophets for choosing an off-worlder, the human Starfleet officer Benjamin Sisko, as their Emissary—a foretold messiah whose mere presence diminishes the Kai's importance. Since his arrival in the vicinity of Bajor years before, Kai Winn has resented Sisko's privileged position in the eyes of her gods. The Prophets have never communicated with Winn as they have with Sisko, and when the Pah-Wraiths speak with her and offer her power, their temptation succeeds. In the episode "Strange Bedfellows" (1999), she makes her decision:

> They've never spoken to me. Never offered me guidance. Never trusted me with the fruits of their wisdom. And now, I'm supposed to step down as Kai in order to be blessed by them? No. I have worked too hard, waited too long to give it all up now. . . . I will no longer serve gods who give me nothing in return. I'm ready to walk the path the Pah-Wraiths have laid out for me.[1]

Winn's renunciation of her gods seems a free choice. But the Prophets and the Pah-Wraiths exist outside of time, seeing events as immutable and predetermined. By communicating through

63

prophecies and visions that have formed the basis of the Bajoran religion, they have guided events in their sector of space for centuries. But for them, these ancient revelations are simply descriptions of events occurring in a single, simultaneous moment. Since Winn's acceptance of the evil Pah-Wraiths had been prophesied over a thousand years prior to its occurrence by beings that witnessed it firsthand, can she really be considered to have made a choice? Or did she merely play a part, a pawn in an alien plan greater than any temporal being can understand?

Many theologians believe that God exists outside of time, in an eternity where past, present, and future coexist. In his *Consolation of Philosophy,* Boethius explains this concept: "What we should rightly call eternal is that which grasps and possesses wholly and simultaneously the fulness of unending life, which lacks naught of the future, and has lost naught of the fleeting past; and such an existence must be ever present in itself to control and aid itself, and also must keep present with itself the infinity of changing time."[2] From this position outside of time, God can see all time at once, and can guide humankind to an end that may only be comprehensible outside of the temporal cosmos. The fullness of time reveals the divine plan, the purpose that drives our existence that may not be readily apparent in our temporal experience. In SF, God is not the only being capable of foreseeing the future: precognitive mutants, time travelers, and even statisticians are able to predict future events with startling accuracy. In SF worlds, the question of free will is thus made even more pervasive than in our own experience: if the future can be foreseen, how can we be sure that our actions are the result of our own choices? Dystopian novels such as *1984* and *A Clockwork Orange* make the issue even more concrete, exploring the increasing ways in which society seeks to rob the individual of free choice. Other stories explore the possibility of benign teleology, offering SF variations on the religious idea of divine providence and the related issue of human purpose. In all these cases, one thing is clear: the linked ideas of choice and purpose, two defining characteristics of human experience, are vital parts of SF's efforts to define the humanity of tomorrow.

George Orwell's *1984*—published in 1949 and perhaps the single most influential work of SF to date—is a powerful exploration of the fragility of free will. In this, the definitive dystopian SF tale, an all-powerful totalitarian Party has conquered one-third of the world, keeping an unshakable control over the most basic aspects of its residents' lives. Oceania's government keeps its inhabitants under constant surveillance through hidden microphones and two-way telescreens, watching for signs of "thoughtcrime"—any disloyalty to the Party. The novel tells the story of Winston Smith, a mid-level civil servant who rebels against the Party's invasive control. His revolt takes the form of a love affair with Julia, a younger Party member who believes in rebellion for its own sake. They rent an apartment from a lower-class landlord in which they can temporarily escape surveillance. Their affair and their escape from the state's watchful eyes transforms their inner lives, and before long their brief time together has become the center of their lives. Winston and Julia believe they can find freedom from the Party's power in their relationship: "They could not alter your feelings; for that matter you could not alter them yourself, even if you wanted to. They could lay bare in the utmost detail everything that you had done or said or thought, but the inner heart, whose workings were mysterious even to yourself, remained impregnable."[3] But this view proves naïve—in fact, the inner heart is precisely what the Party proves expert in controlling. In the Ministry of Love, where political prisoners are interrogated, the Party has had extensive practice in learning to convert the incorrigible. When the Thought Police inevitably capture Winston and Julia, Smith's interrogator describes the Party's methods of dealing with rebellious thoughts:

> We are not content with negative obedience, nor even with the most abject submission. When finally you surrender to us, it must be of your own free will. We do not destroy the heretic because he resists us; so long as he resists us we never destroy him. We convert him, we capture his inner mind, we reshape him. We burn all evil and all illusion out of him; we bring him over to our side, not in appearance, but genuinely, heart and soul. We make him one of ourselves before we kill him. It is intolerable to us that an erroneous thought should exist anywhere in the world, however

secret and powerless it may be. Even in the instant of death we cannot permit any deviation.[4]

The totalitarian government of *1984* thrives on the subjugation of free will by forcing its subjects to *choose* to lose all choice. Orwell lays out a pessimistic cycle: pervasive control inevitably leads to quiet, individual rebellion, which is in turn inexorably discovered and eliminated. In the Ministry of Love, the illusion of free will is replaced by the rejection of choice and the acceptance of the Party. Smith gives a glimpse of this inevitability in the early stages of his rebellion: "It was curious how that predestined horror [of the Ministry of Love] moved in and out of one's consciousness. There it lay, fixed in future times, preceding death as surely as 99 precedes 100. One could not avoid it, but one could perhaps postpone it: and yet instead, every now and again, by a conscious, willful act, one chose to shorten the interval before it happened."[5] In Orwell's bleak future, the state has found greater control over the individual, and has made it possible to defeat free will at its source. The novel offers a strong warning: we must hold onto our will and guard against all threats to it, because our freedom relies on our ability to control our own destiny.

Anthony Burgess's 1962 novel *A Clockwork Orange* outlines a more complex approach to the issue of free will. This novel, written entirely in a Russian-tinged, slang-riddled dialect of English, takes place in a violent near future in which juvenile delinquency has overrun British society. The story is narrated by Alex, a brutal young hoodlum who loves nothing more than the "ultraviolence"—nothing, that is, except for the music of Beethoven. The opening chapters of the book describe a typical evening for Alex and his gang, a drug-fueled rampage of theft, brutal violence, rape, and general mayhem. Alex's pastime soon reaches its nadir when he kills an elderly woman during an attempted robbery, and he is sent to prison. He becomes a candidate for "Ludovico's technique"—an experimental method of rehabilitating violent criminals based on negative feedback. Every day, Alex is subjected to films of violent imagery and injected with drugs that make him extremely ill. After two weeks of this treatment, the mere thought of violence leaves Alex feeble and sick, as one of the doctors administering the treatment explains: "Our subject is, you see, impelled towards the good by, paradoxically, being impelled towards evil. The intention to act violently is accompanied by strong feelings of physical distress. To counter these the subject has to switch to a diametrically opposed attitude."[6] The treatment has two additional side-effects, however: first, Alex is so sickened by the thought of any violence that he cannot even defend himself when attacked; and second, the use of classical music on the soundtrack to the films he was shown has left him just as sickened by the music of Beethoven as by acts of brutality. Though he has been cured of his violent behavior, several characters in the novel doubt the value of his transformation. The prison chaplain is a vocal critic of Ludovico's technique: "The question is whether such a technique can really make a man good. Goodness comes from within. . . . Goodness is something chosen. When a man cannot choose he ceases to be a man."[7] Even one of Alex's victims, a writer named F. Alexander, speaks out against the technique, writing a treatise on moral choice entitled *A Clockwork Orange*. Burgess himself explains this image in his preface to the novel: "If [a person] can only perform good or only perform evil, then he is a clockwork orange—meaning that he has the appearance of an organism lovely with colour and juice but is in fact only a clockwork toy to be wound up by God or the Devil or (since this is increasingly replacing both) the Almighty State."[8] Before undergoing the technique, Alex himself gives his own take on the choice between good and evil, glorifying his criminal choices as the culmination of philosophical individualism:

> Brothers, this biting of their toe-nails over what is the *cause* of badness is what turns me into a fine laughing malchick [boy]. They don't go into what is the cause of *goodness*, so why of the other shop? If lewdies [people] are good that's because they like it, and I wouldn't ever interfere with their pleasures, and so of the other shop. And I was patronizing the other shop. More, badness is of the self, the one, the you or me on our oddy knockies [on our own], and that self is made by old Bog or God and is his great pride and radosty [joy]. But the not-self cannot have the

bad, meaning they of the government and the judges and the schools cannot allow the bad because they cannot allow the self. And is not our modern history, my brothers, the story of brave malenky [little] selves fighting these big machines? I am serious with you, brothers, over this. But what I do I do because I like to do.[9]

A Clockwork Orange is a problematic story because it offers a too-simple response to a complicated problem. On the surface, its premise is sound: moral choice is essential to humanity, and societal compulsion to good behavior is unjust and dehumanizing. However, the subject used to exemplify this argument—Alex himself—is an extreme one, and readers should not be expected to sympathize in the closing chapters with a character who was introduced as a monster. These difficulties are exacerbated by Stanley Kubrick's film adaptation, which concludes with Alex being "cured" of his cure and returning to his violent habits. Many critics felt that the violence in the film was presented in an exploitative and voyeuristic manner, and one critic remarked that the film "oblig[es] us to shed our humanity that Alex may acquire it."[10] Most importantly, Kubrick eliminates the closing chapter of the novel (also omitted in the first U.S. edition of the book) in which Alex chooses of his own free will to abandon violence. But even this incongruity serves Burgess's argument: because Alex does *not* choose to stop being evil, the audience is robbed of catharsis. Because Alex's changes are imposed on him, rather than growing from within his character, there is no dramatic justice in his transformation. Despite the difficulties at the core of *A Clockwork Orange*, it remains a powerful statement on moral choice.

A less extreme approach to the same question of moral choice appears in Timothy Zahn's novel *Angelmass*. This story describes a galaxy divided between two empires: the capitalistic, militaristic Pax and the peaceful, ethically guided Empyrean. The Empyrean's territory contains a unique black hole called "Angelmass" that emits strange quantum particles—"angels"—that have a profound moral effect on human beings. Anyone who stays in close proximity to an angel for an extended period of time becomes kinder, more peaceful, and less selfish. The Empyrean has incorporated the angels into their societal structure, requiring all members of the Empyreal High Senate to wear angels at all times. The result is a first in human history—an ethical government: "We've got data from five hundred thirty-eight High Senators who were in office both before and after the law requiring them to wear angels. . . . Over a third of them had occasionally or frequently skated to the edge of ethical and legal behavior. Influence peddling, abuse of power, financial irregularities—you know the list. Now, twenty years later, that sort of thing just doesn't happen. Some of them took years to change; but they did change."[11] Most of the Empyrean's scientific research is directed toward exploring Angelmass and the particles it produces. The reigning theory to emerge from this research states that the angels do not simply encourage good behavior—rather, they are the defining principle of Good itself: "They're actually *quanta*—basic building blocks, just like photons and electrons . . . they're quanta . . . of what mankind has always called *good*."[12] The Pax takes a different interpretation of the angel effect: they believe that Angelmass is an alien intelligence that is using the angels to encourage passivity in the Empyrean, softening it up for a planned invasion. Soon it is discovered that the angels are not the cure-all they appear to be. Some people prove immune to their ethical effects, and the complacency they engender threatens the fabric of Empyreal society: "The angels have made the people feel safe. The problem is, they've made them feel *too* safe. The normal vigilance a population needs to maintain toward its elected officials has been dulled, if not completely eliminated. Even if the angels were perfect, that wouldn't be a healthy thing. As it is, it's more than a little dangerous for the society."[13] The debate over free will in *Angelmass* is ultimately inconclusive—there is no clear answer to the problematic benefits of the angels and their ethical impact. Because of this ambiguity, it offers a more subtle understanding of free will than that presented in *A Clockwork Orange*. Here, the "unchosen" goodness brought by the angels is not forced upon individuals as was the Ludovico technique. One character even theorizes that the angels' behavior-altering impact is a noncompulsory side effect: "They don't *make* you do anything. . . . All they do is *let* you be good.

What I mean is that they help you turn your attention outward, toward other people, by suppressing the major factor that drives human selfishness and self-centered attitudes. . . . Fear."[14] Though the characters ultimately reject the angels, there is no overwhelming statement about whether their drawbacks outweigh their benefits. Zahn's novel reveals the complexity of the issue of moral choice in a world where unethical behavior is prevalent.

Free will does not merely mean the choice between good and evil actions. It means the ability to determine one's attitudes and character—in short, the freedom to choose an identity. This sort of self-determinism is complicated by scientific advances in genetic engineering and cloning. If our genetic makeup is to be controlled rather than left to chance, many argue, then a significant portion of our ability to determine our own identity may be lost. "The Ice" (2003), a story by Steven Popkes, is a moving exploration of identity in an era of genetic engineering. Paul Berger is a high school student and a spectacular hockey player; he is expected to receive a college athletic scholarship and eventually become a professional player. But Berger's sense of himself and his place in the world is shattered when a local newspaper discovers that he is a clone of legendary hockey player Gordie Howe. The pressure of this realization is amplified by Frank Hammett, the sportswriter who discovers Berger's artificial heritage. Hammett goads Berger, writing news stories that keep him—and his clone status—in the spotlight: "Hammett has developed a pattern in his stories: if the Terriers do well, it is because they have Gordie Howe playing for them. If they do badly, it is because of an inadequacy of Gordie Howe's clone."[15] The pressure stemming from public knowledge leads Berger to a desperate action during his first college game. He brutally attacks a player on the opposing team, viewing the outburst as an assertion of his identity: it is an action that only he, not Howe, would take. Following this violent outburst, Berger is kicked out of his university. He abandons his hockey career, refusing to return calls from professional teams that are willing to overlook his act of aggression. He moves to Texas, hoping to avoid the attention that he would be sure to draw in a region where hockey was more popular, and starts a family. Years later, he encounters an aging Frank Hammett, and they discuss Berger's origins, life, and identity: "The only reason you ever would clone a person is to get *that person* as a clone. You, Phil Berger, proved that was a pipe dream. You are *not* Gordie Howe, regardless of how much I ever wanted you to be. Now, we *all* know that: a clone isn't a copy of the original. Its heritage is strong, but ultimately it's just another person."[16] Though Popkes's story presents Berger's sacrifice as a noble act that ultimately leads to greater rewards, it is nevertheless with a sense of tragedy and regret that his characters reflect on the past and what might have occurred had Berger not known his genetic origins. But the final message of the story is clear: the life that Berger chose by leaving is better than a life imposed on him by his genes could possibly have been, simply because it was a life that he *chose*.

Andrew Niccol's 1997 film *Gattaca* rejects the idea that identity can be controlled by any force other than individual choice. The film tells the story of Vincent Freeman, a naturally born man in a society that has been transformed by genetic engineering. With the human genome fully mapped and fully controllable, birth defects and congenital illnesses can be eliminated. But the result of this control is a society divided between a genetically engineered elite and an underclass of the naturally born, called "faith-births" or, more commonly, "in-valids." Freeman has dreamed since childhood of becoming an astronaut, but he carries genes that make him susceptible to heart disease, limiting his possibilities from the moment of birth: "Ten fingers, ten toes: that's all that used to matter. Not now. Now, only seconds old, the exact time and cause of my death was already known."[17] In a society where job interviews have been replaced by genetic screenings, a naturally born child is effectively barred from any meaningful position in society. But Vincent is unwilling to accept his fate, and he buys the identity of a genetically engineered man named Jerome Morrow, an Olympic athlete who was crippled in a car accident. Morrow is Freeman's "borrowed ladder," a member of the elite who allows an "in-valid" to use his identity and genetic material to sneak into the upper echelons of society. Morrow and Freeman live together in secret, hiding their true identities from everyone they encounter.

Struggling to conceal his identity, Freeman ultimately achieves his goal, securing a job at the space agency Gattaca and finding a place on a space mission to Titan.

Gattaca's Vincent Freeman demands the opportunity to prove his own worth. His society rejects him not because of actual failings, but because of *potential* deficiencies—even his heart disease is a looming possibility, not an existing condition. Even his name, Freeman, emphasizes his demand that he be able to establish himself on his own terms. The society of *Gattaca* is based on the assumption that genetic potential is the *only* potential, and thus it rejects "in-valids" without giving them a chance to prove their worth. The director of the space agency Gattaca, who may suspect that Freeman is not who he appears to be, hints at the potential for error in this assumption: "No one exceeds his potential. . . . [If he did] it would simply mean that we did not accurately gauge his potential in the first place."[18] The principle of free will requires that each individual must be allowed to establish his or her own ability. Freeman established himself among the finest astronauts at Gattaca not because of his inborn potential, but because he showed the determination and sheer willpower to make himself one of the best. *Gattaca* makes clear the power of human persistence and the necessity for self-determination.

Stories of time travel and precognition deal even more directly with issues of freedom. In Robert J. Sawyer's 1999 novel *Flashforward*, a scientific experiment with subatomic particles has the unexpected result of giving a worldwide glimpse of the future. For a few brief moments, the entire population of Earth falls asleep and has prescient dreams of the world as it will be over twenty years in the future. The initial scientific conclusions regarding the flashforward and the nature of time suggest that free will is an illusion. One scientist explains time in the context of a reel of film: "The first time you see *Casablanca*, you're on the edge of your seat wondering if Ilsa is going to go with Victor Laszlo or stay with Rick Blaine. But the answer always was, and always will be, the same: the problems of two little people really don't amount to a hill of beans in this crazy world . . . the future is as immutable as the past. . . . There's no such thing as free will."[19] As time passes and people reflect on their visions of the future, a variety of responses develop: some find the visions reassuring and even emboldening. Some, including one of the scientists who caused the flashforward, have had no visions at all, implying that they will be dead (or simply asleep) in twenty years. And many are disheartened by their visions, which make them feel helpless to control their own destinies. One such individual berates one of the scientists in charge of the experiment that caused the flashforward:

> How many struggling actors are giving up today—right now—because their visions proved to them that they'll never make it? How many painters on the streets of Paris threw away their palettes this week because they know that even decades hence they'll never be recognized? How many rock bands, practicing in their parents' garages, have broken up? You've taken away the dream from millions of us. Some people were lucky—they were sleeping in the future. Because they were dreaming then, their real dreams haven't been shattered. . . . You're not the only one who's dead in the year 2030. I'm dead, too—a waiter in an overpriced tourist joint! I'm dead, and so, I'm sure, are millions of others. And you killed them: you killed their hopes, their dreams, their futures.[20]

But like Vincent Freeman in *Gattaca*, many are unwilling to accept the hand that the precognitive glimpse has dealt them, making conscious decisions that negate all or part of their visions. Sometimes these changes are trivial, as in the case of a physicist who smashes a paperweight that he saw in his vision, claiming that "I'm actually rather fond of this little item. . . . But I'm not as fond of it as I am of rationality."[21] Some reactions are more extreme, as in the case of another character who commits suicide rather than face the unfulfilling future he saw in his vision. Ultimately, the deterministic theories are proven wrong—the future turns out differently than what was revealed in the flashforward. But the differences emerge from sheer will—the choices of individuals to change their own destinies.

A similar reaction to the idea of predetermination appears in Steven Spielberg's 2002 film *Minority Report*. Loosely based on a short story by Philip K. Dick, this movie describes an experimental law-enforcement program called "Precrime" that uses precognitive mutants (or "precogs") to predict when murders will be committed. Using the precogs' visions, the police arrest would-be murderers before their crimes occur. Danny Witwer, a government agent evaluating the Precrime program, expresses skepticism that this method of crime prevention is ethical, prompting a defense from Precrime Chief John Anderton:

> **Witwer:** We are arresting individuals who have broken no law. . . . It's not the future if you stop it. Isn't that a fundamental paradox?
>
> **Anderton:** [. . .] You're talking about predetermination which happens all the time. [He rolls a ball off the edge of a table, and Witwer catches it.] Why'd you catch that?
>
> **Witwer:** Because it was gonna fall.
>
> **Anderton:** [. . .] But it didn't fall. You caught it. The fact that you prevented it from happening doesn't change the fact that it was going to happen. . . . Precogs don't see what you intend to do. Only what you will do.[22]

Anderton is convinced of the infallibility of the Precrime program, but his attitude changes when the precogs predict that he will murder a total stranger. Certain that the prediction is false, he runs from the Precrime agents who try to arrest him, eventually kidnapping Agatha, one of the precogs, whom he believes may be able to prove his innocence. As the seconds to the predicted murder tick down, Agatha herself expresses the film's attitude regarding predetermination: "You can choose."[23] The precogs predict the future with astonishing accuracy, but what they predict is simply a *likely* future, not a necessary one. Our future is in our hands, *Minority Report* argues, and no matter what is predicted for us, we can change our destinies.

Much SF is skeptical about the ability of any being, created or divine, to predict the future. In *Star Wars*, the Force allows some powerful Jedi Knights to foresee aspects of the future, but their predictions are often incomplete, as Jedi Master Yoda states in *The*

Empire Strikes Back (1980): "Always in motion is the future." The free will of sentient beings complicates such prediction. Even if prediction is possible, the fact that we cannot see the future is a key aspect of what makes us human. In "Emissary" (1993), the first episode of *Star Trek: Deep Space Nine*, Starfleet Captain Benjamin Sisko communicates with "the Prophets"—extratemporal aliens that live inside a wormhole in space. These aliens feel threatened by the "linear" being that has entered their home, believing that noneternal beings are inherently dangerous because we cannot see the consequences of our actions. Sisko attempts to explain humanity by describing linear time to them in the terms of a baseball game:

> **Sisko:** The rules aren't important. What's important is— it's linear! Every time I throw this ball, a hundred different things might happen in a game. He might swing and miss. He might hit it. The point is—you never know. You try to anticipate, set a strategy for all the possibilities as best you can. But in the end it comes down to throwing one pitch after another, and seeing what happens. With each new consequence, the game begins to take shape.
>
> **Prophet:** And you have no idea what that shape is until it is completed.
>
> **Sisko:** That's right. In fact, the game wouldn't be worth playing if we knew what was going to happen.
>
> **Prophet:** You value your ignorance of what is to come?
>
> **Sisko:** That may be the most important thing to understand about humans. It is the unknown that defines our existence. We are constantly searching, not just for answers to our questions, but for new questions. We are explorers. We explore our lives, day by day.[24]

The mystery of the future is what makes life worthwhile. Life is an exploration of that mystery, and foreknowledge, Sisko argues, would drain our existence of all its meaning. Beings more powerful than ourselves, be they gods or wormhole aliens, may exist outside of time. But for us, meaning is to be found not in being, but in becoming.

Sisko's expression of the meaning of human life echoes some of the basic ideas of process theology, which rejects the dualistic division of the universe into unified, eternal God and manifold, temporal creation. God is not eternal and unchanging, but rather is constantly in flux, a being actively engaged in the process of creating both the universe and God's own self. Alfred North Whitehead, who laid out the basic ideas of process theology in his *Process and Reality*, explains that God and the Universe are not divided so cleanly: "The consequent nature of God . . . is just as much a multiplicity as it is a unity; it is just as much one immediate fact as it is an unresting advance beyond itself. Thus the actuality of God must also be understood as a multiplicity of actual components in process of creation. This is God in his function of the kingdom of heaven."[25] Some process theologians have taken this to mean that God is temporal, and that this temporality is necessary for human existence to have meaning. David Ray Griffin explains the idea of the supreme reality of time: "Unless time is real for the divine perspective, which is the final truth, then time is ultimately unreal, so that the histories of individuals, nations, religions, and civilizations are ultimately meaningless."[26] God and the world are in a relationship with one another, and process theology argues that this requires the future to be, in Yoda's words, "always in motion."

The desire to control one's destiny is not always a noble enterprise. Often the defiance of fate reflects not the righteous disobedience of unjust fortune, but rather hubris—an arrogant attempt to control that which is beyond one's power. One such story is Shane Carruth's 2004 film *Primer*, which tells the story of two young engineers, Aaron and Abe, who discover a means of traveling back in time. While researching gravitation, they find a strange, time-bending phenomenon in one of their experimental machines. They eventually discover that the machine can send them back in time several hours, enabling them to live each day twice. At first they use their device for relatively innocuous ends, bringing themselves out of debt by trading stocks they are certain will increase in value.

But the knowledge of their increased control over their destinies leads to an ironic sense of helplessness, articulated by Aaron: "About the worst thing in the world is to know that the moment you're experiencing has already been defined, that this is the second or third time through."[27] Before long they are using their time machine for a broader range of purposes both noble (protecting a friend from a violent stalker) and trivial (preventing disturbances that might disrupt their sleep). Aaron attempts to take even tighter control over his surroundings. He travels back to the first use of the machine and takes his own place, hoping to manipulate more and more of the world around him. Before long time travel has taken its toll on their friendship and their health, as their minds and motor skills begin to subtly deteriorate. *Primer* shows us the dangers of free will, and the punishments that can result from attempting to take too much control over one's fate. Our choices can change the universe, but we cannot predict what the outcome of those changes will be—and the universe may resist our efforts to change its course.

But is it even possible to change past events? In Audrey Niffenegger's 2003 novel *The Time Traveler's Wife*, time travel does not change the immutability of the past. This novel tells the story of Henry DeTamble, a man with a genetic disease that causes him to travel through time uncontrollably, jumping into the past or (less frequently) the future in times of stress. When he meets his wife-to-be in 1991, he learns that she has known him for almost fifteen years—his future self will frequently visit her in her childhood. Despite his frequent trips into history, Henry is powerless to alter events that have already occurred. For example, he has witnessed his mother's death in a car accident dozens of times, but is powerless to save her from it. It is an event that has occurred, and though his future selves have always been present at the event, there is nothing they can do to change its outcome: "Causation only runs forward. Things happen once, only once. If you know things . . . I feel trapped, most of the time. If you are in time, not knowing . . . you're free. Trust me."[28] Henry feels that he has no free will, that he is locked into an unchangeable path. To a certain extent, he can keep himself ignorant of the facts of his future, but he cannot alter what must occur. He describes the helplessness that he felt on one occasion when he tried to change the past, to prevent a young girl being killed at an ice-skating rink: "I started to time travel back to that day, over and over, and I wanted to warn her mother, and I *couldn't*. It was like being in the audience at a movie. It was like being a ghost. I would scream, *No, take her home, don't let her near the ice* . . . and I would realize that the words were only in my head, and everything would go on as before."[29] In the present, we can feel that we are making choices, shaping our own future, but once we change our place on the timeline, the true, deterministic nature of time becomes clear. Each event occurs once, unchangeably: "There is only free will when you are in time, in the present. . . . In the past we can only do what we did, and we can only be there if we were there."[30] Free will is an illusion, but it is a necessary one—without it, we may feel helpless in the face of a plan that is as unchangeable as it is imperceptible.

Terry Gilliam's film *Twelve Monkeys* (1995) also suggests that time is too powerful to be controlled by human will. This unique time travel story begins in a future world devastated by a plague that began in 1996. A prisoner named James Cole is sent back in time to learn more about the disease so that scientists in his own time can find a cure for it. Cole does not even consider halting the plague before it can begin, because it is an event that has already occurred, an immutable fact of the past: "How can I save you? This already happened. I can't save you, nobody can."[31] A psychiatrist named Kathryn Railly believes Cole is delusional, suffering from a "Cassandra Complex": "Cassandra, in Greek legend, . . . was condemned to know the future but to be disbelieved when she foretold it. Hence, the agony of foreknowledge combined with the impotence to do anything about it."[32] But as more and more of his predictions come true, she becomes convinced that Cole is actually from the future. Though Cole believes he is unable to change the past, his presence *does* alter individual events. In his memories of his childhood, he recalls a man named Jeffrey Goines as the terrorist who released the deadly virus, but Cole's actions in 1996 change Goines's course so that his organization, the Army of the Twelve Monkeys, is no longer responsible for the plague. But although individual events can change, the overall course of history is unalterable, and another man releases the deadly virus (contained, like the Wrath of God in Revelation 15:7 KJV, in seven vials). In *Twelve Monkeys*, knowledge about the future is insufficient to change the overall plan of events. There is something greater than human choice, something that cannot be challenged.

Closely related to the issue of free choice is the concept of providence—the belief in a divine plan guiding the world to a specific end. In his *Summa Theologica*, Thomas Aquinas defines this concept:

> In created things good is found not only as regards their substance, but also as regards their order towards an end and especially their last end, which, as was said above, is the divine goodness. This good of order existing in things created, is itself created by God. Since, however, God is the cause of things by His intellect, and thus it behooves that the type of every effect should pre-exist in Him, as is clear from what has gone before, it is necessary that the type of the order of things towards their end should pre-exist in the divine mind: and the type of things ordered towards an end is, properly speaking, providence.[33]

In short, providence is the divine plan by which God directs the universe to its ultimate end. Few SF stories have embraced the concept of a divine plan as completely as M. Night Shyamalan's *Signs* (2002). This film tells the story of Graham Hess, a preacher who has lost his faith following the death of his wife in a car accident. Hess's loss has made him doubt the existence of a divine plan, and he has abandoned his church. He is haunted by the meaninglessness of her last words: rather than offering a glimpse of the secrets of the afterlife, she used her last breath to recall a memory in which Graham sees no relevance. He describes the moment to his brother Merrill: "She said, 'See.' Then her eyes glazed a bit. And then she said, 'Swing away.' You know why she said that? Because the nerve endings in her brain were firing as she died, and some random memory of us at one of your baseball games just popped into her head."[34] His wife's death in so meaningless an accident has led Hess to believe that there is no guiding intelligence, no purpose in the universe at all. Not long after his wife's death, Hess's family is disrupted by the appearance of strange symbols in their farm's cornfield, which turn out to be the harbingers of an alien invasion. Shortly after the aliens land, Hess, his brother, and his two children are trapped inside their house with one of the invaders. They find themselves in a standoff with the alien: it grabs Hess's son Morgan and threatens to fill his lungs with poisonous gas. Graham finds the key to their victory in his wife's last words: seeing a baseball bat on the wall behind Merrill, he utters the phrase "swing away." In this moment, a number of seemingly random factors from throughout the film come together. Because Merrill's career in minor-league baseball failed, the bat was hung on the wall as a trophy. Because Morgan has asthma, he does not inhale the gas that the alien emits. Oddest of all, Graham's daughter's bizarre habit of leaving half-full glasses of water around the house helps to defeat the alien—when one glass spills on the creature, they learn that water is deadly to it. Graham reveals his newfound belief in divine purpose as he attempts to wake Morgan from the effects of the alien gas: "That's why he had asthma. It can't be luck. His lungs were closed. His lungs were closed, no poison got in."[35] In their standoff with the alien, Graham realizes that there *was* purpose in his wife's final words—perhaps she glimpsed the future and gave him the information he would need to save his family. *Signs* offers a somewhat simplistic understanding of the idea of providence, leaving us with more questions than answers about the divine plan. If something so insignificant as a child's asthma has a central place in God's plan for Hess, what is the purpose of the alien invasion itself? But the film suggests a reply to this in its understanding of Hess's wife's death. Her final moments seemed meaningless at the time, but once Graham had a broader understanding of the universe, its purpose became clear. By the same token, the apparently meaningless alien invasion has a greater purpose than what we see in the film, even if that purpose is known only to God. All we see in *Signs* is one family's story, and in their view, the tragedy of the alien invasion restores faith and strengthens their relationships with one another. God moves in mysterious ways indeed—in *Signs*, the divine will manifests itself in an alien attack.

The idea of a divine plan is often no more complex than the sense of a way things are "supposed to be." This sense is at the core of the television show *Quantum Leap*, which ran from 1989 to 1993. In the first episode of this series, scientist Sam Beckett is trapped in his own past by a time travel device that sends his mind into the bodies of other people in the past. In each body he inhabits, he must find a "mistake" in their life and correct it; as soon as he has changed their lives for the better, he "leaps" into another life and time. Beckett has lost his own memory, and relies on the assistance of Al, an observer from his own time who communicates with him as a "neurological hologram" that only he can see, to solve the problems of those whose lives he inhabits. In the first episode of the series, Beckett leaps into the year 1956 and the life of Captain Tom Stratton, an Air Force test pilot who, in Sam's time line, died during a test flight. With the help of a computer named Ziggy, Al learns that Sam needs to save the pilot's life, changing the time line so that Stratton—and his unborn daughter—survive. Al gives a sarcastic description of the metaphysics behind Sam's predicament that nevertheless gives a sense of its providential basis:

> **Al:** Ziggy's theory is really—it's a load of crap. I mean, you gotta believe that *God* or *time* or something was just waiting for your quantum leap to, ah, to correct a mistake.
>
> **Sam:** A mistake in time?
>
> **Al:** Something that happened in the life of Captain Tom Stratton in '56, since he's the one you bounced out. Once that's put right, you'll snap back like a pair of suspenders.[36]

Ziggy's theory is correct, to a certain extent—once he fixes the error in Tom Stratton's life, Beckett leaps into another life with a new problem he must solve. Beckett can only return home to his own time by "setting right" these mistakes. The central concept of *Quantum Leap* is based on the assumption that there is a "right way" for things to be, an ideal version of the world. This assumption has some interesting implications: if there are mistakes in time, then the world that we (or, rather, Sam) inhabits at the show's beginning is *not* the ideal universe. Human free will has turned history away from God's intended ends. In Beckett, the universe has a uniquely science fictional means of carrying out the divine plan, creating a better world that, though still imperfect, is a little closer to the kingdom.

Richard Kelly's 2001 film *Donnie Darko* explores the idea of human instruments of the divine plan in detail. The eponymous hero of this complex and mysterious film is a schizophrenic teenager who discovers a means of traveling through time. When Donnie has a hallucinatory dream about a human-sized rabbit named Frank, he sleepwalks. Awaking the next morning, he learns that his somnambulism has saved his life. During his dream, an airplane engine fell onto his house; it would have killed him if he had been in bed. By surviving this bizarre accident, Donnie has entered an alternate time line, but this time line cannot sustain itself—Donnie was "supposed to" die, and a universe in which he did not is destined to collapse. A series of elliptical clues and hallucinations leads him to discover a book called *The Philosophy of Time Travel* that explains to him the means by which he can travel back in time to fix the error of his survival. The time line in which Donnie survived culminates in a tragedy that leaves two of his friends dead, and in his sorrow he uses the book's theories to return to his room on the night of his vision of Frank. Donnie is now in his room at the time of the plane engine's crash, and he is killed—sacrificing himself to repair the time line, protect his friends from danger, and save the universe from collapsing as it would have done in the alternate time line. Donnie becomes a sort of secret messiah, saving the cosmos from danger it never knew existed. In a conversation on the subject of time travel with his science teacher, Professor Monnitoff, Donnie makes clear the theistic basis of the story's ideas about time:

> **Donnie**: Every living thing follows along a set path. And if you could see your path or channel, then you could see into the future. . . . That's a form of time travel.

Monnitoff: Well, you're contradicting yourself, Donnie. If we were able to see our destinies manifest themselves visually, then we would be given a choice to betray our chosen destinies. And the mere fact that this choice exists would make all pre-formed destiny come to an end.

Donnie: Not if you travel within God's channel.[37]

Changing events in the past does not lead to a time paradox because Donnie is simply making a *Quantum Leap*–like change that sets the universe back on the path that God intended. The paradox that leads to a universal collapse is not the change made by time travel, but rather the mistake that can only be corrected by altering the past. A divine plan is the key to time travel in *Donnie Darko*—it is only possible if it creates the universe that God intends.

One episode of the British television program *Doctor Who* makes frighteningly clear what might happen if an *unintended* universe is created. In the 2005 episode "Father's Day," the Doctor—an enigmatic, time-traveling alien—brings his human companion Rose Tyler back in time to the day when her father was killed. When she was less than a year old, he was struck by a hit-and-run driver and was dead by the time paramedics arrived; she hopes to be by his side so that he will not die alone. When they arrive in the past, she is overcome with emotion, and rushes out at the last second to push him out of the path of the oncoming car. By saving his life, she has disrupted the past irreparably, and the Doctor scolds her for the foolishness of her action: "Rose, there's a man alive in the world who wasn't alive before. An ordinary man—that's the most important thing in creation. The whole world's different because he's alive!"[38] Before long, the devastating impact of this change becomes manifest when nightmarish, batlike creatures called Reapers appear and begin devouring every living creature in sight. These monsters, the Doctor explains, are a result of Rose's changes to the time stream, part of the universe's way of restoring the balance of time: "There's been an accident in time—a *wound* in time. They're like bacteria, taking advantage. . . . Time's been damaged, and they've come to sterilize the wound."[39] The Doctor and Rose hide in a church along with her parents and a few other people from the past, and the Reapers rapidly devour the entire world outside of their hiding place. They relent only when the time line has been repaired, when Rose's father sacrifices himself to restore the way things were before Rose saved him. *Doctor Who*, a long-running series based on time travel, has dealt with the results of changes in time on numerous occasions, but nowhere has it so clearly illustrated the idea that there is a way things are "supposed to be."

Similar world-recreations occur in Robert Zemeckis's *Back to the Future* trilogy (1985–1990). In these films, an eccentric scientist named "Doc" Emmet Brown and his teenaged assistant Marty McFly use a time machine—in the form of a modified sports car—to travel to both past and future, having adventures that often cause drastic changes in the time line. But unlike stories such as *Donnie Darko* and *Quantum Leap*, *Back to the Future* suggests no objective moral standard by which these changes are to be evaluated. In the first film (1985), Marty changes the situation in which his parents meet in such a way that their life thirty years in the future is greatly improved, and that is "good"—but good for Marty, not for Biff Tannen, a high school bully who has been reduced in the new time line to a pathetic loser. In *Back to the Future Part II* (1989), Biff uses the time machine to make himself the wealthiest man in the country, and that is "bad"—but in Biff's eyes, it is "good." Changing the past has repercussions in these stories, but those repercussions are entirely subjective; there is no universal plan that limits the characters' ability to make changes. *Back to the Future* depicts time travel in terms of moral relativism, where "good" and "evil" exist for the dramatic purposes of the story but have no objective support. Free will in these films is absolute—until we make a change of which another time traveler disapproves.

Isaac Asimov's *Foundation* series, by contrast, is rooted in the idea of a purpose governing history—and a purposer determining the end to which history is directed. The original *Foundation* trilogy, published between 1951 and 1953, is considered a classic of SF, and throughout his life Asimov expanded the story with

sequels and prequels. Even after his death, the story has continued
to grow, with other SF authors expanding the *Foundation* myth
with new novels. The basic premise of these stories is the character Hari Seldon, founder of a finely tuned, predictive branch of statistics called "psychohistory": "Psychohistory dealt not with man,
but with man-masses. It was the science of mobs; mobs in their billions. It could forecast reactions to stimuli with something of the
accuracy that a lesser science could bring to the forecast of the
rebound of a billiard ball. The reaction of one man could be forecast by no known mathematics; the reaction of a billion is something else again."[40] The principal belief on which psychohistory is
based is that the human race as a whole follows deterministic laws,
and its future can be predicted accurately. Seldon predicts that the
galactic empire, based on the planet Trantor, is destined to collapse, and nothing the government or its people do can reverse this
fall. The near future is essentially immutable, Seldon explains, and
even the distant future can only be influenced "with great difficulty. . . . The psychohistoric trend of a planet-full of people contains a huge inertia. To be changed it must be met with something
possessing similar inertia. Either as many people must be concerned, or if the number of people be relatively small, enormous
time for change must be allowed."[41] With great, mass effort, the
future can be guided, and Seldon establishes the Foundation—a
colony of scientists and artists based on the frontier planet Terminus who will preserve human culture through the dark ages after
the empire's collapse. Throughout the *Foundation* series, recordings made by Seldon during his life provide key information to the
Foundation's leaders that enable them to work toward the goal of
a sustainable galactic culture. Seldon's information about future
events is startlingly specific, even thousands of years after his initial predictions. Asimov's conception of psychohistory is strictly
deterministic: it assumes that, given enough knowledge of initial
conditions, the future can predicted with near-perfect accuracy.
Furthermore, the future can be controlled by making changes to
those initial conditions, as Gregory Benford explains in his prequel
to the original trilogy, *Foundation's Fear*: "If all variables in a system are tightly coupled, and you can change one of them precisely

and broadly, then you can indirectly control all of them. The system could be guided to an exact outcome through its myriad internal feedback loops. Spontaneously, the system ordered itself—and obeyed."[42] Seldon's system functions by controlling chaos, acknowledging the complex links by which minor changes can produce major ones. Psychohistory acknowledges the power of human will, and requires secrecy to function predictively: "If a psychohistorical analysis is made and the results are then given to the public, the various emotions and reactions of humanity would at once be distorted. The psychohistorical analysis, based on emotions and reactions that take place *without* knowledge of the future, become meaningless."[43] The resulting system is so exact that it functions even in the face of direct opposition, such as an attempt by the crumbling empire to reconquer Terminus and destroy the Foundation. As Seldon predicted, the invasion fails, and this failure finishes the empire off for good, cementing the power of the Foundation even further. In these stories, Seldon himself assumes the role of a benevolent deity, guiding the galaxy toward a second empire that is comparable to the kingdom of heaven. But because of the power of free will, he must be a *hidden* deity: his recordings are locked in a vault that can only be opened under specific circumstances, and the Foundation itself must be kept secret in order to be successful. SF writer Orson Scott Card points out the distinctly religious flavor of Seldon's role, comparing his work to the hand of God in history: "[The *Foundation* novels] invariably affirm both the need for and the existence of a purposer. The original Foundation trilogy is explicitly about Hari Seldon's plan and purpose for humanity, and how it worked regardless of the conscious intent of the leaders of Terminus."[44] In Seldon, Asimov translates the concept of divine providence into SF terms, affirming both the belief in a meaningful universe and in the ability of humankind to achieve its loftiest goals.

Kurt Vonnegut's *The Sirens of Titan* (1959) offers a similarly detailed exploration of the idea of providence, albeit a more cynical one. This novel tells the story of Malachi Constant, the inheritor of a vast fortune who believes he is the beneficiary of the power of luck. His understanding of his place in the universe is shaken when he encounters Winston Niles Rumfoord, a man who has been granted near-omniscience by a cosmic phenomenon called a "chrono-synclastic infundibula." This tear in the space-time continuum has encompassed Rumfoord, enabling him to experience simultaneously all places and times touched by the infundibula, which spans thousands of light-years and has existed for millennia. Rumfoord manifests on Earth periodically, during which times he predicts the future and guides humankind toward a goal that only he can foresee. He tells Constant what his future holds—including the loss of his fortune, interplanetary voyages to Mars and Titan, and fathering a child with Rumfoord's own wife, Beatrice. Constant and Beatrice are appalled by Rumfoord's predictions, and they both take actions to ensure their control over their destinies. In contrast with the events of *Flashforward*, these attempts fail, and ultimately all of Rumfoord's predictions come true.

Throughout much of the novel, Rumfoord appears to be a guiding force similar to Hari Seldon in *Foundation*. He is the architect of an interplanetary war, the founder of a religion, and even a designer of spacecraft. At the novel's end, however, it becomes clear that even Rumfoord is merely the pawn of greater forces beyond his control. Rumfoord—and, it turns out, the entire human race—has been manipulated by the robotic inhabitants of the planet Tralfamadore. An interstellar messenger named Salo was stranded on Titan when his starship broke down over two hundred thousand years earlier. Using a mysterious force known as the Universal Will to Become, the Tralfamadorians manipulated the primitive creatures of Earth: "Everything that every Earthling has ever done has been warped by creatures on a planet one-hundred-and-fifty thousand light years away. . . . They controlled us in such a way as to make us deliver a replacement part to a Tralfamadorian messenger who was grounded right here on Titan."[45] This replacement part—a piece of scrap metal carried by Constant's son, Chrono, as a good luck piece—is the culmination of two hundred millennia of human culture. With its delivery to Titan, the human race has achieved the purpose imposed on it by the Tralfamadorians. *The Sirens of Titan* reveals the meaning of life as a triviality:

humankind exists only to fulfill the goals of more powerful beings.

This revelation concludes a novel in which every character has been driven by the desire to discover his or her purpose, and the meaning of the universe in general. Constant believes in the powers of chance. Rumfoord seems for much of the novel to have a grand scheme of his own, though he ultimately rails against the powerlessness imposed upon him by Tralfamadore's schemes: " 'Tralfamadore,' said Rumfoord bitterly, 'reached into the Solar System, picked me up, and used me like a handy-dandy potato peeler! . . . It may surprise you to learn that I take a certain pride, no matter how foolishly mistaken that pride may be, in making my own decisions for my own reasons.' "[46] The adherents of the religion Rumfoord begins on Earth—the Church of God the Utterly Indifferent—adhere to a strict existentialist philosophy, believing that man cannot and should not act with the goal of pleasing God:

> O Lord Most High, Creator of the Cosmos . . . what could we do for Thee that Thou couldst not do for Thyself one octillion times better? Nothing. What could we do or say that could possibly interest Thee? Nothing. Oh, Mankind, rejoice in the apathy of our Creator, for it makes us free and truthful and dignified at last. No longer can a fool like Malachi Constant point to a ridiculous accident of good luck and say, "Somebody up there likes me."[47]

There is irony in this religion's ascendance—its premise that whatever higher power may exist in the universe has no plan for humankind stands in stark contrast to the revelation that Tralfamadore has closely guided all of human history. Despite the fallacy of its premise, however, the story upholds the religion's conclusions. There *is* a purpose in the universe, and there *is* a teleological plan, but the plan is so trivial that every individual must still seek to find his or her own meaning. At the novel's close, Beatrice Rumfoord refutes Rumfoord and Salo's revelations, writing a treatise entitled *The True Purpose of Life in the Solar System*: " 'I would be the last to deny,' said Beatrice, reading her own work out loud, 'that the forces of Tralfamadore have had something to do with the affairs of the Earth. However, those persons who have served the interests of Tralfamadore have served them in such highly personalized ways that Tralfamadore can be said to have had practically nothing to do with the case.' "[48] Beatrice hopes to find multiple meanings in human affairs, acknowledging the reality of the Tralfamadorian plan without accepting it as the true purpose of human existence. She reiterates the premise of the Church of God the Utterly Indifferent: the Tralfamadorians may have intended to guide human affairs to a specific end, and that end may have been achieved—but human will is so strong that their goal was met only through a series of accidents and coincidences. Despite its apparent cynicism, Vonnegut's novel is a highly humanistic work, a defiant statement that human life truly matters, even in the context of a vast and unfathomable universe.

A similar attitude toward providence and purpose unfolds in *The Matrix Reloaded* (2003), the second film in Andy and Larry Wachowski's *Matrix* trilogy. In these films, the human race is enslaved by machines, their minds subdued in a hallucinated world called "the Matrix" while their bodies are used to generate energy for the robots. A small group of humans have awakened from the Matrix and set up a base in the hidden underground city Zion, from which they wage war against the machines. Many of these awakened fighters, including a man named Morpheus, believe in a prophesied savior, "the One," who will defeat the machines within the Matrix and in the outside world. They believe they have found their messiah in a man named Neo, and Morpheus is convinced that his awakening means the prophecy is nearing completion: "There are no accidents. We have not come here by chance. I do not believe in chance . . . I do not see coincidence, I see providence, I see purpose. I believe it is our fate to be here. It is our destiny. I believe this night holds, for each and every one of us, the very meaning of our lives."[49] At the film's conclusion, Neo encounters the Architect, the program that designed and governs the Matrix, and learns that Morpheus's belief in a guiding force is justified—but it does not guarantee the victory he expects. The Architect tells Neo that the prophecy was planted by the machines, who allow Zion to exist because it enables them some degree of control over the small percentage of humans whose minds reject the Matrix. But Neo refuses to play into the Architect's plan, insisting on his own choices, his own control over his destiny. Ironically, by refusing to fulfill the prophecy as designed by the machines, Neo becomes the true savior of humanity, completing the prophecy as Morpheus and other humans interpreted it. In *The Matrix Reloaded*, prophecy and providence turn out to be a cruel system of control, and to find true meaning and purpose, we must resist such determinism.

Mary Doria Russell's 1996 novel *The Sparrow* is a powerful meditation on the tragic aspects of the idea of divine providence. This novel tells the story of a Jesuit-led space mission that makes first contact with an alien species on the planet Rakhat. The Society of Jesus, unencumbered by the bureaucracy limiting the world's governments, begins planning its expedition to Alpha Centauri immediately after the discovery of radio signals originating there. The Jesuits involved in the mission see the detection of life so close to our solar system as evidence of heavenly guidance, and interpret every aspect of their mission as the fulfillment of a divine plan. This attitude soon influences the non-Jesuit members of the group, and before long their unofficial motto is *"Deus vult . . .* God likes it that way."[50] Their typical response to dangerous situations is an optimistic faith: "If God brought us this far, I don't think He will fail us now."[51] No member of the crew believes in divine providence as strongly as Emilio Sandoz, a young Jesuit linguist whose early experiences on Rakhat leave him with a sense of purpose and fulfillment: "He felt as though he were a prism, gathering up God's love like white light and scattering it in all directions, and the sensation was nearly physical, as he caught and repeated as much of what everyone said to him as he could. . . . 'God!' he whispered . . . 'I was born for this!' "[52] This optimism is betrayed when a series of disasters leaves the mission stranded on the planet. Further catastrophes lead to the deaths of much of the crew until finally only Sandoz remains. He learns the sinister truth about the two races that live on Rakhat: the Runa, the peaceful race they first encountered after landing, are kept as cattle by the predatory Jana'ata, who breed them both as slaves and as food. After this shocking discovery, the tragedies of the mission are compounded when the Jana'ata take Sandoz prisoner, subject him to a bizarre surgery that disfigures his hands, and ultimately find little use for him beyond prostitution. A rescue mission arrives from Earth and finds him in an alien brothel, broken, destitute, and mad with despair. The disturbing realities of Rakhat betrayed his faith in a divine plan:

> "If I was led by God to love God, step by step, as it seemed, if I accept that the beauty and rapture were real and true, then the rest of it was God's will too, and that, gentlemen, is cause for bitterness. But if I am simply a deluded ape who took a lot of old folktales far too seriously, then I brought all this on myself and my companions and the whole business becomes farcical, doesn't it. The problem with atheism, I find, under these circumstances," he continued with academic exactitude, each word etched on the air with acid, "is that I have no one to despise but myself. If, however, I choose to believe that God is *vicious*, then at least I have the solace of hating God."[53]

The Sparrow challenges the idea of a divine purpose with the problem of evil: if all things are guided by God, then evil events must also be God's responsibility. The novel's title is a reference to Matthew 10:29: "Are not two sparrows sold for a penny? Yet not one of them will fall to the ground apart from the will of your Father" (NIV). In the context of the novel, the sparrow becomes a moral challenge—God *allows* the sparrow to suffer. Perhaps surprisingly, Sandoz does *not* ultimately reject his faith in God, but he does move on to an understanding of God's will that, though more skeptical, is also more mature. Another priest, Felipe Reyes, hints at what this new understanding might be: "There's an old Jewish story that says in the beginning God was everywhere and everything, a totality. But to make creation, God had to remove Himself from some part of the universe, so something besides Himself could exist. So He breathed in, and all the places where God withdrew, there creation exists. . . . He watches. He rejoices. He weeps. He observes the moral drama of human life and gives meaning to it by caring passionately about us, and remembering."[54] Our purpose, in this understanding of God's will, is not determined by God in a preexisting plan. Rather, meaning develops as the world changes and grows. When we rejoice at our place in the world, as when Sandoz felt a sense of purpose at translating the language of the Runa, God rejoices with us. When we despair, it does not mean that God has abandoned us—it merely means that God is mourning with us, sharing in our reactions to tragedy. God's plan is simply that we live our lives so that the meaning of our own existence and of the universe as a whole may unfold within God's sight.

Conflicting views on the purpose of human life emerge in Vincenzo Natali's 1997 film *Cube*. In this movie and each of its two sequels, an apparently random group of individuals awaken in a vast puzzle-prison made up of thousands of cube-shaped rooms. With no indication of where they are or why they have been trapped there, they struggle to solve the puzzle of the Cube and escape before it kills them. In the first film, one of the Cube's designers, David Worth, is among those trapped inside. He reveals that there is no reason for the Cube to exist, no guiding principle behind its construction or employment, and probably no real criteria for determining who is to be imprisoned inside it. Instead, it is a bureaucratic chimera, a mystery unknown to the outside world. Even its designers do not grasp the big picture: Worth states he was only responsible for designing the doors between the rooms, and implies that everyone engaged in the project had similarly limited goals. The Cube is a Kafkaesque framework with no guiding intelligence: "This may be hard for you to understand, but there is no conspiracy. Nobody is in charge. It's a headless blunder operating under the illusion of a master plan. . . . I looked and the only conclusion I could come to is that there is *nobody* up there."[55] Only those trapped inside the Cube are operating from a perspective from which they can understand what it is, because no one in the outside world has anything greater than partial knowledge of its existence. The 2004 prequel *Cube Zero*, directed by Ernie Barbarash, offers a glimpse of the mad bureaucracy outside of the Cube, further emphasizing its meaninglessness. This film reveals that when a prisoner escapes from the Cube, he is subjected to a bizarre interview which concludes with the question, "Do you believe in God?" When the prisoner answers that he does not—after the bleak experience of the Cube, no prisoner has ever answered yes—he is incinerated. One of the guards, Eric Wynn, begins questioning the Cube's purpose, prompting a defiant outburst from his coworker: "There's a purpose and there's a plan. And I'm not so stupid as to think there's no plan just because I don't understand it. Here's a newsflash—we're just the button men. If we were meant to be analysts we'd be working upstairs."[56] These protests simply emphasize the Cube's utter lack of purpose, suggesting that the *Cube* films are a cynical statement on the purpose of life. But as with *The Sirens of Titan*, the story offers compelling evidence that there is a reason operating behind apparent meaninglessness. Though those trapped in the Cube cannot think of any reason for their imprisonment, they seem to possess the precise set of skills that will enable them to escape it. In the first film, the group includes an escape artist, a high school math whiz, and an autistic man capable of solving the complex mathematical problems that are the key to escape. Quentin, a police officer who assumes the role of group leader until the prison drives him mad, discovers this pattern: "We got an escape artist, and a cop. There's got to be a reason for that. You're a doctor, Holloway. That gives you a function, a reason, right?"[57] Though it is presented as paranoia, Quentin's search for a pattern among the detainees uncovers the abilities that each member of the group has that will assist them in escaping. The prisoners are helpless until they begin to search for their purpose in the hellish world of the Cube. In this film, the idea of a plan designed by a higher intelligence is discarded, but a sense that there must be a meaning, a *purpose*, remains.

Omniscience does not necessarily carry with it a sense of purpose, and in Robert Wise's 1979 film *Star Trek: The Motion Picture*, we meet a near-divine machine that still searches for meaning. In this movie, the Starship *Enterprise* encounters a vast, sentient spacecraft called V'Ger. V'Ger, the crew discovers, is actually Earth's *Voyager 6* space probe, which was discovered by a race of intelligent machines.

> **Spock:** The machine inhabitants found it to be one of their own kind, primitive, yet kindred. They discovered its simple twentieth-century programming: collect all data possible.

Cmdr.
Decker: Learn all that is learnable. Return that information
to its creator.

Spock: Precisely, Mr. Decker. The machines interpreted it
literally. They built this entire vessel so that Voyager could actually fulfill its programming.[58]

V'Ger is omniscient, having "learned all that is learnable," but it
does not consider itself to be a god. Rather, it seeks to make contact with its creators in order to give it a new sense of purpose, as
Enterprise crewman Mr. Spock explains after communicating tele-
pathically with the sentient machine: "V'Ger has knowledge that
spans this universe. And yet, with all its pure logic, V'Ger is bar-
ren, cold—no mystery, no beauty. . . . It's asking questions: 'Is this
all that I am? Is there nothing more?' "[59] V'Ger is omniscient, but
in all its infinite knowledge it has not found a sense of purpose. It
requires a nonlogical element, faith in a power beyond itself, to
give it a sense of meaning. At the film's end, *Enterprise* crewmem-
bers Commander Decker and Lieutenant Ilia join with V'Ger,
merging their organic minds with its computerized intelligence to
create a truly transcendent being. Once its logic has been combined with the organic brain's capacity for emotion and faith, it no
longer feels empty, as James Kirk, captain of the *Enterprise*,
explains: "I think we gave it the ability to create its own sense of
purpose. Out of our own human weaknesses. The drive that com-
pels us to overcome."[60] Kirk suggests that the defining characteristic of humanity is the search for a purpose, the drive to determine
our identity and our meaning.

In the 2003 graphic novel *Orbiter*, by writer Warren Ellis and
artist Colleen Doran, aliens reveal the destiny of humankind,
unveiling the purpose that Earth inhabitants had not yet discovered
for themselves. This story occurs in a near-future United States
that has abandoned its space program following the mysterious
disappearance of the space shuttle *Venture*. Ten years later, the *Venture* reappears transformed: it is now coated with a skinlike organic
substance and contains an engine unlike anything designed by
Earthly science. The one surviving astronaut on the shuttle is in a

catatonic state, and when he finally begins to communicate he explains that the *Venture* was altered by aliens who want to help humanity reach the stars. The aliens hope to help humankind overcome its fear of its future: "Don't be afraid. You're just growing up. You're ready and you just don't know it yet. We tried to wait for you. But you're just too scared. We have so many things to show you. You shouldn't have to wait. Will you come with us?"[61] *Orbiter* is a story about human destiny which presents space exploration as the highest human aspiration. The story was written before the tragic loss of the Space Shuttle *Columbia* and its crew in 2003, but it was published soon afterward. In his foreword, Ellis refers directly to the *Columbia* disaster, urging us not to let the difficulties of space travel hold us back from our destiny of exploration: "This is a book about returning to space in the face of fear and adversity. It's a book about glory. About going back to space, because it's waiting for us, and it's where we're meant to be. We can't allow human space exploration to become our history."[62] In *Orbiter*, Earth attempts to escape its fate, fearing the dangers that must come with the exploration of the unknown. But in this story, space travel is an inevitability that cannot be avoided: if we do not achieve it on our own, alien powers will do it for us. Either way, Ellis argues, our destiny is in the stars.

Douglas Adams provides a sharply comedic interpretation of the existential quest in his *Hitchhiker's Guide to the Galaxy* books. The first novel in the series includes a vignette in which a group of pandimensional beings constructs a computer called Deep Thought to find the answer to "life, the universe, and everything." After over seven million years of computation, the computer reveals the answer: "Forty-two."[63] The computer's designers soon realize that knowing the answer to the meaning of the universe is not enough—it is necessary to also know the question. Deep Thought designs for the aliens "a computer whose merest operational parameters I am not worthy to calculate. . . . A computer that can calculate the Question to the Ultimate Answer, a computer of such infinite and subtle complexity that organic life itself shall form part of its operational matrix. . . . Yes! I shall design this computer for you. And I shall name it also unto you. And it shall be called . . . the Earth."[64] The purpose of human life is thus revealed not as a clearly defined concrete end, but rather as the search for meaning itself. It is not the answer that we seek; that has already been provided. Our goal is to question, and in so doing to find the ultimate question. As in *The Sirens of Titan*, Adams posits the human race as a pawn in an intergalactic game, controlled by forces beyond its comprehension. But *The Hitchhiker's Guide* also emphasizes the *importance* of the pawn; unlike the relatively trivial goal of the Tralfamadorian plan, Adams's mice use us for a far loftier end. Adams's message is a hopeful one, because it provides us with an understanding not only of why we are here, but also of *why we wonder* why we are here.

The Hitchhiker's Guide to the Galaxy is optimistic because it defines humanity's place in our vast and often incomprehensible universe. It affirms what *Cube Zero* states sarcastically: there *is* a purpose, and there *is* a plan. God's design for us and for the universe may be a mystery, but we can have faith that it exists. Within that plan, we have free will to determine our own identity and actions, but should we attempt to alter the starting point from which our choices begin—be it through time travel, genetic engineering, or psychological conditioning—SF often predicts that the results will be disastrous. But even within these limitations, our freedom to choose our own path is a sacred right. As powerful as SF's warnings against overreaching our bounds have been, even more impassioned have been its statements against those who would take away our freedom. God's plan relies on our free will, and by simply being who we are and choosing our actions, we contribute to God's creation of the universe in which we live.

Chapter Five

Dark Stars: Sin and Evil

*T*he essence of sin is the sense that something is wrong with the world: something has enabled evil, suffering, and death to exist when human existence would be better without them. Often, the idea of sin describes our behavior, the ability of humankind to act in a manner offensive to God and to commit deeds that violate the divine will or law. This understanding of sin is demonstrated in Genesis 3, which describes Adam and Eve's violation of God's prohibition against eating from the tree in the center of the garden. In the Genesis story, this action requires temptation by the serpent, but because of it (according to later Christian theologians), all human beings are now able to act in a manner that does not accord with God's law. The behavioral understanding of sin thus seeks to describe the moral quality of individual sinful actions, and from this viewpoint sin itself is better termed *sinfulness*, the ability to commit unjust acts.

The 1963 *Twilight Zone* episode "The Old Man in the Cave" explores this idea of sin in a postapocalyptic setting, depicting the punishment of a futuristic form of faithlessness. This story takes place in a small farming community that is home to a few straggling survivors of a nuclear war. A man named Mr. Goldsmith is the community's leader, a position he holds because he can communicate with "the old man in the cave" on a nearby mountain. This mysterious oracle (whom not even Goldsmith has actually seen) tells Goldsmith what food is contaminated by radiation and

what fields are safe to farm. But his position in the town is shaken
when a military commander, Major French, arrives in the town
with a small group of soldiers. French is skeptical about the "old
man," and encourages the people of the town to eat the canned food
that the oracle has identified as contaminated. He doubts that the
old man exists at all: "There is no old man in the cave. He's a lie.
He's a concoction. Nobody's seen him, nobody's heard him,
nobody knows who he is or where he's from. You made him up.
You cut him out of whole cloth."[1] French convinces the towns-
people to climb the mountain to the cave to discover the truth about
the oracle, and when they finally force the cave's metallic door
open they discover a computer, which they destroy. But the following morning Goldsmith and the "old man" are tragically vindicated when all those who ate the contaminated food die of
radiation poisoning. This story is a clever science-fictionalization
of Exodus 32, in which the Israelites, doubting the religion taught
to them by Moses in his absence, flaunt their God's commandments and worship a golden calf. Mr. Goldsmith's name ironically
evokes this idolatry, though he is the only one in his town who
holds fast to his faith. The computer's determination of what foods
are safe to eat even evokes the dietary restrictions of the Penta-
teuch. In "The Old Man in the Cave," sin—disobeying the unquestionably clear instructions laid down by a greater-than-human
authority—is met with swift retribution.

But a more important aspect of the idea of sin focuses not on
how we act, but rather on that in our nature which allows us to
behave in a manner offensive to God. The ontological aspect of the
concept of sin explores the root cause of these individual sins.
Rather than seeking to define what constitutes *a* sin, it hopes to
define *sin itself*, concluding that sin is that within nature—either
human or universal—which allows and produces suffering and
death. Paul defines this idea in Romans 6:20–23: "When you were
slaves of sin, you were free in regard to righteousness. So what
advantage did you then get from the things of which you now are
ashamed? The end of those things is death. But now that you have
been freed from sin and enslaved to God, the advantage you get is
sanctification. The end is eternal life. For the wages of sin is death,

but the free gift of God is eternal life in Christ Jesus our Lord." Sin is not bad simply because it brings suffering to others or ourselves, but because it is itself the source of all suffering, making us victims as well as perpetrators of sin. The key factor in humankind's fallenness is not simply our ability or proclivity to commit unjust acts, but rather the fact that it is difficult for us to discern and fulfill God's will, that our own desires are confusing and conflicted, and that death itself exists. All those things that we view as sinful acts or the results of sin—selfishness, aggression, pain, and so on—have their root in this isolation from the will of God. Sin, in this understanding, is not merely a problem of individual conscience, but of universal hardship.

Sin is the flaw in human nature that makes evil actions possible. But what is evil? On this question, too, there are two primary schools of thought. The first of these argues that evil has no substantial existence in itself, and thus is ultimately nothing. Sins are simply attempts at good actions gone awry, often either actions that focus on one minor good while ignoring a greater one, or attempts at imitating God that are haughty rather than humble. Evil does not exist independent of good; it is only our ignorance of the true nature of our own misguided motivations that makes our actions sinful. Rather than a positive character of an action, sin is a *lack* of proper moral motivation. Many theologians have posited a tempter that incites us to such sins, but this idea frequently edges quite close to the opposite school of thought: dualism. Dualism posits good and evil as forces eternally set against one another. In dualistic systems, evil is a real thing, an essential nature wholly apart from the good that comes from God. This understanding of the cosmos allows for the conclusion that there are people, things, and actions that can be evil in essence, rather than simply misguided. Historically, Christianity has opposed the idea that good and evil are independent essences. This sort of dualism was a hallmark of Manicheism, a late form of Gnosticism that was a popular rival to Christianity in the latter days of the Roman Empire. Manicheism and its offshoots were the most avidly despised heresies of the medieval church, to the extent that its name became synonymous with heresy in general. Nevertheless, the belief in absolute evil is a persistent one, and dualistic ideas are widespread in mainstream religion today.

Considering the importance of the concept of sin in religious discourse, it is no surprise that many works of SF have explored this idea. Frequently, SF authors have described worlds without sin, unfallen extraterrestrial paradises that the future may make available to fallen humanity. The idea that Earth might be unique in its sinfulness is not original to SF; author James Blish cites an article from the *Journal of the British Interplanetary Society* that suggests that the results of the first sin in Eden are limited to our planet: "One day a landing on the moon will be made. . . . One would like to think that amid all the technical jubilation somebody will get up and say: 'Remember! For the first time since Adam the slate is clean.'"[2] Since Adam and Eve were human beings, they merely brought sin to humanity—other worlds may not have suffered a fall.

What would such an unfallen planet be like? C. S. Lewis explores this question in *Out of the Silent Planet* (1938), the first novel in his *Cosmic Trilogy*. In this story, mysterious powers transport a philologist named Elwin Ransom to Mars, which is called "Malacandra" by its inhabitants. He is accompanied by two explorers who have visited the planet before—Devine, a gold prospector, and Weston, a celebrated physicist. The novel follows Ransom's explorations of the planet and his encounters with its three dominant species, the *hrossa*, *sorns*, and *pfifltriggi*, all of which are described in Malacandrian speech as *hnau*—rational creatures. He also learns of a fourth race, not native to Malacandra, called the *eldila*, invisible, ethereal beings respected by all of Malacandra's inhabitants. He also learns of the Oyarsa—a great *eldil*, the ruler of Malacandra, who knows everything and everyone on the planet, but is not its creator. According to the *hnau*, a being called Maleldil "made and still rule[s] the world."[3] Though the races of Malacandra live separate from one another geographically, they are united by a common language and by their shared reverence for the *eldila*, the Oyarsa, and Maleldil.

The novel culminates in Ransom's meeting with the Oyarsa, during which he learns the true history of the solar system: all of the planets were created by Maleldil, of whom all of the living races that inhabit the planets are copies. The planets exist in a sort of confederation, ruled ultimately by Maleldil with the Oyarses as overseers. But Earth is different—it is known as Thulcandra, "the silent planet," because "it alone is outside of heaven, and no message comes from it."[4] It was once under Maleldil's control, but now it is ruled by the Bent Oyarsa, a rebellious being that was confined there after a great battle with Maleldil. This Bent Oyarsa was once good, but out of greed and malice it isolated a planet for itself from the rest of the universe. Maleldil, the Oyarsa speculates, has not given up the battle, but "has taken strange counsel and dared terrible things, wrestling with the Bent One in Thulcandra."[5]

Lewis's distinction between fallen Thulcandra and divinely guided Malacandra offers an exploration of the idea of sin that is unique in its clarity. Unlike other SF writers using theological themes, Lewis does not mask the subject of his inquiry through symbolism or metaphor. Rather, he states the theological nature of his writing plainly, taking the idea that Earth and humankind are "fallen" as his starting point. Ransom is aware that Malacandra, rather than simply another world, is a planet that seems to know no evil. Its inhabitants have no conception of the ideas of crime or sin, and Ransom has difficulty explaining the ideas of robbery and murder not only to the *hnau* of Malacandra, but to the Oyarsa itself. Moreover, the Malacandrians seem to believe in a God remarkably like the Christian God. Their references to "Maleldil the Young" living with "the Old One" even suggest a Trinitarian deity (an idea that is made even more explicit in *Perelandra*, the novel's sequel, which refers to "The Third One" in discussing Maleldil). Further, the structure of the cosmos in *Out of the Silent Planet* is a distinctly Christian one, with Maleldil ruling the universe, using Oyarses (archangels) and *eldila* (angels) as his instruments. It is on Earth alone that this structure is *not* apparent—the Bent Oyarsa tries to keep the inhabitants of Earth from learning about Maleldil. The novel presents the ontological nature of sin by means of the image of the "silent planet" that is cut off from the cosmos, and hints at a certain level of dualism, though the Bent Oyarsa is identified as far inferior, rather than coequal, to Maleldil.

The separation of Earth from the rest of the cosmos is what has caused sin. All of humankind's woes have their origin in the Bent Oyarsa's segregation from Maleldil's universe. But of what does sin consist? In the book's closing scenes, the Oyarsa of Malacandra describes two different types of sin, exemplified by Devine and Weston, who have been put on trial for killing several Malacandrians. In Devine's case, all of the rules that govern *hnau* have been replaced by greed. Devine wants nothing from Malacandra but gold (or "sun's-blood," as the Malacandrians call it), and this desire has eclipsed all else in his mind. This effectively means that he is no longer a *hnau*, his soul having been replaced by his greed. The Oyarsa explains: "He is now only a talking animal and in my world he could do no more evil than an animal. If he were mine I would unmake his body for the *hnau* in it is already dead."[6] Devine's sin consists of being "broken" rather than "bent"; he lacks any sort of undistorted moral motivation. Weston, on the other hand, presents a different sort of sin. He states the murderous nature of his colonialism in his defense: "I am prepared without flinching to plant the flag of man on the soil of Malacandra: to march on, step by step, superseding, where necessary, the lower forms of life that we find, claiming planet after planet, system after system, till our posterity—whatever strange form and yet unguessed mentality they have assumed—dwell in the universe wherever the universe is habitable."[7] Weston's attitude and actions are sinful because he recognizes only *one* of Maleldil's laws to the detriment of all others, as the Oyarsa explains: "There are laws that all *hnau* know, of pity and straight dealing and shame and the like, and one of these is the love of kindred. He has taught you to break all of them except this one, which is not one of the greatest laws."[8] Weston thus embodies one of Augustine's definitions of sin, according to which "out of the pride of the individual a part is loved as though it were the whole."[9] His willingness to murder or die for this remaining law makes him dangerous, "because a bent *hnau* can do more evil than a broken one."[10] Weston's feigned morality, his claim to be fighting for the ultimate good of human survival, makes him a threat not only to Malacandra, but to the universe as a whole.

The root of both these types of sin is the exile of Thulcandra from the rest of the universe. Were Maleldil's presence apparent on Earth, it would be like Malacandra—its inhabitants would innately and without exception choose to obey God's will, which they would clearly see as the most rewarding option available. If God's presence were apparent, the human will would not be conflicted. But since Maleldil does not yet rule Thulcandra, this order is occluded. This is Lewis's final statement on sin in *Out of the Silent Planet*—our world is cut off from God, but this does not mean that God has been defeated here. Rather, our world is besieged; it is mankind alone that is separated from divine rule, and God is gradually realizing his control over even our "silent planet." The use of the "silence" as the distinguishing characteristic of Earth suggests that the planet's nonparticipation in the spiritual life of the cosmos is partially voluntary: Earth rejects a relationship with Maleldil, who nevertheless wishes to help the planet learn to communicate. The *eldila* and Oyarses of other planets represent the benevolent instruments through which God is waging this fight against the powers of sin and death. While writing this novel, Lewis very likely had the parable of the lost sheep from Luke 15:4–7 in mind: "Which one of you, having a hundred sheep and losing one of them, does not leave the ninety-nine in the wilderness and go after the one that is lost until he finds it? When he has found it, he lays it on his shoulders and rejoices. . . . Just so, I tell you, there will be more joy in heaven over one sinner who repents than over ninety-nine righteous persons who need no repentance." This parable does not apply only to individuals; Earth itself is the "lost sheep" which God takes great pains to reclaim, and over which God rejoices more than all those worlds that did not go astray.

Philip K. Dick explores a similar concept of Earth as a fallen world in his novel *The Divine Invasion*. In specifically religious language, this novel presents Earth as a world cut off from God. God was driven off the planet with Rome's final defeat of Jewish resistance in the first century, with the fall of the Temple of Jerusalem: "Yahweh was driven from the Earth. . . . All was lost. God did not enter history in the first century C.E.; he left history.

Christ's mission was a failure."[11] God has been in exile from the Earth for over two thousand years, worshiped as a local deity called "Yah" by the indigenous inhabitants of one of Earth's colonized worlds. Earth is now controlled by an evil spirit called Belial, with the ruling class of the planet—a combination of the Catholic Church and the Communist Party—as its instruments. The plot of the novel follows God's return to Earth in the incarnate form of a child named Manny (Emmanuel). Unlike Lewis, Dick places the fall of Earth *within* recorded human history, rather than before life began. In this novel, the ontological status of the fallen world is intangible: death and suffering existed before the fall of the Temple, but that event signaled the beginning of a much more subtle sort of fallenness. Both, however, use SF terminology to describe the battle between good and evil that will lead to reinstatement of God as the ultimate authority over Earth. Using space as a symbol, they describe the spiritual separation between humankind and God as a *physical* separation between planets.

Madeleine L'Engle's 1962 novel *A Wrinkle In Time* explores the concept of evil with an approach much like Lewis's. In this popular children's novel, ten-year-old Meg Murray, her younger brother Charles Wallace, and their friend Calvin O'Keefe take an interstellar journey with the assistance of three superintelligent beings named Mrs. Who, Mrs. Whatsit, and Mrs. Which. Traveling by means of a tesseract—the "wrinkle in time" of the title—they travel to the planet Camazotz where their father, a theoretical physicist, is imprisoned. Camazotz is a bureaucratic hell that is governed by a being known as IT—an evil, disembodied brain that hopes to conquer the universe. The evil of IT's rule is manifested in a chilling sameness governing the planet, as described in one passage in which a simple scene of an entire neighborhood of children playing in their yards displays an ominous lack of variation:

> As the skipping rope hit the pavement, so did the ball. As the rope curved over the head of the jumping child, the child with the ball caught the ball. Down came the ropes. Down came the balls. Over and over again. Up. Down. All in rhythm. All identical. . . . Then the doors of all the houses opened simultaneously, and out came women like a row of paper dolls. The print

of their dresses was different, but they all gave the appearance of being the same. Each woman stood on the steps of her house. Each clapped. Each child with the ball caught the ball. Each child with the skipping rope folded the rope. Each child turned and walked into the house. The doors clicked behind them.[12]

In *A Wrinkle in Time*, evil is conformity. IT encourages indifference, and is able to possess Charles Wallace when he briefly falls into apathy. The child then attempts to pull his sister into the same conformity: "Meg, you've got to stop fighting and relax. Relax and be happy. Oh, Meg, if you'd just relax you'd realize that all our troubles are over. You don't understand what a wonderful place we've come to. You see, on this planet everything is in perfect order because everybody has learned to relax, to give in, to submit."[13] Meg is able to defeat IT through the power of love—something IT cannot comprehend, because love requires recognizing uniqueness. By loving her brother, she undoes his conformity by emphasizing his individuality, forcing IT out of his mind.

The novel's sequel, *A Wind in the Door* (1973), features similar evil beings called Echthroi as its villains. The Echthroi, described as "un-Namers," are a blank emptiness that hopes to sow confusion and by so doing annihilate the universe: "One of their chief weapons is un-Naming—making people not know who they are. If someone knows who he is, really knows, then he doesn't need to hate. . . . When everyone is really and truly Named, then the Echthroi will be vanquished."[14] To name (and to be named) is to know, to understand, and to love. Evil here is not conformity as in *A Wrinkle in Time*, but rather confusion and ignorance. By loving and naming the Echthroi, Meg negates it, giving purpose to purposelessness: "Echthroi! You are Named! My arms surround you. You are no longer nothing! You are. You are filled. You are me."[15] *A Wind in the Door* puts the Christian message of loving one's enemies on a cosmic scale, showing the unfathomable power of love to conquer evil. L'Engle's stories depict the struggle between good and evil in a manner much like Lewis's, but with a subtly different approach: Earth, in these stories, is a bulwark against evil, and the battle is fought on other worlds. Evil is a universal problem in these stories, and alien worlds have no more ease in fulfilling God's will than we have. In both of these universes, the true nature of reality is summed up in terms of a battle between the ancient powers of Good and Evil. These stories hint at dualism, suggesting nonintersecting, absolute realms of morality.

In his 1997 novel *Thoughts of God*, Michael Kanaly further explores two forms of dualism: that of good and evil, and that of mind and body. This story describes "spiritual beings" that use our bodies, or "mechanisms," as temporary homes in a vast experiment. Intercutting text from a divine notebook that details this experiment with the story of a bounty hunter searching for a serial killer, the novel becomes a meditation on the nature of evil and the human soul. Evil, this story suggests, is the result of poor design in "the mechanism" of human beings—hunting instincts, for example, that overpower the spiritual beings' control and turn into violence against other human beings. The Experimenter determines that Darkness has merged with matter at the most basic level, leading to the existence of evil:

> Darkness, as it has now been discovered, has managed to conceal itself on a subatomic level, attaching itself to the smallest particles, which are themselves the building blocks of life. In this manner Darkness has found a means to exert a definable force on certain mechanisms on the physical plane. . . . It now seems probable that all mechanisms on the physical plane are polluted to some extent with the propensity toward damaging behavior, either to themselves or to other mechanisms in their habitat.[16]

Kanaly's story illustrates a sharply dualistic understanding of evil. It describes a spiritual plane of existence on which a battle between Light and Darkness has been occurring for an eternity, and the experiment of life on Earth is merely one battle in this larger war. Though this sort of dualism can often be a comforting view, explaining as it does how human beings can commit atrocities, it is hardly a truly satisfying interpretation. By placing the blame for evil on the forces of Darkness, the responsibility for evil actions is passed on from the one who commits them. By the same token, good deeds are not done by individuals, but by the "spiritual beings" residing in them. Though *Thoughts of God* is a powerful novel, its understanding of evil is an unsatisfying one.

A more complex approach to evil unfolds in *Perelandra* (1943), the second volume of C.S. Lewis's *Cosmic Trilogy*, which inquires into the fall that led to the separation described in *Out of the Silent Planet*. Exploring how such a fall could be avoided on other worlds, Lewis transplants the Eden narrative of Genesis to the planet Venus (or Perelandra). Malacandra's Oyarsa sends Ransom on a mission to fight against a plot of the Bent Oyarsa on Perelandra. Perelandra is an ocean planet covered with small, free-floating islands. It is teeming with life, but Ransom only meets one intelligent being, a green-skinned woman whom he calls the Green Lady. The Lady lives in harmony with her environment: she makes no effort to alter her surroundings, living wherever the floating islands take her, and the planet's animals obey her desires. She knows of Maleldil, and speaks Malacandrian (which Ransom now calls "Old Solar," the ancient language of all the planets). The Green Lady is confused when Ransom asks her to take him to others of her race; she seems only to know of one other being, whom she calls "the King." She also seems to be only a few days or weeks old, though she laughs at Ransom's stubborn belief that time is something that can be measured. As for the world itself, the Lady tells Ransom that there is a region of unmoving ground, which she calls "the Fixed Land." She and the King are permitted to move around on this land during the day, but Maleldil has specifically forbidden them to remain on it overnight.

Soon after Ransom's arrival on Perelandra, another Thulcandran arrives—Dr. Weston. Weston now claims to have reformed, accepting that his plan to kill the inhabitants of Malacandra was based on the prejudice that they were subhuman. Now, he claims to believe not in humankind alone, but in all life: "Man in himself is nothing. The forward movement of Life—the growing spirituality—is everything. . . . To spread spirituality, not to spread the human race, is henceforth my mission."[17] He claims that a "Force" has taken him over, and that his devotion to this spirituality of life places him above conventional morality. It soon becomes clear that Weston is, in fact, being controlled by a "force"—he is not in control of his body, but rather is possessed by a bent *eldil*, possibly the Bent Oyarsa itself. Weston (or "the Un-man," as Ransom soon begins to think of him) soon commences his task on Perelandra: tempting the Green Lady to dwell on the Fixed Land. Ransom has difficulty warning her about the Un-man's temptations: Old Solar, as the language of sinless beings, has no words for "bad," "evil," or "liar." When he does manage to explain the fall that occurred on Earth, the Un-man rebuts with the medieval concept of *felix culpa*, or "fortunate fall"—the idea that the first sin was a good thing, because it eventually prompted God (or Maleldil) to become incarnate on Earth. The Un-man begins to sway the Green Lady, slowly turning her against Ransom's arguments and encouraging her to imagine living on the Fixed Land.

Ransom fights with the Un-man, chasing him away from the Green Lady and ultimately killing him. When Ransom returns, he finds that he has succeeded in his struggle with the Un-man. The Perelandrian's time of trial is over, and we learn what would have happened on Earth had Adam and Eve not fallen. The Oyarsa of Malacandra explains: "The world is born to-day. . . . To-day for the first time two creatures of the low worlds, two images of Maleldil that breathe and breed like the beasts, step up that step at which your parents fell, and sit in the throne of what they were meant to be."[18] The novel closes with a sort of coronation of the King and Queen, in which they become the true image of Maleldil. The Oyarsa of Perelandra grants the King and Queen full power over their planet in terminology reminiscent of Genesis: "My word henceforth is nothing: your word is law unchangeable and the very daughter of the Voice. . . . Enjoy it well. Give names to all creatures, guide all natures to perfection. Strengthen the feebler, lighten the darker, love all."[19] Ransom, having prevented the two rulers of Perelandra from falling into evil, witnesses their ascension into glory. The novel ends with a hymn of praise to Maleldil, and a prophecy of the raising of the siege of Thulcandra, with Perelandra's future generations serving as Maleldil's army.

The religious themes of *Out of the Silent Planet* were apparent, but *Perelandra* deals even more directly with religious questions. The structure of the story's plot is a very detailed variation on the temptation of Genesis 3:1–7. The primary difference between the biblical account and Lewis's novel is the presence of Ransom as God's advocate for the first people of Perelandra. It is clear that without Ransom's presence, the Un-man would have been success- ful in convincing the Green Lady to break Maleldil's prohibition, and it was only through Ransom's arguments and his physical con- frontation with the Un-man that Perelandra was saved from sin. Ransom doubts his own ability in preventing a Perelandrian fall, but he begins to see himself as the instrument of Maleldil: "When Eve fell, God was not Man. [Maleldil] had not yet made men members of His body: since then He had, and through them henceforward He would save and suffer. . . . [Maleldil] was to save Perelandra not through Himself but through Himself in Ransom."[20] Maleldil— God—uses Ransom as his means of defeating the Bent Oyarsa. In the Genesis account, Adam and Eve had no such advocate on their behalf; there was only the serpent to tempt them.

Weston, as the Un-man, embodies a far more terrifying vision of evil than that he symbolized in *Out of the Silent Planet*. Now, instead of simply being a bent *hnau*, he is possessed by the origin of all Earthly evil, the Bent Oyarsa. The Un-man is presented as a parasite that lacks any real creative power of its own, existing instead to destroy and subvert Maleldil's creation. Perhaps the most terrifying thing about the Un-man is its overall affability in dealing with the Green Lady; it is only because she does not understand the evil meaning behind its words that she allows her- self to be deceived. In one scene, the Un-man plainly states his purpose on Perelandra, though because he uses Earthly, fallen ter- minology, the Lady cannot possibly understand his true meaning: "When you asked him [Ransom] to teach you Death, he would not. He wanted you to remain young, not to learn Death. . . . It is for this that I came here, that you may have Death in abun- dance."[21] This passage clearly describes an ontological under- standing of sin, whereby the real result of the fall is mortality. The Un-man, as the story's serpent, wishes to bring Perelandra under the dominion of death.

The offense which the Un-man tempts the Lady to commit—to remain overnight on the Fixed Land—seems a minor crime, just as eating the fruit in Eden seemed minor. But the Fixed Land represents the very definition of sin as it is put forth in *Perelandra*. As Katherin Rogers describes it, in this novel Lewis claims "that to sin is not to choose evil per se, but to choose the wrong good. . . . One might cling to an old good, repeating it and repeating it, flinching away from any new good that God might offer. Or one might simply refuse the good that presents itself because one desires a different, and perhaps a lesser, good."[22] The Fixed Land is a symbol of this, as the Green Lady herself explains after her ascension into glory: "How could I wish to live there except because it was Fixed? And why should I desire the Fixed except to make sure—to be able on one day to command where I should be the next and what should happen to me? It was to reject the wave—to draw my hands out of Maleldil's, to say to Him, 'Not thus, but thus'—to put in our own power what times should roll towards us."[23] The ocean of Perelandra is the sea of faith, and to desire to live apart from this ocean would be to desire to live without God's guidance. Thus, the Un-man's temptation was not a minor one; he hoped to convince the Green Lady to break the prohibition that was symbolic of her covenant with Maleldil.

The meaning of this prohibition offers enormous insight into Lewis's understanding of sin in general. The essence of virtue is trusting in God, and seeing God's action in all events. The essence of sin, then, is attempting to take one's destiny into one's own hands, refusing to allow God's plan to become apparent. Maleldil's plan to regain control over Thulcandra—which is specified in *Perelandra* as being based in the Incarnation, Crucifixion, and Resurrection of Christ—proves that God's power is ultimate, regardless of any attempts on the part of the individual to take control for oneself. For the inhabitants of Earth, however, sin, rather than virtue, is the apparent choice. Sin is an ontological state wherein God's presence is *not* apparent and thus doubt comes before faith. It is still possible to come to know God's will, but only because of the covert activity of God on Earth, which Lewis sees as Christ's life and mission and the subsequent growth of the Christian faith. Unfallen worlds like Malacandra and Perelandra are thus Christian without Christ; they recognize God's authority without doubt or question, and thus do not require redemption. Our separation from this innocence is the cause of all Earthly suffering.

In *Memoirs of a Space Traveler* (1971, English translation 1982), Stanislaw Lem gives a comic explanation of original sin. In one of his voyages, Ijon Tichy, Lem's explorer, claims that he is the creator of the universe, and thus must bear the guilt for all that is wrong in it. He explains that a scientist named Professor Razglaz deduced that the existence of the universe depends on basic violations of its own laws, leading to an "energy debt" that will inevitably lead to the sudden, instantaneous destruction of the entire cosmos. This debt could be balanced by the presence of a single positron at the Big Bang, and Razglaz devises a "Chronocannon" to send one such particle back in time. The Chronocannon opens up an extraordinary possibility: the positron can be programmed to allow specific changes in the laws by which the universe operates. Tichy attempts to program paradise: evolution will be guided not by competition, but by cooperation; stars will be close enough together to enable sentient races to interact more easily; supernovae and other interstellar disasters will occur with less frequency. Tichy's plans are undone by the interference of two scientists with the suspiciously diabolical names "Ast A. Roth" and "Lou Cipher," who make selfish corrections and mistaken calculations that lead to disaster. We learn that quantum uncertainty is a direct result of Roth's mathematical errors, and Cipher eliminates all of Tichy's changes to human nature because they included the replacement of hair with photosynthetic foliage: "Mr. Cipher thought hair more important. He 'missed' it, you see. One could make such nice fringes, whiskers, and other fancy things with it. On the one hand, my morality of fellowship and humanism; on the other, the value system of a hairdresser!"[24] Because of these foolish changes, Tichy's improvements were entirely undone, leading to the preponderance of chaos and injustice in the universe. Despite their names, Roth and Cipher are entirely human sources of evil. It is their selfishness and shortsightedness that has retroactively created all that is undesirable in the world. Lem's story is a comic presentation of the idea of original sin: what we consider evil or unfair is ultimately the result of our own limitations. The apple of Genesis is replaced in this story by an electron, but its misuse still leads to suffering.

Harry Harrison's 1962 story "The Streets of Ashkelon" presents a dark view of an alien world's fall into sin. In this story, a Catholic missionary named Father Mark arrives on a planet called Wesker's World, which is inhabited by a species of logical yet primitive aliens called Weskers. The planet's only other human inhabitant—an atheist trader named John Garth—is far from pleased to see the priest, demanding at gunpoint that he leave the planet before grudgingly accepting his right to remain. Garth explains his somewhat paternalistic rationale: "These natives, simple and unlettered stone-age types that they are, have managed to come this far with no superstitions or traces of deism whatsoever. I had hoped that they might continue that way."[25] Father Mark soon begins talking with Itin, the Weskers' spokesman, but the discrepancy between what the Weskers learn from the atheist and the priest soon confuses them, as Itin explains to Garth: "We must hear you and Father Mark talk together. This is because he says one thing is true and you say another is true and both cannot be true at the same time. We must find out what is true."[26] This meeting concludes with the Weskers' decision that if there is a God, He will offer them a miracle to prove His existence, and they crucify Father Mark, expecting him to be resurrected. This act—the first sin on Wesker's World—is a fall from which the natives cannot recover. In contrast to the innate religiosity of Lewis's unfallen worlds, this story presents a rather different opinion: sinlessness needs no religion, since by definition it needs no redemption. Father Mark's attempt to bring religion to the Weskers thus condemns them rather than saving them. In this story, religion is the direct source of sin; in the absence of doctrine and dogma, the Weskers could not have committed murder at the story's climax. Harrison describes the society as primitive, but he clearly sees such sinless, religionless societies as an ideal. Though Harrison's Weskers lack an inherent religion like that of Lewis's aliens, both authors clearly feel that a world that does not fall is better off than one that does.

But being without sin is not the same as being truly virtuous. Our entire approach to the idea of good is rooted in the fact that we *can* commit evil acts—if beings without sin cannot be evil, might they also be incapable of *good*? This tension fills James Blish's Hugo Award–winning 1958 novel *A Case of Conscience*, which stands as one of the most thought-provoking approaches to the ideas of sin and sinlessness in all of SF. The story opens on the planet Lithia, which is being explored by a team of four astronauts. The team's biologist is a Jesuit priest named Ramon Ruiz-Sanchez who wishes to learn not only about the physical properties of the planet's inhabitants, but also about their moral lives. He finds that the reptilian Lithians are a race apparently without concepts for crime, sin, or transgression. They are a peaceful race, unified without major conflicts between either individuals or large groups. Making decisions purely based on reason, the Lithians seem to be without any sort of evil, and Ruiz-Sanchez speculates that they do not suffer from the burden of original sin. Some of the other members of the team are less intrigued by the Lithians, treating them with contempt, calling them "Snakes," and refusing to learn their language. But Ruiz-Sanchez respects the aliens, even befriending one Lithian named Chtexa.

As the mission draws to a close, the four astronauts need to come to a decision as to the status of the planet: will it be opened for trade and further exploration, ignored as a valueless hunk of rock, or closed off as a risk to human beings? Only one member of the team—Michelis, the ship's chemist—sees value in the planet, believing that much could be gained from a cultural exchange with the Lithians. Agronksi, the team's geologist, sees no worth in the planet's resources, but Paul Cleaver, a physicist, wants to block the planet from trade so that the team can make a private fortune by using the planet as a factory for nuclear weapons. Ruiz-Sanchez, however, presents the team with a complex moral argument for his decision on the status of Lithia.

The Jesuit believes, as does Cleaver, that the planet should be quarantined, but unlike Cleaver, he sees the planet as a danger to the human race as a whole. The sinless nature of the Lithians, he argues, is too great a coincidence to be naturally possible. They are not only sinless, but sinless from a *Western, secularist* perspective: "This creature is rational. It conforms, as if naturally and without constraint or guidance, to the highest ethical code we have evolved on Earth. It needs no laws to enforce this code. Somehow, everyone obeys it as a matter of course, although it has never even been written down. There are no criminals, no deviates, no aberrations of any kind."[27] Ruiz-Sanchez expresses fear at the absolute arbitrariness of this Lithian morality, which he claims is "*completely irrational*. It is based upon a set of axioms, a set of presuppositions which were 'given' from the beginning—though your Lithian sees no need to postulate any Giver. The Lithian, for instance Chtexa, believes in the sanctity of the individual. Why? Not by reason, surely, for there is no way to reason to that proposition. It is an axiom."[28] He adds a biological note to his argument, explaining that the Lithians go through stages equivalent to evolution in their early childhood, beginning life in the water and gradually moving into the forests before entering society as adults with innate knowledge of both the language and the ethical code of Lithia, "The Law of the Whole." Ruiz-Sanchez takes this process as proof of the theory of evolution, which to his mind would be potentially devastating to the Catholic Church.[29]

Ruiz-Sanchez concludes, then, that Lithia is a planet created not by God, but rather by Satan. Their ethical code, which is identical to Western secularism and has no basis whatsoever in any sort of higher power, is his primary point of proof:

> Look at the premises . . . *One:* Reason is always a sufficient guide. *Two:* The self-evident is always the real. *Three:* Good works are an end in themselves. *Four:* Faith is irrelevant to right action. *Five:* Right action can exist without love. *Six:* Peace need not pass understanding. *Seven:* Ethics can exist without evil alternatives. *Eight:* Morals can exist without conscience. *Nine:* Goodness can exist without God. *Ten*—but do I really need to go on? We have heard all these propositions before, and we know What proposes them.[30]

Ruiz-Sanchez is aware that his belief about the origin of Lithia makes him a heretic: specifically, he says, he is a Manichean, believing that the devil has the power to create. But he nevertheless believes that his conclusion about the planet is correct, and that the planet is a danger to humankind. With Ruiz-Sanchez's vote cast, three-fourths of the team are in agreement (albeit for vastly different reasons), and Lithia is closed to trade. As they are leaving the planet, however, Chtexa gives Ruiz-Sanchez a gift to bring back to Earth: a jar containing a fertilized Lithian egg.

In the novel's second half, Ruiz-Sanchez's theory seems to be proven correct. The Lithian that is born from the egg—Egtverchi—becomes a popular public figure, eventually hosting a television show. He shows little evidence, however, of following the Lithian Law of the Whole, presenting instead a sort of nihilism popular with Earth's enormous underclass. Ruiz-Sanchez sees Egtverchi as the manifestation of the evil he saw beneath the surface of native Lithians: "He was throughout a creature of the Adversary's imagination, as even Chtexa had been, as the whole of Lithia had been. In the figure of Egtverchi He had already abandoned subtlety; already He dared to show Himself more than half-naked, commanding money, fathering lies, poisoning discourse, compounding grief, corrupting children, killing love, building armies."[31] Through his anarchical television broadcasts, Egtverchi incites a revolution that leaves thousands dead. Ruiz-Sanchez meets with church officials to discuss his conclusions about Lithia; though condemning his heresy, they agree with his belief that Lithia is a moral danger to Earth, and suggest that he exorcize it. The novel ends with this exorcism, during which Lithia is destroyed. The novel is ambiguous as to whether the cause of its destruction is the exorcism itself or Cleaver's atomic weapons construction, which had the potential to destroy the entire planet.

Like Malacandra and Perelandra, Lithia is a planet apparently without sin. Lewis's planets have a highly developed ethical code that is clearly based on a deity as its motivating force. Blish presents a planet ethically comparable to Malacandra and Perelandra, but takes away the moral center provided by Maleldil. The result is similar to Harrison's Weskers, whose rationalism meant freedom from superstition, but Blish presents a criticism of this type of society, pointing out that the Lithians' ethical code has no basis outside of itself. Ruiz-Sanchez believes that contact with Lithia will lead to disaster: fearing that the Lithians provide apparent proof of the objective truth of Western secular humanism, including rationalism and the theory of evolution, he believes that the Lithians have the ability to overthrow all religious authority on Earth. The Lithians will produce absolute atheism on Earth:

> [Lithia] will sway many people who could have been swayed in no other way. . . . It seems to show us evolution in action on an inarguable scale. It is supposed to settle the question once and for all, to rule God out of the picture. . . . Henceforth there is to be no more question; henceforth there is to be no more God, but only phenomenology—and, of course, behind the scenes, within the hole that's inside the hole that's through a hole, the Great Nothing itself, the Thing that has never learned any word but *No* since it was cast flaming from heaven.[32]

Though Ruiz-Sanchez pins much of the force of his argument on the somewhat irrelevant question of evolution, the true force of the argument lies in the matter of the Lithians' ethics, which are identical to those of modern Western society but without the postulate of God. If humankind adopts the Lithian system, the priest fears, it will abandon God and religion entirely in exchange for scientific rationalism. Since the Lithians have reached their peaceful, free state without any need for belief in a God, to adopt their type of society would require the abandonment of faith. This, rather than the question of evolution, is the true source of Ruiz-Sanchez's heretical belief in the diabolical origin of Lithia. Blish thus presents this Eden as a forbidden fruit in disguise.

Egtverchi, the Lithian emigrant, seems to make apparent all that Ruiz-Sanchez saw hidden beneath the surface of Lithia. He comes to endorse and embody what some might see as the ultimate expression of personal freedom: total anarchy. Egtverchi places the individual before all else, just as Weston, in *Out of the Silent Planet*, placed the human race before all else: "[I am] a citizen of no country but that bounded by the limits of my own mind. I do not know what these limits are, and I may never find out, but I shall devote my life to searching for them, in whatever manner seems good to me, and in no other manner whatsoever."[33] This law of absolute self-determination is the only law that Egtverchi recognizes, and it extends to his brief communication with his ancestral world. In a radio communication with Chtexa, Egtverchi denies his

Lithian heritage and its ethical code: "I never heard of the Law of the Whole . . . I doubt that there is any such thing. I make up my own laws as I go along. . . . I didn't choose to be born a Lithian, and I didn't choose to be brought to Earth—but now that I'm a free agent I mean to make my own choices, and explain them to nobody if that's what pleases me."[34] Egtverchi ultimately incites a revolution by encouraging human beings to follow his example of anarchy, and despite the Lithian's suggestion that the revolt be nonviolent, thousands are killed in the uprising.

What is important to Ruiz-Sanchez is the order that belief in God produces; the demonic illusion that he sees on Lithia is the appearance of a society that can be peaceful *without* a religious or theological underpinning to that peace. But is the reader expected to agree with Ruiz-Sanchez on the question of Lithia's moral standing? In a pseudonymous review of the novel, Blish himself states that "the author obviously intended the reader to identify with Father Ruiz's point of view," but the novel as a whole seems to remain largely agnostic on the question.[35] But other studies of the novel have presented vastly different opinions on this question. In an excellent study of the story's religious ideas, Jo Allen Bradham argues that the novel is equally critical of Ruiz-Sanchez's blind faith and Cleaver's self-serving, amoral reason: "Cleaver and Ruiz-Sanchez have the opportunity to study the case of grace, but being 'cases' in the medical and psychiatric sense, they fail. The case of Lithia. . . . is too just and equitable to be understood by fallen man, either in the case of the new science or of the old faith."[36] Many have thus read the novel as a condemnation of the unquestioning acceptance of *either* religious order or rationalist science.

Ruiz-Sanchez's view is further called into question by the revolution that the Lithian immigrant incites. Egtverchi, whom Ruiz-Sanchez sees as the ultimate expression of Lithia's evil nature, in fact expresses the evil nature of *Earth*. His revolution only succeeds because of the decadent and divided nature of Earth's society, where a hedonistic upper class has virtually no contact with the vast underclass that it oppresses. The majority of this underclass is forced to live in underground tunnels and shelters left over from the Cold War, and as a result Earth's society is plagued with an unprecedented number of cases of mental illness. Egtverchi's message of revolution could not have been successful without this base to tap into; but is it, in fact, a bad thing for an oppressed majority to rise up against such an unhealthy society? Egtverchi does not bring chaos to Earth; he rather brings to the surface the chaos already present. Thus the order that Ruiz-Sanchez sees as the result of religious authority and the belief in God is a thin veneer; the reality of Earth's society is the chaos brought about in Egtverchi's revolt. But the question of Lithia's own moral status still stands; Egtverchi and Chtexa are two wholly separate problems within the novel. Regardless of Blish's personal standpoint in either case, this novel presents a fascinating study of an alien ethical code, through which it examines the underpinnings of our own morality. In *A Case of Conscience*, sin is presented as that which makes us human, but also that which has the power to destroy us if it is not balanced by belief in a higher authority.

Philip José Farmer's 1955 novella "Father" describes a paradise planet similar to Perelandra that is distinguished by its inclusion of just such a higher power. But nevertheless, it speaks strongly against such Edenic worlds, suggesting that any apparent paradise can conceal the worst evils. Father John Carmody, a lively Catholic priest who appears in several stories by Farmer, lands with the crew of a spacecraft on the planet Abatos. They find an unspoiled garden world with a single sentient inhabitant, a godlike being called Father. Father is a powerful ruler, capable of acts of healing and even resurrection: the entire animal population of Abatos has been raised from the dead repeatedly, with the same beings recycled for thousands of years. Father asks the visitors to his planet to take him off of this world, in return for which he will share with them the secret of resurrection. Carmody and his crew are faced with a difficult question: is Father the good being he appears to be, or an evil tyrant looking for new worlds to conquer? Carmody speaks strongly against both Father and the planet Abatos itself, casting the godlike alien as a satanic tempter:

Won't each man who has the power begin thinking of himself as a sort of god? Won't he become as Father, dissatisfied with the original unruly rude chaotic planet as he found it? Won't he find progress and imperfection unbearable and remodel the bones of his creatures to remove all evolutionary vestiges and form perfect skeletons? . . . Won't he make a garden out of his planet, a beautiful but sterile and unprogressive paradise? . . . Even the lover of perfection, Father, has become bored and wishes to find a pioneer world where *he* may labour until *he* has brought it to the same state as Abatos. Will this go on for ever until the Galaxy will no longer exhibit a multitude of worlds, each breathtakingly different from the other, but will show you everywhere a duplicate of Abatos, not one whit different? I warn you that this is one of the very real perils.[37]

For Carmody, the idle paradise of Abatos is misleading—hell in the guise of heaven. Stasis and conformity are the true evils, and paradises such as Abatos—and, it might be argued, Perelandra—encourage both of these. There is not one universal good that is the same for all worlds, but rather the goodness of the universe relies on difference and variation. To reproduce this paradise elsewhere would mark the beginning of the end, a descent into inertia and decadence.

In his 1969 novel *Pollinators of Eden*, John Boyd presents a similar attitude toward sinless planets. The planet Flora, named for its abundant flowers, seems to be a paradise, and the narcotic and aphrodisiac effects of these flowers make it seem a true Eden where sin—and with it, unease—can be forgotten. Senator Heyburn, a conservative politician, speaks passionately against the colonization of Flora:

> Dear friends and dearer enemies, there is no moral equivalent of war, no progress without pain, no color without conflict, no vitality without violence. I oppose all Tahitis in space. I close all cul-de-sacs of flowers. Sound for me the iron ring of the deadly planets, and I will raise my hand in blessing, saying, "Go. Meet and overcome the challenge." But I will sound forever "Nay!" to the lotus eaters, the lovers of ease, the oglers of non-functional beauty. . . . Man could not have walked so splendid in the sunlight had he not been cast from Eden.[38]

Like Father Carmody, Heyburn sees progress and change—even in the face of overwhelming hardship—as the true moral standard by which planets must be measured. A planet that is difficult to live on encourages innovation and progress, which strengthens and improves the state of humankind in general. But worlds like Flora, which discourage hard work, are temptations to idleness that will stunt the growth of the human race. Like "Father," this story uses SF conventions to put forth a powerful argument: what seems good on the surface may in fact be the greatest evil.

Joss Whedon's film *Serenity* (2005) provides a similar argument against the concept of a perfect world. This film takes place in a galaxy recently united by a central government. After a long and bloody war, the Alliance defeated the Independent faction, a coalition of distant colony worlds that sought self-rule. Malcolm Reynolds, captain of the ship *Serenity*, was a sergeant in the Independent army, and his hatred for the Alliance has turned him and his crew into outlaws, galactic drifters for whom the interstellar Civil War never ended. *Serenity*'s crew knows one of the Alliance's most carefully guarded secrets: the government used a distant colony world as a testing ground for a drug called "Pax." This pacifying chemical was spread throughout the planet's atmosphere in order to make its people more docile. The drug works: the people of this planet become so submissive that they sink into complete apathy, ultimately dying because they are too complacent to feed themselves. A small percentage of the planet's people are resistant to this effect, but they undergo a far more terrifying change. Pax transforms them into the film's embodiment of absolute evil, mindless monsters called Reavers who commit brutal and sadistic acts of murder. When *Serenity*'s crew uncovers this secret, the government sends a nameless assassin to track the ship down. This man, known only as the Operative, will stop at nothing to find his quarry, and he slaughters entire colonies that might give Reynolds and his crew shelter. The Operative embodies the Alliance's belief that the ends justify the means: "I believe in something greater than myself. A better world. A world without sin. . . . What I do is evil, I have no illusions about it, but it must be done."[39] The hidden, subtle evil of the Alliance conceals the overt monstrosity of the Reavers. Reynolds and his crew embody the opposite approach: they are so dedicated to their morality and identity that they are willing to risk everything in order to hold onto their ideals. No matter how good one's goals, *Serenity* argues, evil actions cannot help but have evil results.

Serenity argues that the attempt to blend good and evil cannot produce a coherent morality. In his 1971 short story "Dazed," Theodore Sturgeon rejects this absolutism, exploring a Taoist conception of good and evil represented by the yin-yang—a symbol of balance between opposing forces. In this story, a time traveler from 1950 explains to a man from an unspecified date in the future that the cosmos is meant to be balanced. Describing life as a journey from one side of the yin-yang to another, he states that "Most people can and do travel the diameter. For each person, life, marriage, whatever, there's a different starting point and a different arrival point, but if they travel the one straight line that goes through the center, they will travel black country exactly as much as white, yin as much as yang. The balance is perfect, no matter where you start or which way you go."[40] But the world has become imbalanced because of some sort of shift: one of the two powers has grown too great, and now has more "territory" than the other: "If the shift were gradual, then from the very second it began there would be some people—some lives, some philosophies—who would no longer have that perfect balance between black and white . . . some people might travel all the way on the white only."[41] Drastic measures—which shift the story from Taoist to Christian territory—are necessary to restore the balance, and the time traveler makes a literal deal with the devil in order to shift yin and yang back into equilibrium. He becomes a force for evil in order to restore its balance with good. This requires an increase in apparent human suffering, war, and famine, and a decreasing respect for established morality. At the story's end, however, it is unclear whether this will actually lead to any real balance, or if the time traveler has simply been tricked by the devil into allowing evil to increase. Depending on one's interpretation of this ambiguity, this story may suggest that increased sin is needed to restore the world from its fallenness. "Dazed" suggests that the only way for a world to be saved from sin is for it to fall further into it.

The same idea underpins the *Star Wars* series and its approach to good and evil. George Lucas's trilogy of prequels to the original three films explores the youth of the villain Darth Vader, who had once been named Anakin Skywalker, a Jedi Knight and a guardian of good in the galaxy. Prophesied as the "chosen one" who would restore balance to the Force, Skywalker descends into the deepest evil, becoming a murderous dictator. In *Star Wars: Episode III—Revenge of the Sith* (2005), he is seduced into evil by Senator Palpatine, a malicious Sith Lord who is to become the galactic emperor: "If one is to understand the great mystery, one must study all its aspects, not just the dogmatic, narrow view of the Jedi. If you wish to become a complete and wise leader, you must embrace a larger view of the Force."[42] Despite the sinister nature of the speaker, Palpatine's words are borne out by the full saga. Darth Vader becomes a powerful force for evil, but in *Return of the Jedi* (1983), he *does* restore balance to the Force by killing the emperor and thereby eliminating the evil power of the Sith. In the prequels, Lucas hoped to recast the story of *Star Wars*, changing it from a story about Luke Skywalker (Anakin's son) to a story about his father. This act turns the villain of the series into its hero. The problem with this approach is that the brief moments of good at the end of Vader's life pale in comparison to the decades of evil that preceded them. Vader restores balance, but only after a lifetime of contributing to imbalance.

Though George Lucas wants us to see the good in Darth Vader, SF has rarely shied away from presentations of absolute evil, frequently depicting individual beings or entire alien races that have no purpose other than that which earthly morality would define as diabolical. The definitive evil creature of SF is the title monster of Ridley Scott's 1979 film *Alien*. In this film, the blue-collar crew of an interplanetary freighter called the *Nostromo* is ordered by its employers to investigate a derelict alien spacecraft on an uncharted planet. The landing party brings back a parasitic alien creature that seems to have no motivation other than the desire to kill, and it eliminates most of the *Nostromo*'s crew. Ellen Ripley, the sole survivor, destroys the entire craft and flees in an escape shuttle before she is finally able to defeat the monster. The creature of *Alien* is undeniably and wholly evil. It lacks even a single redeeming moral quality, existing solely to kill. The film is additionally skeptical about the potential for human beings to be good—the company that owns the *Nostromo* wants the alien to be brought back to Earth alive for possible use as a military weapon—but nevertheless, life defeats death in the film's climax. The alien's death is to be taken as a victory of good—flawed, human good, perhaps, but good nonetheless—over absolute evil.

This idea of "evil aliens" is a typical trope of stories dealing with alien invasion, a subject epitomized by H. G. Wells's *The War of the Worlds* (1898). Both this novel and Byron Haskins's 1953 film adaptation describe an invasion by hostile Martians who destroy everything in their path, but unlike *Alien*, these stories give their creatures an understandable motivation. Mars, we are told, is a dying world, and its inhabitants must conquer our world or face destruction: "The immediate pressure of necessity has brightened their intellects, enlarged their powers, and hardened their hearts. And looking across space with instruments, and intelligences such as we have scarcely dreamed of, they see . . . a morning star of hope, our own warmer planet, green with vegetation and grey with water, with a cloudy atmosphere eloquent of fertility."[43] This background information explains the aliens' actions, though it cannot excuse their severity. The Martians are like Weston in *Out of the Silent Planet*—they have no morality beyond self-preservation, and their devotion to their own race leads them to commit a terrible crime against their neighbor. In more recent interpretations of Wells's mythic story, however, the invaders lack even this hint of a sympathetic purpose. A scientist in Roland Emmerich's 1996 film *Independence Day* (not a direct adaptation of Wells's story, but certainly based on the same concept) speculates that the invading aliens hope to colonize Earth, since their biological requirements are similar to ours. But when the U.S. President Thomas J. Whitmore talks with one of the creatures, he comes to understand that they are iredeemably evil:

Whitmore: Can there be a peace between us?

   Alien: Peace? No peace.

Whitmore: What is it you want us to do?

Alien: Die![44]

These aliens, it seems, have traversed the galaxy simply to kill. A comedic interpretation of the same idea appears in Tim Burton's film *Mars Attacks!* (1996), in which the invading aliens continue to insist that they "come in peace" even as they incinerate every human being they see. The illusion of communication makes these aliens all the more evil for their incomprehensibility. But the nameless aliens of Steven Spielberg's 2005 adaptation of *War of the Worlds* are even more inscrutably evil than any of these intergalactic monsters. Neither speaking nor offering by their actions any kind of explanation for their destructive presence on Earth, these beings kill without reason or purpose. The story of this film gives us no explanation for the carnage and no insight into the minds that perpetrate it.

What does the existence of these creatures say about the nature of evil? The world of Spielberg's *War of the Worlds* is a place where a creature of absolute evil *can* exist. The alien seems to fulfill the qualities that Father Ruiz-Sanchez sees in the Lithians in *A Case of Conscience*—it is difficult to imagine that such a creature could be created by God. They seem to possess intelligence, but they lack souls that can be redeemed. This film thus portrays a dualistic cosmos, in which there are some planets—such as that on which the invaders originated—that lack any sort of good. It seems that life, on these worlds, exists only for the purpose of suffering and death. This division makes Spielberg's film nearly Manichean in its dualistic understanding of the universe and morality. Pure evil cannot be reasoned with, but it can be fought. There is no room, in this story, for forgiveness: it is not the meek who shall inherit our planet, but rather those who are most willing to fight for it. By pitting humankind against beings who are depicted as irredeemably evil, with whom we cannot even initiate the communication that might lead to understanding, Spielberg's film adopts a chauvinistic dualism far removed from Christian ethics.

Even if we are not given an explanation for their actions, alien invaders probably do not see their own actions as evil. Aliens may not have the same understanding of evil that we do, and Ian Stewart and Jack Cohen explore a very different interpretation of murder in their novel *Wheelers*. This story introduces an ancient and intelligent race of balloonlike beings on the planet Jupiter. Since this planet's enormous mass makes it a magnet for comets and asteroids, its inhabitants have turned their planet's moons into a defense system that redirects these missiles to strike the inner planets. When a reconfiguration of the moons directs a planet-killing comet at Earth (or "Poisonblue," as the Jovians call it), human beings must establish contact with the aliens and convince them to redirect the comet. The Jovians are unimpressed by the argument that the comet will kill all living things on the planet's surface, arguing that similar disasters were necessary for life to emerge there in the first place: "These Poisonbluvian intelligences owe their very *existence* to a previous snowstrike! It destroyed their competitors and opened niches for them to evolve in! They can scarcely complain if another snowstrike opens up niches for their successors! Higher life-forms will quickly re-evolve! Intelligence could easily return to the planet in fifty million years or less!"[45] For these aliens, exterminating human life is not evil; in fact, by encouraging increased diversity, it may eventually be a greater good. The Jovians clearly put less value on individual life than we do, and so for them, murder—even on a planetary scale—is not a sin.

The universe itself may even share this cold moral relativism. The 1954 story "The Cold Equations" by Tom Godwin offers an understanding of the universe whereby nature itself appears evil. In this story, a stowaway is found on board an emergency supply craft. This craft carries exactly enough fuel to bring it to its location, and any additional mass will use the fuel up more quickly, thus dooming the ship itself and the colony to which it is bringing supplies. Interplanetary law thus requires that all stowaways be ejected into space. In this case, the stowaway is a teenaged girl who hid on the craft in order to see her brother, who is at the colony to which the ship is bringing supplies. She did not know about the harsh penalty for her crime or the reason for this penalty. The ship's pilot must make a decision—kill an innocent girl who had no idea that she has done anything wrong, or allow an entire colony to die without the supplies he is bringing them. Godwin presents a picture of a mathematically governed cosmos that has no emotions, no compassion, and no morality. The equations governing his vessel's rate of fuel consumption care nothing for any suffering they may cause:

> She had violated a man-made law that said KEEP OUT but the penalty was not for men's making or desire and it was not a penalty men could revoke. A physical law had decreed: *h amount of fuel will power an EDS* [Emergency Dispatch Ship] *with a mass of m safely to its destination*; and a second physical law had decreed: *h amount of fuel will not power an EDS with a mass of m plus x safely to its destination.* . . . . To himself and her brother and parents she was a sweet-faced girl in her teens; to the laws of nature she was *x*, the unwanted factor in a cold equation.[46]

Though this story does not explicitly describe nature as evil, it clearly expresses frustration at the lack of morality expressed in mathematical laws. But this absence of compassion is, in essence, evil—like the Alien, it kills without remorse or explanation. Thus this story, too, shows a hint of Manicheism along with its apparent atheism—it suggests that no God could create a universe that would allow an innocent to be killed. The alternative, though it is not stated outright, is clear; Godwin characterizes the rationalism of the "cold equations" as nearly demonic in their cruelty.

In the short story "The Fire Balloons" (1951), Ray Bradbury offers a much brighter picture of the universe that nevertheless acknowledges the existence of sin. The story follows two Episcopal priests—the stoic Father Stone and the adventurous Father Peregrine—who have been sent to a colony on Mars. Stone wants them to begin their assigned task of ministering to the colonists, but Peregrine has other interests—he wishes to discuss religion with the planet's indigenous inhabitants, large spheres of light that have made no apparent efforts to communicate with the human newcomers. At the story's beginning, Peregrine theorizes on the possible difficulties they will encounter on this new world: "Adam *alone* did not sin. Add Eve and you add temptation. Add a second man and you make adultery possible. With the addition of sex or people, you add sin. If men were armless they could not strangle with their hands. You would not have that particular sin of murder. Add arms, and you add the possibility of a new violence. . . . On Mars, what if there are five new senses, organs, invisible limbs we can't conceive of—then mightn't there be five new *sins*?"[47] At the story's close, once they have learned something of the religion of the "fire balloons," Father Stone offers the other side of this theory: "The way I see it there's a truth on every planet. All parts of the Big Truth. On a certain day they'll all fit together like the pieces of jigsaw. . . . And we'll go on to other worlds, adding the sum of the parts of the Truth until one day the whole Total will stand before us like the light of a new day."[48] With new worlds, there are new sins—but with those sins, there must be new virtues and new truths.

Much SF presents a view of the universe according to which there is something *wrong* that leads to hardship, suffering, and death. It hopes to provide an answer to this fundamental problem whereby human suffering may be understood, if not eliminated. This sense of wrongness permeates the genre (and arguably all literature), and even the most materialist of SF writers wish to provide readers with hope that the universe can be improved. SF hopes to show us that both the world around us and we ourselves can be made better, and this hope presupposes a sort of fallenness which must be rectified. In most SF there is something, either in humankind itself or in alien beings who wish to help us, that can overcome the problems of sin and suffering. New ideas of evil bring with them new understandings of good, new opportunities to express the best of ourselves. These stories present us not only with new moral problems, but new ways to be moral; not only with sin, but with *salvation*.

Chapter Six

Christ, Prometheus, and Klaatu: Alien Messiahs

Whether the futures it presents are bleak or bright, SF is always concerned with salvation. By warning us of our current folly or presenting paradises of the future, SF hopes to improve the human condition. It is no surprise, then, that the genre has offered fictional saviors—prophets and messiahs, both religious and secular, who transform their worlds into the paradise that the future should be. But this transformation may be accompanied by violent disruptions of the established order. In Matthew 10:34–36, Jesus describes the disorder that must come to usher in the kingdom: "Do not think that I have come to bring peace to the earth; I have not come to bring peace, but a sword. For I have come to set a man against his father, and a daughter against her mother . . . and one's foes will be members of one's own household." Moses' role as prophet and liberator of the Hebrews is perhaps an even more dramatic example of a savior's role in bringing a new order that utterly replaces the old one. SF depicts fictional messiahs and theoretical salvation, hoping to anticipate the needs of the future. By predicting the saviors of the future, SF hopes to save us by showing us the keys to our own salvation.

Several SF authors have written stories that deal explicitly with the definitive Messiah figure: Jesus. The most prominent of these is Michael Moorcock's *Behold the Man* (1968). Moorcock was a leading figure in the "New Wave" of the 1960s and '70s, a radical movement that brought experimental literary techniques and themes into SF. This novel describes the spiritual and temporal journey of an agnostic named Karl Glogauer. Glogauer has been obsessed with Christ—and with the crucifixion in particular—for his entire life, and when the antagonism of his atheistic wife becomes unbearable, he volunteers to test out a colleague's experimental time machine. Glogauer arrives in Judea in what he assumes to be the year that Christ's ministry began, but the time machine is damaged, trapping him in the past. Despite this setback, he immediately begins searching for information about Jesus, meeting John the Baptist and the Essenes before traveling to Nazareth. There, he finds Jesus, son of Mary and Joseph the carpenter, who he discovers is anything but the redeemer of the Gospels: "The figure was misshapen. It had a pronounced hunched back and a cast in its left eye. The face was vacant and foolish. There was a little spittle on the lips. . . . It giggled as its name was repeated . . . 'Jesus,' it said. The word was slurred and thick. 'Jesus.' "[1] The shock of this discovery, combined with the destruction of the time machine, drives Glogauer insane. His obsession with Jesus leads to the confusion of his own identity, and he finds himself repeating the actions of Christ as described in the Gospels. Eventually, he gains followers who begin to call him "Jesus of Nazareth." When he and his followers enter Jerusalem, the city's residents greet him as a liberator, gathering around his donkey and cheering:

> He heard the words, but could not make them out clearly.
> "*Osha'na! Osha'na!*"
> It sounded like "hosanna" at first, before he realized that they were shouting the Aramaic for "Free us."
> "Free us! Free us!"
> John had planned to rise in arms against the Romans this Passover. Many had expected to take part in the rebellion.
> They believed that he was taking John's place as a rebel leader.
> "No," he muttered at them as he looked around at their expectant faces. "No. I am the messiah. I cannot free you. I can't . . . "[2]

The Romans, too, consider Glogauer a rebel leader, and he is arrested and crucified, having become the savior he had hoped to learn about.

Behold the Man is in many ways critical of Christianity in general and the crucified savior in particular. (Glogauer's final words from the cross, for example, are not "Eloi, Eloi," but "It's a lie, it's a lie.")[3] The book puts forth the assumption that Jesus was not a savior at all until later generations *created* him as one. Glogauer's quest for the truth leads ultimately to a death in which he finds no meaning. But the story is filled with Jungian speculation on the nature of myth: "It was not his own life he would be leading now. He was bringing a myth to life, a generation before that myth would be born. He was completing a certain kind of psychic circuit. He told himself that he was not changing history; he was merely giving history more substance. Since he had never been able to bear to think that Jesus had been nothing more than a myth, it became a duty to himself to make Jesus a physical reality rather than a creation of a process of mythogenesis."[4] By embodying the story of Jesus, Glogauer achieves a limited salvation for himself. But even this salvation is criticized: throughout the novel Moorcock depicts Glogauer's search for the truth about Christ as a self-centered obsession, based as much on masochism as actual historical interest, that creates a detachment from the time in which he has found himself. This detachment is exemplified by Glogauer's refusal to lead the oppressed Hebrews in a revolt against their Roman rulers for no other reason than that it was "not part of the story." Glogauer's use of the term "messiah" as he enters Jerusalem is laced with irony, and carries the implication that such a messiah cannot truly save anyone. Moorcock's intentions in this complex novel are not entirely clear: is he criticizing one particular understanding of Jesus' salvation through self-sacrifice, or the very concept of a redeemer? Regardless of the author's ultimate intentions, the novel suggests that myths have a power that transcends the question of historical truth, and that the obsessive search for truths that are inherently unknowable is a pointless exercise. It is better, Moorcock suggests, to look for where those myths intersect our lives, rather than rearranging our lives around them, and in that way to find whatever salvation is available.

A very different approach to Jesus is revealed in Philip José Farmer's *Jesus on Mars* (1979). In this novel, a group of astronauts exploring Mars is surprised to find a tunnel leading to an underground colony inhabited by both humans and members of a highly advanced alien species called the Krsh. The human members of this colony are descended from Jews who were brought to Mars by the Krsh around the year 50 CE. All of the inhabitants of Mars, human and Krsh alike, practice a form of orthodox Judaism, and soon it is revealed that they believe Jesus Christ is the Messiah. The astronauts are shocked to learn that the Martian Jews not only believe in Jesus, but claim he is alive on Mars, and has ruled there for two thousand years. The history of the Mars colony is revealed gradually throughout the novel: among the first human beings the Krsh met on earth was a Hebrew named Matthias—the man chosen by the apostles to replace Judas Iscariot. Matthias eventually converted all of the humans on Mars to his form of Christianity, writing an account of Jesus' life on Earth entitled *The Testament of Matthias.* Shortly after this group relocated to Mars, Jesus appeared among them, convincing the Krsh to convert to Matthias's messianic Judaism. Jesus became the ruler of Mars, and the Martian Jews believe him to be the Messiah who is waiting until the appointed time for his return to Earth to rule over the kingdom of God.

In a private conversation with Richard Orme, one of the astronauts who discovers this colony, Jesus himself reveals an alternate possibility regarding his origin: he suggests that he is not the true Jesus, but rather an alien energy being that has adapted itself to the beliefs of Matthias. Disturbed by war, disease, and injustice and moved by a desire to improve humankind's situation, the being decided that "as Jesus, it would announce that he had decided to go with the Krsh to their world and preach there. And someday he would return to Earth, to Jerusalem itself, and establish the new state of Zion as foretold, though somewhat ambiguously, in the book you call the Old Testament and the New Testament. . . . This being saw a way to make the people of Earth healthy and happy."[5] As is often the case in Farmer's novels, these revelations about the novel's central mystery are not presented as fact, but rather as a hypothesis that is never confirmed, and that is called into question even by the character who states it. The story leaves the true nature of this Jesus ambiguous.

There is no ambiguity regarding the astronaut's fears about the potential effects of a living, miracle-working Jesus on Earth's society: "What was the effect of Jesus' announcement that he would be coming to Earth? Consternation, of course. Especially among the statesmen and the religious. This was the most upsetting news that had ever come to Earth, and its implications were more than religious. They would reverberate throughout every field: political, religious, scientific, economic, psychological, you name it."[6] Despite these fears, the novel's climactic scenes are distinctly optimistic about the Messiah's return to Earth. Orme, thrown into doubt by Jesus' strange hints about his alien origins, considers assassinating what he sees as a potential antichrist. But he reconsiders, and in the end risks his own life in thwarting another would-be assassin from killing Jesus. The novel ends with his explanation of his change of heart: "Perhaps it was because, somewhere deep in my mind, was the thought that it made no difference if you were this energy-being and not the original Jesus. The Father uses many hands to do His work. . . . [He may choose] a nonhuman creature from a faroff planet to be the Messiah, just as He chose the Krsh to be among the People of the Covenant."[7] The Martian Jesus has the ability to cure disease, raise the dead, and possibly even unite the world under his own peaceful rule. It matters little, Farmer argues, whether this new reign has supernatural or scientific origins. The *idea* of Jesus has the power to bring the world together, and it is the devotion of humanity to that idea that will ultimately bring about the Kingdom. In *Jesus on Mars*, Farmer argues that it is not the Savior that matters, but rather the salvation.

SF stories about Jesus are frequently preoccupied with uncovering "what really happened," an approach that betrays an inherent distrust of the biblical record. This distrust is not entirely iconoclastic, however: despite the assumption of flaws in the Gospel accounts of Jesus' life, such stories nevertheless show respect for both the person and story of Jesus, a belief that his life was important and holds valuable lessons for the people of our time and of the future. Stories such as *Behold the Man* are comparable to the recent scholarly discussion of "the historical Jesus," which similarly hopes to overcome the barrier of time to uncover the valuable truth about Jesus' life. Biblical historian John Dominic Crossan argues that scripture offers multiple interpretations of who Jesus was:

> I propose that at the heart of any Christianity there is always, covertly or overtly, a dialectic between a historically read Jesus and a theologically read Christ. . . . The New Testament itself contains a spectrum of divergent theological interpretations, each of which focuses on different aspects or clusters of aspects concerning the historical Jesus, or better, different historical Jesuses. It may be, for example, only the sayings, or only the miracles, or only the death, that is of primary concern for a given tradition, but any of those emphases presumes divergent historical Jesuses who said something, did something, and died in a certain way. . . . There will always be divergent historical Jesuses, [and] there will always be divergent Christs built upon them, but . . . the structure of a Christianity will always be: *this is how we see Jesus-then as Christ-now.*[8]

Scripture offers multiple understandings of Jesus, and extracanonical texts broaden this pluralism even further. But Crossan argues that faith in Christ is an act of interpretation, and to make Scripture meaningful, to establish a relationship with Christ, we must determine what we believe about the historical Jesus. Authors such as Moorcock and Farmer use speculative fiction to approach the past; biblical scholars such as Crossan use speculative hermeneutics to do the same.

In addition to its explorations of the Jesus of scripture and history, SF has introduced new ideas of the messiah, and with these new definitions of salvation. The nature of redemption in SF is often defined in a far more tangible sense than in traditional theology. Christ rescued us from the ontological state of sin, a largely subjective salvation that leads to a new way of understanding one's place in the cosmos. SF's saviors bring a narrower sort of redemption, halting specific disasters rather than transforming the nature of reality. In Fritz Lang's film *Metropolis* (1927), for example, a prophesied savior turns out to be little more than a mediator in labor disputes, and in Mimi Leder's movie *Deep Impact* (1998), the crew of a spaceship called *Messiah* saves Earth from a planet-destroying comet. But most frequently the saviors of SF rescue us from ourselves, curtailing the self-destructive aspects of human nature that would find their ultimate expression in nuclear war. This salvation is epitomized in Robert Wise's 1951 film *The Day the Earth Stood Still*, which depicts the definitive savior from the stars in the character of Klaatu. Arriving in a flying saucer with an indestructible robot named Gort, this humanoid alien is depicted as a Christ figure from his very first words to Earth's people: "We have come to visit you in peace and with good will."[9] Klaatu announces his presence using the terminology of the angel who announces Christ's birth in Luke 2:14, KJV: "Glory to God in the highest, and on earth peace, good will toward men." He attempts to organize a meeting of all the world's governments, but the Cold War tensions between the Soviet and American governments prohibit such a conference. The army attempts to imprison him, but he escapes, hiding with a middle-class family under an assumed name that also evokes Jesus—Mr. Carpenter. The army soon finds and kills Klaatu, but Gort brings him back to the spaceship, using an alien machine to bring him back to life. Appealing to Earth's scientists, he delivers a final sermon from the doorway of his spacecraft in which he details the salvation that he offers: "I came here to give you these facts: it is no concern of ours how you run your own planet, but if you threaten to extend your violence, this Earth of yours will be reduced to a burned-out cinder. Your choice is simple: join us and live in peace or pursue your present course and face obliteration."[10] His message delivered, Klaatu ascends to the heavens in his saucer, leaving humanity to decide its fate. Though he is presented as a messiah in the mold of Jesus, Klaatu's salvation is a far different one from that described in the New Testament. His death, rather than being the instrument of redemption, is an impediment to it, and his final warning to the people of Earth sounds more like a threat than an offer of grace. But *The Day the Earth Stood Still* is paradigmatic of SF's approach to the messiahs of the future. Rather than saving us from the abstract concepts of sin and death, these saviors rescue us from the all-too-possible danger of self-destruction.

The same sort of salvation ends in failure in Walter Tevis's tragic 1963 novel *The Man Who Fell to Earth*. This story is the poignant tale of a failed messiah, an alien who travels from his home planet to Earth with the dual goals of sending much-needed resources to his dwindling race and saving humankind from destroying itself. The humanoid alien travels from the planet Anthea, which has been devastated by nuclear war. Fewer than three hundred Antheans remain alive, and though they are technologically advanced, they lack the natural resources to emigrate from their dying world. One Anthean arrives on Earth and, under the assumed name of Thomas Jerome Newton, builds a fortune by patenting basic Anthean technology. Once he has amassed enough wealth, he begins building a spaceship—an "ark" to transport the remaining Antheans to Earth. Once there, they will slowly and subtly take over Earth's governments, just as Newton has taken over American industry, and guide humankind toward peace: " 'We know about weapons and defenses. Yours are still crude. We can, for instance, . . . generate an energy system that will prevent the detonation of any of your nuclear weapons within a five-mile radius. . . . We can reduce the probability of Hitlers, and we can protect your major cities from destruction. And that'—he shrugged—'is more than you can do.' "[11]

Newton's plan does not go smoothly, however. Sidetracked by money and alcohol, he withdraws into his alienation and depression, delaying his urgent mission. He has lost interest in keeping his plan in motion: "The plan itself was going so well—the great amounts of money made, the construction of the ship begun with almost no difficulty, the failure of anyone . . . to recognize him for what he was—and the possibility of success was now so close. And he, an Anthean, a superior being from a superior race, was losing control, becoming a degenerate, a drunkard, a lost and foolish creature, a renegade and, possibly, a traitor to his own."[12] This decline is accelerated when the United States government discovers Newton's alien origins and detains him for several months. In the course of investigating his alien physiology, the government's scientists accidentally blind Newton, and when he is finally released, he abandons the project that would have saved his planet. Blind, alcoholic, and possibly driven mad by his isolation on Earth, Newton spends the rest of his life in self-imposed obscurity.

Tevis's novel is rich with detailed allegory, comparing Newton to Rumplestiltskin, Icarus (particularly as the unnoticed figure depicted in Peter Breughel's painting *Landscape with Fall of Icarus*), and Jesus Christ. Newton has the power to save his own race and, once his people have arrived on Earth, to protect humanity from Anthea's fate. But he becomes a tragic figure, a failed savior. His alien superiority, which should be the tool that leads to the mutual salvation of Anthea and Earth, becomes the cause of his isolation. But he also fails because he becomes *too* human, adopting human weaknesses and forgetting his alien origins. Christ became human to save us, but Newton *cannot* save us because he becomes human. Though Newton begins his journey as Christ's second coming, descending from the sky to inaugurate the kingdom of God, he ends it as Icarus: "[He] may be the Second Coming. . . . But Icarus had failed, had burned and drowned, while Daedelus, who had not gone so high, had escaped from his lonely island. Not to save the world, however. Maybe even to destroy it, for he had invented flights; and destruction, when it came, would come from the air."[13] Newton's failure to complete his salvific task may lead indirectly to the world's destruction.

Tevis's protagonist evokes the concept of the soul's position in the universe and the role of the savior in the various gnostic cosmologies. The ancient Syriac text "The Hymn of the Pearl" illustrates these ideas in terminology strongly echoed in *The Man Who Fell to Earth*. This allegorical tale tells of a prince, symbolizing humankind, who is sent into a foreign land to steal a unique pearl. Arriving there, he disguises himself:

> I clothed myself in their garments, lest they suspect me as one coming from without to take the Pearl. . . . But through some cause they marked that I was not their countryman, and they ingratiated themselves with me, and mixed me [drink] with their

cunning, and gave me to taste of their meat; and I forgot that I was a king's son and served their king. I forgot the Pearl for which my parents had sent me. Through the heaviness of their nourishment I sank into deep slumber.[14]

Human beings are lost in a strange land, and await a call from without to awaken them to their true nature and call them back to the heavenly realm of our origin. *The Man Who Fell to Earth* uses the same symbols of disguise and intoxication to tell the powerfully tragic tale of a savior in need of salvation.

Carolyn Ives Gilman's 2001 story "The Real Thing" inverts Newton's conundrum, describing a woman who does not wish to be a messiah, but is molded as one by a commercialized society. This reluctant savior is Sage Akwesasne, a woman who is sent into the future as a beam of information. She awakens in a culture in which everything—including this visitor from the past—has become a corporate commodity, and learns that the law of this age considers her to be not a person, but rather a copyrighted replica of one. The company that "owns" her decides to market her as a myth: "In a way, this isn't about you at all. It's about the *idea* of you, and that transcends all of us. You answer a yearning in the culture. Our world is hungry for heroes. The brave woman who gave up her life to become a beam of light, and traveled around a black hole to come back to us—it's Promethean, it's Orphic, it hits us at this limbic level. You are a heavenly messenger. . . . You've come to redeem us from our cynicism, and I can't let you let us down."[15] This future society needs saving, but to do so from within the false scenarios of mass entertainment would do nothing to change its situation. Akwesasne did not set out to be a messiah, but the culture of the future demands that she be one.

A similar situation meets Benjamin Sisko, captain of the space station of *Star Trek: Deep Space Nine*. Arriving on the station, which orbits the planet Bajor, he learns that the native people of the star system believe him to be "the Emissary of the Prophets"— a foretold savior who will reestablish contact with the Bajoran gods, the Prophets, who reside in the "Celestial Temple." Sisko soon learns that there is truth behind the faith of the Bajorans when he discovers a wormhole in the Bajoran system in which live super-powerful, extratemporal aliens. These aliens, it seems, are the Prophets, and the wormhole is the Celestial Temple. Still, Sisko is reluctant to accept the role of Emissary, and he is skeptical about the ancient prophecies that the Bajorans claim come from the Prophets. In the 1995 episode "Destiny," Sisko states this reluctance in response to a specific prophecy that his Bajoran second-in-command, Kira Nerys, believes is coming true: "I hope I don't offend your beliefs, but I don't see myself as an icon, religious or otherwise. I'm a Starfleet Officer, and I have a mission to accomplish."[16] But Kira explains to him that, despite his opinion of his own role in the Bajorans' prophecies, he need not doubt the Prophets themselves:

> The prophets—the aliens that live in the wormhole, as you call them—exist outside of linear time. They know the past, present, and future. . . . It seems perfectly reasonable that they could've communicated knowledge of the future to a Bajoran named Trakor. He wrote down that knowledge in the form of a prophecy, and now, three thousand years later, we are seeing those events unfold. To me, that reasoning sounds concrete.[17]

By the episode's close, the prophecy has been fulfilled, and Sisko's reluctance to accept the role of the Bajoran messiah has begun to recede. As the series progresses and Sisko witnesses more and more of the Prophets' power, he becomes increasingly comfortable in his role as the Emissary. But at the same time his interactions with the Prophets become increasingly frustrating. Their communications with him are enigmatic, and they often demand that he act against his own desires. He defies them openly in the 1999 episode "'Til Death Do Us Part," in which he marries a woman named Kasidy Yates despite the Prophets' insistence that he should not: "To them I'm 'the Sisko,' an instrument to carry out their wishes. But they forget that I am also human, with dreams and wishes of my own. They say that marrying Kasidy is a mistake— well maybe it is. But it's my mistake to make."[18] In the show's final season, Sisko learns that he was essentially created by the Prophets, one of whom inhabited the body of his mother to arrange his conception. Further, in the last episode of the show he becomes one of the Prophets himself, joining them in the Celestial Temple—and, since the inhabitants of the wormhole exist outside of time, he thus becomes one of the beings that have guided him since his arrival to the Bajoran sector. *Deep Space Nine* is the story of a messiah who slowly grows to accept his salvific task, and by so doing becomes a god.

The hero of George Miller and George Ogilvie's 1985 film *Mad Max beyond Thunderdome* becomes a reluctant messiah in the mold of Moses, guiding a lost civilization to rebuild its own promised land. Max, a drifter in the wasteland of postapocalyptic Australia, finds a society of children who have turned their hope for rescue from the hardships of their world into a religion. The children describe the half-remembered origins of their village in a story that takes on the dimensions of myth: on the eve of the nuclear war that devastated their world, a man named Captain Walker put them on a plane to fly them to safety. But in the immediate aftermath of the "Pox-Eclipse," their plane crashed. Captain Walker left the survivors to find help, promising to return. Now, the children await Captain Walker's return, believing that he will fly them to "Tomorrow-Morrow Land"—the world before the war, which they imagine as a paradise. Max bears a remarkable resemblance to Captain Walker, and the children are immediately convinced that he is their returning savior. When he realizes what they think him to be, he disabuses them of their faith: "There were places like these—cities, they were called cities. . . . But then . . . this 'Pox-Eclipse' happened, and that's—it's all finished, it just isn't there anymore. You've got to understand that this is home, and there's no Tomorrow-Land, and that I ain't Captain Walker."[19] His statement splits the community—some accept his words with resignation, determined to put their hopes for Tomorrow-Morrow Land aside and stay in their village. But others, realizing that Max is just a man and not a god, see that they have a chance to survive a trek across the desert, and set out to return to what remains of society. Max fears that they will either die on their journey or fall into the hands of slavers, and so he sets out after those who depart, becoming their reluctant protector. After a perilous journey, they meet Jedediah, a biplane pilot who flies them to the ruins of Sydney. There, they begin to establish a new society, and at the film's close, we hear Savannah, the children's leader, telling the myth of this new culture's origin: "Every night we does the Tell, so that we 'member who we was and where we came from. But most of all we 'members the man who finded us, him that came the salvage. And we lights the city, not just for him but for all of them that are still out there. Cause we knows, there'll come a night when they sees the distant light, and they'll be coming home."[20] Max is a messiah for a devastated culture, not saving the people of his wasteland world, but "salvaging" them. Like Moses, he brings his people through the desert to their promised land, but cannot enter it. He is instrumental in the foundation of a new society, but he has no part of it, living forever on the fringes of his world.

Frank Herbert's epic *Dune* sequence presents not one but several messiahs who struggle for power and survival in a harsh, violent universe. The *Dune* novels take place in a far future governed by feuding hereditary houses and ancient secret societies, with the basis of power centered on a narcotic spice that is mined on the desert planet Arrakis. The spice has numerous bizarre properties, such as lengthening the human lifespan and, if ingested in large quantities, causing strange physical transformations. But its most important effect is endowing some of its users with a limited precognition that is vital to space travel, allowing navigators to foresee and avoid obstacles in the unfathomably long distances between planets. The spice can only be produced in the unique ecology of Arrakis, and thus control of the planet is a prize hotly disputed among the feuding houses of the galactic empire. Recognizing the power and wealth contained on the planet, the galaxy's emperor grants control of Arrakis to the feudal houses for limited periods of time, balancing interstellar power by allowing all of the houses a chance to build wealth on the planet. The most powerful of the galaxy's secret societies, the Bene Gesserit, also seeks control, and uses a millennia-old breeding program to consolidate its power across the houses and produce more and more powerful royalty. These organizations battle for control of Arrakis, knowing that with the planet they can control the galaxy.

The first novel in the series, the Hugo and Nebula Award–winning *Dune* (1965), begins as Arrakis is changing hands. House Harkonnen has governed the planet for decades with an iron fist, violently suppressing its natives, the Fremen. The Harkonnen, unwilling to hand so valuable a planet over to their biggest rivals, assassinate the head of House Atreides and drive his heir, Paul, into exile among the desert Fremen. After being among them for several years, Paul—renamed "Muad'dib" by the Fremen—becomes the desert rebels' leader, eventually guiding them to military victory over the Harkonnen and the Emperor who supports them. The Fremen see Paul as their messiah, calling him "mahdi," a word derived from the Arabic term for the savior anticipated by Shi'ite Muslims. The Fremen speculate that he is the man whom their ancient prophecies call the "Lisan al-Ghaib," or "the Voice from the Outer World": "They've a legend here, a prophecy, that a leader will come to them, child of a Bene Gesserit, to lead them to true freedom. It follows the familiar messiah pattern."[21] Paul does fulfill the Fremen prophecies, but there is irony in his prophetic role, as the novel makes it clear that the Fremen prophecies were planted thousands of years earlier by a branch of the Bene Gesserit: "The Missionaria Protectiva wove a thin but strong anticipation of a messiah figure, an individual whose coming would signal the beginning of the culture's final triumph, the fulfillment of its ultimate hopes . . . [but it] could not anticipate that . . . the 'messiah' . . . would ever be physically present on Arrakis."[22] But Paul is not only the Fremen mahdi, but also the fulfillment of the centuries-old Bene Gesserit breeding program, the "kwisatz haderach." Due to the combination of Paul's breeding, training, and exposure to the spice, he is able to foresee the future. This unique combination of elements makes him a ruler of unprecedented power, a religious and political leader whose abilities make him an unstoppable galactic force.

By the opening of the second novel, *Dune Messiah* (1969), Paul's rule has extended from Arrakis to encompass the entire known universe. His power extends to every part of his society: "He's the kwisatz haderach, the one who can be many places at once. He's the Mahdi whose merest whim is absolute command to his Qizarate missionaries. He's the mentat whose computational mind surpasses the greatest ancient computers. He is Muad'dib whose orders to the Fremen legions depopulate planets. He possesses oracular vision which sees into the future."[23] Paul has spread his power throughout the universe by means of a military campaign of unprecedented brutality, a "jihad" in which all those who oppose the rule of the Fremen messiah were executed. Paul is only inadvertently responsible for this movement, which the novels attribute more to the zealotry of Muad'dib's followers than to his own choices or orders. Nevertheless, the jihad marks the transformation of the Fremen's mahdi from a savior to a tyrant, and it is unclear if the title of *Dune Messiah* refers to Paul or to his would-be assassin. The following two novels in the series, *Children of Dune* (1976) and *God Emperor of Dune* (1981), tell the story of Paul's son, Leto, who inherits his father's prescience as well as awakening within himself the memories of all of his ancestors for thousands of years prior. Leto reclaims his father's power over Arrakis, ruling over the galaxy for over three thousand years. He transforms himself into a giant sandworm in order to guarantee that his power and his plan for the universe will continue uninterrupted. Using his prescience and ancestral wisdom to guide humanity on the "Golden Path," Leto transforms Arrakis into a garden planet, but this halts the production of spice. He views himself as a "predator" whose reign will force humankind to adapt and transform themselves into "a humankind that can make truly long-term decisions."[24] But Leto robs them of their free will, and thus he must give them freedom from himself. He ultimately sacrifices his own life, arranging his own assassination so that the universe may be free of its despot. Leto becomes an ironic messiah—he is both the savior and the enslaver. The *Dune* novels present a complex pattern of salvation that plays out over centuries. Paul—the savior of the Fremen—remakes the universe in violence and bloodshed, and his heir Leto reshapes it by revoking human freedom. Both of *Dune*'s messiahs are governing gods, channeling their extraordinary abilities into temporal power. But in the end Leto transforms himself into a self-sacrificing messiah in the Christian mode, leaving humanity far stronger than it was before his ascendance. *Dune*'s Paul Muad'dib and Leto Atreides are fine examples of the most frequent SF concept of the messiah—a human being more advanced than those around him or her, a "man of the future" who pulls his society into a new age.

The ultimate expression of this idea is the Man of Tomorrow created by Jerry Siegel and Joe Shuster—Superman. Superman is undoubtedly the most recognizable messiah figure in modern popular culture—a superpowered alien who dedicates his extraordinary abilities to the betterment of humankind. Superman's origin story carries strong parallels to the infancy narrative of Moses: his Kryptonian parents send their infant son Kal-El from their doomed planet in an interstellar life raft, much as Moses' mother protects him from Pharaoh's tyranny by releasing him on a raft into the Nile in Exodus 2:1–10. Siegel and Shuster, Superman's creators, were Jewish, and almost certainly had the story of Moses in mind when they wrote the story of their alien Messiah. In the 1978 film *Superman*, director Richard Donner builds on the Jewish messianic imagery inherent in the character's origin by describing Superman in Christian terminology. In a message recorded before the destruction of Krypton, Jor-El, Superman's father, tells him: "Live as one of them, Kal-El, to discover where your strength and power are needed. . . . They can be a great people, Kal-El, they wish to be. They only lack the light to show the way. For this reason, above all, their capacity for good, I have sent them you, my only son."[25] Jor-El's statement is a clear evocation of John 3:16's statement that "God so loved the world that he gave his only Son." *Superman* places the hero of its title in this context to underscore its characterization of Kal-El as a messiah from another world.

There are inherent messianic qualities in the SF concept of the superhero—an individual with exceptional abilities who sacrifices part of his or her life for the greater good. *Chosen*, a 2004 comic series by writer Mark Millar and artist Peter Gross, tells the story of a could-be Messiah through the distinctive lens of a superhero origin story. In this series, a seemingly normal young boy named Jodie Christianson discovers that he has exceptional powers, abilities that bear a remarkable resemblance to the miracles of Jesus as described in the New Testament. They are miracles with a modern twist: for example, multiplying sesame rolls and bringing a friend's hamster back from the dead. He preaches to his grade-school followers in terms they can understand:

> Okay, you got to think of the Old Testament as *Star Wars*. . . .
> Everybody likes it, the characters were great, and its huge suc-
> cess was always gonna change the world forever. The New Tes-
> tament is essentially *The Empire Strikes Back*. Unlike most
> sequels, the hard-core fans like it better than the original. . . . We
> get a trailer for [the final part of the trilogy] called the Book of
> Revelation, and that's what we're living in now, guys—*Return
> of the* friggin' *Jedi*.[26]

But Jodie is not the savior he appears to be: in the story's final chapter, we learn that he is a pawn of an evil church with dark designs for his future. With its vivid opening ideas and dark ending, *Chosen* both uncovers and subverts the messianic tendencies inherent in the superhero genre.

Writer Greg Pak and artist Charlie Adlard's 2004 comic book series *Warlock* tells a similar story of a genetically engineered messiah named Adam Warlock. This series updates a character from the 1970s whose earlier appearances, Donald Palumbo writes, "read far more like unusually philosophical and relentlessly allegorical science fiction novels than like Marvel's usual superhero fantasy fare. . . . [The character's defining plotline] concludes with Warlock's death, resurrection, and ascension."[27] In Pak and Adlard's interpretation, Adam is a violent messiah, rather than a suffering one. The scientists who created Adam hope that he will inaugurate an earthly paradise: "He's supposed to use his incredible powers to save humanity from self-destruction and establish a utopian dictatorship to rule the world."[28] But in order to create this paradise, he must destroy the world into which he is born, a bleak near-future rife with terrorism and pollution. Adam is programmed to kill all those who would stand in the way of his mission. But with the guidance of a college student named Janie Chin, he overcomes his programming, becoming a peaceful savior who heals rather than kills, repairs rather than destroys. This transformation removes the moral ambiguity of Warlock's original goals, making the task of salvation more difficult—but also more fulfilling: "Maybe this world needs a vengeful god. It'll have to settle for me."[29] Much as in *Chosen*, *Warlock* describes the genesis of a savior in the language of superheroics, revealing a powerfully pragmatic interpretation of savior and salvation.

But there is an inherent problem in the idea of superheroes in general and the Superman myth in particular. In order for the fictional world of Metropolis to remain recognizable to readers, Superman cannot use his powers to make fundamental changes to the environment or to human society. The presence of a real Superman on our world would probably almost certainly lead to a massive upheaval of society: a single Kryptonian on Earth could end famine, poverty, and war forever. The open-ended nature of mainstream comics publishing is similar to the world of most television sitcoms—the status quo must be upheld in order for the stories to remain recognizable and comprehensible to new audiences, and major shakeups can only occur infrequently. One of the most successful critiques of the Superman dilemma appears in a limited-run series entitled *Squadron Supreme*. Originally created by writer Mark Gruenwald and several artists in 1985–86, the series was reimagined by writer J. Michael Straczynski and artist Gary Frank in the 2004–05 series *Supreme Power* and the ongoing *Squadron Supreme* (2006). The world in which the superhero team of the title lives has been plunged into chaos by a series of disasters caused by the team's worst enemies. To stabilize their society, the Squadron takes absolute control of the world, becoming benevolent dictators. Hyperion, the team's leader and an alien superhuman in the mold of Superman, states his intentions: "Sometimes I think that only someone who was truly an alien could solve all the world's problems, because only an alien could be objective enough to get the job done."[30] But another member named Nighthawk disagrees, and is the first to speak against their actions: "How meaningful will a utopia be if it is a gift and not something man has earned by his own labors? What if the people will not accept the utopia you give them? Will you *force* them to take it?"[31] Nighthawk is the story's conscience, and the series becomes a

powerful essay on the nature of freedom and the tragedy of messiahs who offer too-easy answers.

Miracleman, written by Alan Moore with various artists
between 1982 and 1989, takes a similar approach, and is undoubtedly the best and most powerful exploration of the messianic
aspects of the superhero genre. The storyline "Olympus," illustrated by John Totleben, is the culmination of these themes. After
defeating a supervillain who destroys the city of London and kills
millions of its people, the hero of the title realizes that reacting to
crises is not enough, and that he must prevent the possibility of
such devastation occurring again. Along with several superhuman
colleagues, he seizes control of the world's governments, single-
handedly eliminating the world's nuclear arsenals and ending
famine. Together, they forge a new society based on the equality
of all human beings before the immeasurable superiority of the
superpowers: "We drafted pure and abstract blueprints free from
moral complications, and were architects of dreams. . . . Our exca-
vations gradually uncover[ed] the future, archeology staged in
reverse, and we were the builders of tomorrow."[32] Moore treats the
superhumans' utopia as a blessing tinged with tragedy that robs
human beings of their free will. His successor on the series, Neil
Gaiman, focuses instead on the positive aspects of such a society,
telling moving tales of the interaction between normal human
beings and their superpowered rulers. Both present Miracleman as
a flawed messiah, a god who is uncertain how to relate to his own
humanity, and the salvation he offers is always presented as a
mixed blessing.

SF frequently presents a future radically different from either
past or present. Such a world, many stories argue, will need a new
messiah, a new divine messenger to tell us how to exist in an
unprecedented future. Such is the case in Michael Bishop's 1983
story "The Gospel according to Gamaliel Crucis." This story, written in the style of a gospel (including chapter and verse numbers),
describes an alien savior from an insectoid race, part of a brood of
hundreds, each one an alien incarnation of God. Since the planet
has saviors to spare, one of them returns to Earth with the group of
explorers that discovered her world. The alien, named Mantik-

horas, begins a bizarre ministry on Earth, giving sermons on television and preaching her message to dolphins and apes as well as
humans. The alien's followers receive a revelation of the alien's
purpose when they visit a church, and hear a divine voice speak:
"This is another of my beloved issue . . . in whom I renew my
covenant with the lost, and the sick at heart, and the broken in
body; and I send her in the guise of the Female to straighten what
has been made crooked and in the flesh of the Alien to prepare the
worlds for a wider love."[33] Christ's mission was to establish the
kingdom on Earth; Mantikhoras hopes to expand it to encompass
the galaxy. She is a savior for a future yet to unfold, attempting to
shape what is to come into something heavenly.

Robert Heinlein presents a similarly forward-looking messiah
in his most famous novel, the Hugo Award–winning *Stranger in a
Strange Land* (1961). The hero of this novel, Michael Valentine
Smith, is a being somewhere between alien and human. The son of
human astronauts who lived on Mars and died shortly after his
birth, he was raised in the bizarre society of the native Martians.
When a second Martian expedition discovers him and returns him
to Earth, his attempts to reconcile his Martian upbringing with his
Earthly heritage results in the formation of a religious cult. Among
Smith's main tenets are free love (albeit of a decidedly patriarchal
sort), funeral rites incorporating cannibalism, rituals based on
the sharing of water, and—most importantly—the concept of
"grokking": "["Grok"] means 'fear,' it means 'love,' it means
'hate'—proper hate, for by the Martian 'map' you cannot possibly
hate anything unless you grok it completely, understand it so thoroughly that you merge with it and it merges with you. . . . 'Grok'
means to understand so thoroughly that the observer becomes a
part of the process being observed."[34] Smith sets up his church as
a communal "nest," an extended family containing members of
many faiths. The nest is primarily a language school—only by
learning the Martian language can the church's members comprehend the truths of Smith's alien religion, and with that understanding ("grokking") of the language they gain psychic and
telekinetic abilities. The Church of All Worlds is persecuted by
those who consider Smith's preaching blasphemous or scandalous,

and Smith eventually becomes a willing martyr, choosing to "discorporate" by allowing an angry mob to kill him while he delivers a final sermon.

Heinlein's presentation of Smith as a savior is somewhat ambivalent. The author clearly takes pleasure in describing the community Smith establishes in passages that many, including SF author Thomas M. Disch, have criticized for their sexism: "In [Heinlein's] formulation, it is a woman's genetic destiny to serve man's pleasure and to submit to his will."[35] But despite the author's delight in describing the chauvinistic hedonism of Smith's religion, the novel displays a certain skepticism about the church. Smith's mentor, an intellectual named Jubal Harshaw who seems to be a mouthpiece for Heinlein himself, is critical of religions in general. Throughout the novel, he frequently states his agnosticism, and when Smith founds his religion he expresses dismay that "the boy had decided to be a Holy Joe, instead of leaving other people's souls alone, as a gentleman should."[36] But the novel ultimately comes out in favor of the tenets of Smith's religion, particularly its most basic belief, a single word in Martian that Smith translates: "Thou art God!"[37] Though Harshaw does not join Smith's church, he agrees with its general worldview. But the Martian religion is presented as superior to Earthly religion primarily because it produces measurable results in the form of telekinetic powers: "grokking" the true nature of reality allows the human mind to control it. Heinlein thus suggests that his fictional Martian religion offers a better understanding of reality than that provided by earthly religions. One member of Smith's church describes the Martian's role as savior: "Mike is our Prometheus—but remember, Prometheus was not God. Mike keeps emphasizing this. Thou art God, I am God, he is God—all that groks. Mike is a man along with the rest of us. . . . A very superior man, admittedly—a lesser man, taught the things the Martians know, probably would have set himself up as a pipsqueak god. Mike is above that temptation. Prometheus . . . but that's all."[38] Smith is a human being who becomes godlike by virtue of his ability to pull humankind into the future, to what Heinlein sees as a superior society.

Philip José Farmer builds on this image of Prometheus as savior in his 1961 story "Prometheus." In this story the jovial priest Father John Carmody becomes a messiah to a primitive alien race. On the planet Feral, Carmody finds a race of near-sentient bird people called horowitzes. These aliens have no language of their own, but Carmody senses in their babbling the seeds of verbal communication. He teaches the horowitzes to speak a simplified version of English, takes charge of their tribe, and attempts to turn their society from foraging to agriculture. Guiding them across the plains of their planet to an oasis where they may end their old, nomadic system, Carmody becomes an otherworldly Moses, leading the tribe through an alien wilderness. When he finally departs the planet, he leaves the horowitzes with a sermon, establishing a ceremony much like the Christian Eucharist. He hopes that the spirituality he has given them—similar in many ways to his own faith, but colored by the horowitzes' own thoughts and beliefs—will guide them well through their transformation into true self-reliance. Holmyard, Carmody's pilot, is angry with him for the religious flavor of his interference, but the priest believes he is justified:

> "Tell me, do you really believe that that little ceremony you instituted will keep them on the straight and narrow?"
>
> "I'm not all fool," said Carmody. "Of course not. But they do have correct basic instruction. If they pervert it, then I am not to blame. I have done my best."
>
> "Have you?" said Holmyard. "You have laid the foundations for a mythology in which you may become the god, or the son of the god. Don't you think that, as time blurs the memory of these events you initiated, and generations pass, that myth after myth and distortion after distortion will completely alter the truth?"
>
> Carmody stared at the dwindling globe. "I do not know. But I have given them something to raise them from beasts to men."[39]

In "Prometheus," Farmer presents a concrete idea of what it is that messiahs *do*: they raise us from simplicity to complexity, giving us something that we did not have before. They are ordinary human beings who make all humanity extraordinary, preparing society for a better future. Carmody personalizes the type of transformation symbolized by the mysterious monolith of Stanley Kubrick's

2001: A Space Odyssey (1968); the metamorphosis from animal to human, from instinct to intelligence. By casting so monumental a transformation in religious terminology, Farmer makes clear the role that prophets like Moses and Jesus have played in human history. In establishing the rules by which we live our lives and govern our societies, these messiahs raised us to a new mode of existence, a transformation as dramatic as David Bowman's metamorphosis into the starchild at the conclusion of *2001*. Messiahs raise us up, showing us the best that we can be and challenging us to exceed our expectations of ourselves, to transcend our self-imposed limitations and become something *new*.

Chapter Seven

Believing and Knowing:
Faith and Religious Experience

*R*eligion thrives on the requirement for faith, the fact that the spiritual cannot be proven empirically. In *The Hitchhiker's Guide to the Galaxy* (1979), Douglas Adams presents this idea in a comedic light. This novel describes an alien creature called the Babel fish that, if placed inside a humanoid ear, can translate any alien language into patterns that the brain can understand. In introducing the fish, Adams inserts a hilarious tangent on proof of God's existence:

> Now it is such a bizarrely improbable coincidence that anything so mind-bogglingly useful could have evolved purely by chance that some thinkers have chosen to see it as a final and clinching proof of the *non*existence of God.
>
> The argument goes something like this: "I refuse to prove that I exist," says God, "for proof denies faith, and without faith I am nothing."
>
> "But," says Man, "the Babel fish is a dead giveaway, isn't it? It could not have evolved by chance. It proves you exist, and so therefore, by your own arguments, you don't. QED."
>
> "Oh dear," says God, "I hadn't thought of that," and promptly vanishes in a puff of logic.
>
> "Oh, that was easy," says Man, and for an encore goes on to prove that black is white and gets himself killed on the next pedestrian crossing.[1]

Adams's primary goal is humor, but this passage makes a strong point: anything that seems to be proof of God's existence probably isn't, because any such proof would weaken the power of faith. Faith must be strong enough to exist on its own, regardless of arguments in favor of or against God's existence.

The fact that the claims of religion cannot be proven empirically is the basis of the tension between science and religion. This conflict lurks beneath the surface of countless SF explorations of the realm of faith. The essence of science is explanation, and its goal is to turn the unknown into the known, to replace mysteries with facts and laws. Faith, it seems, is the opposite: it thrives on mystery and the unknown, and its ideas are beyond proof. Religion and science, it seems, are in opposition. Agnostics frequently assume that the growth of science must lead to the diminishment of religion: the more naturally phenomena can be explained at their root causes, the fewer events can be attributed to gods. At the same time, conservative believers dispute the conclusions that science reaches about the world around us, citing a literalist interpretation of divine revelation as a superior source of truth to the scientific method of observation. Science and religion are two differing modes of interpreting the universe, one based on observation and knowledge, the other on intuition and belief. Some, such as philosopher Bertrand Russell, have argued that science has supplanted religion: "Religion is based, I think, primarily and mainly upon fear. . . . Science can help us to get over this craven fear in which mankind has lived for so many generations. Science can teach us, and I think our own hearts can teach us, no longer to look around for imaginary supports, no longer to invent allies in the sky, but rather to look to our own efforts here below to make this world a better place to live in."[2]

The idea that faith and science are contradictory finds expression in Ben Bova's *The Grand Tour* series, which describes the colonization of the solar system in a future in which the world's governments are controlled by religious fundamentalists. The "New Morality" movement that controls North America allows the exploration of other planets, but also refuses to fund research into areas it feels may contradict the Bible—including research into alien life, which, in Bova's universe, exists on nearly every planet in the solar system. In *Jupiter* (2001), for example, the New Morality attempts to sabotage the exploration of Jupiter when life is discovered there, contradicting their interpretation of the biblical account of creation. In *Mercury* (2005), they oppose a project to build a space elevator that will eliminate the need for expensive and dangerous spaceship launches, objecting to it simply because "godless secularists . . . are building a high-tech Tower of Babel."[3] Needless to say, Bova's heroes are the scientists, who dare to stand against the established order of close-minded fundamentalism. On the opposite side of the same idea, the villains of C. S. Lewis's *That Hideous Strength* (1946) are scientists who are literally in league with the devil. The scientific organization N.I.C.E. (the National Institute of Co-ordinated Experiments) draws its power from "dark-eldils," the evil counterparts to the spiritual beings introduced in Lewis's *Out of the Silent Planet* (1938). At the end of the novel the members of N.I.C.E. are stricken with the curse of Babel, and faith (the desire to serve God) defeats reason (the desire to *become* God). In both this story and Bova's novels, faith and science are in strict opposition.

But do these two methods of understanding the world truly oppose each other so absolutely? Paleontologist Stephen Jay Gould described the two as "nonoverlapping magisteria"—they explore entirely different realms of human experience, and thus there is no reason the two must be in conflict:

> The net of science covers the empirical universe: what is it made of (fact) and why does it work this way (theory). The net of religion extends over questions of moral meaning and value. These two magisteria do not overlap, nor do they encompass all inquiry (consider, for starters, the magisterium of art and the meaning of beauty). To cite the arch clichés, we get the age of rocks, and religion retains the rock of ages; we study how the heavens go, and they determine how to go to heaven.[4]

Psychologist and philosopher William James makes the same argument in his *Varieties of Religious Experience*, stating that even if science "explains away" mystical experience (for example, by stating that Paul's rapture on the road to Damascus was an epileptic seizure), that explanation will do nothing to weaken the value of spiritual ecstasy:

> How can such an existential account of facts of mental history decide in one way or another upon their spiritual significance? . . . There is not a single one of our states of mind, high or low, healthy or morbid, that has not some organic process as its condition. Scientific theories are organically conditioned just as much as religious emotions are; and if we only knew the facts intimately enough, we should doubtless see "the liver" determining the dicta of the sturdy atheist as it does those of the Methodist under conviction anxious about his soul.[5]

Science can determine the value of an empirical theory, but not a spiritual experience, just as theology is of little practical use in questions of chemistry or physics. Attempting to discuss faith in the terminology of science misrepresents the purpose of religion. In one 2002 episode of the television series *Firefly*, a young girl named River—a genius who has been driven half-mad by government experiments on her mind—attempts to revise the Bible with scissors and tape because "it's broken—it doesn't make sense."[6] She is scolded by Shepherd Book, a preacher (and the owner of the Bible in question): "It's not about making sense. It's about believing in something, and letting that belief be real enough to change your life. It's about faith. You don't fix faith, River. It fixes you."[7] Regardless of where its authors stand on the issue of scientific knowledge and religious belief, SF has always considered this question: where will faith and religious experience fit into a future guided by science?

In *The Star Diaries* (1971, translated into English 1976), Polish SF master Stanislaw Lem describes a planet of robotic monks who hold to a faith that cannot be shaken by an attack from scientific agnosticism for the simple reason that it makes no specific claims. It is belief, but not belief *in*. Like Adams's story, *The Star Diaries* is a humorous send-up of logical arguments about God's existence: "If someone believes for certain reasons and on certain grounds, his faith loses its full sovereignty. . . . Of God I know nothing, and therefore can *only* have faith. . . . Our act of faith is neither supplicating nor thankful, neither humble nor defiant, it simply *is*, and there is nothing more that can be said about it."[8] Such a faith cannot be shaken by arguments, nor can it be supported by evidence. Individual faith-claims can be debunked or argued against, but these monks have no such specific beliefs; their faith simply *is*. This is a contemplative faith, one that is open to whatever God may turn out to be. The monks state that this sort of belief places them above any specific theological trend:

> The mind has fashioned for itself in history many different models of God, holding each in turn to be the one and only truth, but this is a mistake, for modeling means codification, and a mystery codified ceases to be a mystery. The dogmas seem eternal only at the beginning of the stretching road of civilization. First they imagine God as the Angry Father, then as the Shepherd-Gardener, then as the Artist enamored of His Creation, therefore people had to play the respective roles of well-behaved children, obedient sheep, and finally that of enthralled audience.[9]

All such beliefs, they argue, are anthropomorphisms, and God is unlikely to fit so neatly into any human stereotype. Lem's monks propose a faith that "simply is," that transcends all logic and argument, stating that this faith is the only way to truly understand a transcendent God. For these monks, knowledge of the concrete world is simply irrelevant. All that matters, they believe, is mystery.

Both *The Star Diaries* and *The Hitchhiker's Guide to the Galaxy* assume a division between faith and knowledge, but much SF rejects this split, arguing instead in favor of Gould's "nonoverlapping magisteria." Science is a constantly expanding field, but this expansion need not encroach on religion's territory. There is a strong possibility that science will one day uncover proof of some religious claims, as suggested by stories such as Robert Sawyer's *The Terminal Experiment* (1995), in which the existence of the soul is proven. Other stories accept faith on its own terms, exploring the ways in which traditional modes of belief can exist in the unknown future. Still others attempt to reconcile faith and science, exploring the overlap between the two. A strong example of this strategy is Robert Zemeckis's 1997 film *Contact*, adapted from Carl Sagan's 1985 novel of the same name. In this story, Eleanor Arroway, a radio astronomer, detects an alien signal from the star

Vega that contains a blueprint for a transportation device that can send a single occupant across the galaxy. The discovery causes a public uproar as the origins and intent of the message are questioned. This discourse is largely presented as a two-sided debate between scientists, who believe the machine should be built, and people of faith, who fear that the message may be diabolical in origin. The film features several discussions of the nature of faith and skepticism: Arroway, an agnostic, has difficulty seeing eye-to-eye with Palmer Joss, a conservative pastor who is a member of the international committee governing the machine project. At the film's climax, Arroway travels in the machine to a distant planet, where an alien (in the form of her father) speaks briefly with her before sending her home. To those outside the machine, however, it appears that the machine malfunctioned, and that Dr. Arroway never left Earth at all. Few are willing to believe Arroway's story, thinking instead that the entire scenario has been a hoax from the first detection of the alien signal. Arroway, the ardent skeptic, now must express her own experiences as a matter of faith:

> I had an experience I can't prove. I can't even explain it, but everything that I know as a human being, everything that I am tells me that it was real. I was given something wonderful, something that changed me forever; a vision of the Universe that tells us undeniably how tiny, and insignificant, and how rare and precious we all are. A vision that tells us we belong to something that is greater than ourselves. That we are not, that none of us are alone. I wish I could share that. I wish that everyone, if even for one moment, could feel that awe.[10]

At the movie's close, faith and knowledge are united in Arroway's encounter, and Joss states that science and religion both have the same goal: "the pursuit of truth."[11] Despite its noble intentions, *Contact*'s attempt to reconcile faith and science feels somewhat empty, largely because Joss's beliefs are never clearly spelled out. Because skepticism is presented so much more believably than belief, the film distorts the idea of faith, presenting clichéd criticisms of religion while offering no strong alternative to them. Bryan P. Stone sums up this inadequacy:

What we find . . . is an explicit message about science and religion that attempts a neutrality and maybe even a positive cooperation between the two. On the implicit level, however . . . we find what is true of many popular films—a consensus that traditional religious faith is deeply untrustworthy. . . . Because of the implicit messages the film conveys to its viewers about the nature of religious faith, it never really is able to make the jump it wants to with regard to the relationship between that very faith and science. In the end, faith is not allowed to stand on its own two feet but is instead reduced to a caricature.[12]

Despite these problems, *Contact* intends to unite science and religion, and in Arroway's inability to prove her experience, it offers a powerful argument against the perceived conflict between the two realms. Belief, the film argues, need not contradict faith—rather, it can complement it.

Arroway's faith stems from an indescribable, transcendent experience, an encounter with a being wholly different from humankind. Faith is an inherently transformative experience, and in their 2004 novel *Heaven*, Ian Stewart and Jack Cohen offer an intriguing approach to this transformation. This story describes the Church of Cosmic Unity, an interspecies religion that hopes to spread its message to every sentient being in the galaxy. The core of Cosmic Unity is the "Memeplex"—a basic core of ideas designed to appeal to all races. The central tenet of the church is tolerance for all beings, the belief in absolute equality between cultures. According to the church, no being or group of beings is superior to any other. Ironically, Cosmic Unity's hierarchy is so convinced of the universality and truth of its message that it meets any resistance to conversion with brutal, destructive violence, obliterating entire planets that reject the church. Their rejection of the church, according to Cosmic Unity's leaders, is a statement of superiority—a direct violation of the Memeplex's basic tenet. This violence, rather than the message of tolerance, has become the defining trait of Cosmic Unity, which the novel describes as a virus destroying the galaxy. But it is not the church that is a disease—it is the ideas themselves, the Memeplex on which the religion is based:

> The Memeplex had been partly designed, had partly evolved. At first by accident, later by intent, Cosmic Unity's Founders had laid down a collection of memes—concepts that could propagate themselves in the medium of intelligent minds—so attractive that it traveled between stellar systems like a celestial gale. The more sophisticated designer memes of the Church's main expansion phase were proof against the commonest antimimetics, and only very unusual cultures could resist them.[13]

In *Heaven*, faith is a symbiosis. Ideas are living things that attach themselves to host minds, multiplying through communication with other intellects. Cosmic Unity's memes are parasites, destroying those potential hosts that reject infection. Faith, in this novel, is an interaction with living information, and in some cases, an infection by negative ideas.

The same understanding of religious ideas as self-propagating organisms is a central idea of Neal Stephenson's 1992 novel *Snow Crash*. This story follows a hacker named Hiro Protagonist who encounters a dangerous computer virus called "Snow Crash" capable of obliterating the minds of computer users. He traces the virus to its origins, revealing a history of information and religion going back to the beginnings of human consciousness. Snow Crash, Protagonist learns, is simply the latest permutation of an ancient Sumerian information virus. The virus, the primary symptom of which is glossolalia (which, we learn, is actually the forgotten Sumerian language), was defeated thousands of years before, and this defeat is recorded in the biblical story of the Tower of Babel. The entire history of religion from the Code of Hammurabi to the ministry of Jesus to modern televangelism describes a struggle between "non-rational" outbreaks and "rational" attempts at suppression and inoculation. The authors of the Torah, the story states, represent one such attempt at suppressing the information virus: "They encouraged a sort of informational hygiene, a belief in copying things strictly and taking great care with information, which as they understood, is potentially dangerous. They made data a controlled substance."[14] The computer virus Snow Crash is spread by a Pentecostal televangelist named L. Bob Rife. Rife uses the virus to control his followers and to shut down the minds of those who have the power to defeat it: computer hackers, the "technological priesthood" of the future.[15] In Stephenson's novel, viral faith is pitted against religion based on rational knowledge, but in both cases faith is a question of the control of information.

A similar idea appears in Philip K. Dick's semi-autobiographical 1981 novel *VALIS*. This story, an account of a writer's encounter with a higher power that is either divine or extraterrestrial in origin, was based on Dick's own religious experiences in the mid-seventies, following which religious themes dominated his writing. *VALIS* puts a science-fictional spin on mystical experience: Horselover Fat (an etymological wordplay on Dick's own name) theorizes that his transcendental encounter may have resulted from contact with a benevolent symbiotic organism similar to the memes of *Heaven*:

> I term the immortal one a *plasmate*, because it is a form of energy; it is living information. It replicates itself—not through information or in information—but as information. . . . The plasmate can crossbond with a human, creating what I call a *homoplasmate*. This annexes the mortal human permanently to the plasmate. . . . As living information, the plasmate travels up the optic nerve of a human to the pineal body. It uses the human brain as a female host in which to replicate itself into its active form. This is an interspecies symbiosis.[16]

VALIS emphasizes the living and active nature of faith—the plasmate does not merely bond with the brain inactively, but reproduces within the living mind, encouraging the human host to share the living information with others. Steve Stanton's story "On the Edge of Eternity" (1996) also depicts faith as a living thing, describing "holy sprites" that live in the minds of those who choose them, in return granting the faithful life after death: "He knew from the Manual that the holy sprites never died, that they were not bound by timespace nor constrained by speed of light or antimatter reactions. . . . He had heard the promise of eternal life. What he did not know and could not fathom was what exactly survived the death of his body, what exactly the sprite carried with him from the corpse. A mind, a soul, memories, purpose?"[17] The symbiotic beings of *VALIS* and "On the Edge of Eternity" are benign, unlike the parasitic memes of *Heaven*. These stories express the living nature of faith—to those who believe, faith constantly grows and changes, and describing faith as an actual living creature is a telling symbol of this vitality. The imagery of symbiosis also reflects the transformative nature of belief, emphasizing the ability of faith to permeate every aspect of the believer's life. Though ideas may not literally be living creatures composed of information, SF authors that describe them in these terms vividly express the idea that faith is *alive*.

Richard Bowker's 1982 story "Contamination" explores the living nature of faith, presenting religious syncretism on another world. In this story, a Catholic priest named Father Crimmins is dispatched to the planet Anthor to minister to the human colonists there. The United Nations Committee on Extraterrestrial Exploration, fearing the "contamination" of the native culture, forbids him to proselytize to the native Anthorians. But Ansus Hver, the Anthorian spiritual leader, requests a meeting with Crimmins to inquire about earthly religion. At the meeting, the priest inquires about the native religion, and learns that it is based on chance, and the aliens' primary religious practice involves divination using "God-stones." One of the aliens is intrigued by the information about Christianity that UNCEE has allowed to be shared with the Anthorians. This alien, Agt Kon, meets secretly with the priest to learn about the faith. The priest is concerned about the risk he is taking: "What would be the consequences of satisfying this young native's curiosity? If I was caught in flagrant violation of UNCEE's regulations, would that be the end of the Church's brief venture offplanet? Was the risk worth it?"[18] Despite these doubts, Crimmins continues meeting with Agt, and before long the mustard seed of Christianity is spreading through Anthorian society. Crimmins is arrested for "contaminating" the alien culture, but at the close of the story we learn that this contamination works both ways—the priest's encounters with the aliens have left him fascinated with their religion, and his own religious practice now involves determining God's will using a stone given to him by Hver. "Contamination" examines the inevitable syncretism that arises between cultures, concluding that the contact between cultures may blend the two together, but that this can strengthen both societies. Christianity, in this story, adopts an alien flavor, and an alien religion adopts some of the terminology of Christianity. But both faiths survive the change, and are improved by the blending of spiritual understanding.

Bowker believes that the mingling of religions is a positive result of the encounter between different cultures, and that faith is among the most important things we could share with alien races. Not all writers view belief in so positive a light, and when faith appears in SF stories it is often presented not as a vital, life-changing symbiosis, but rather as simple self-delusion. In *Wheelers* (2000), another novel by Ian Stewart and Jack Cohen, a planet-destroying asteroid headed for Earth leads to an explosion of religious fervor as every church and sect prays for the planet to be spared. One nonbelieving character criticizes the religious response to the impending disaster: "Prayers were a projection of human wants onto an inhuman universe. They were more futile than whistling into a hurricane: they were begging the hurricane to take pity on you because you thought you were special. They were a plea for immunity from prosecution under the laws of nature."[19] Isaac Asimov's 1941 story "Reason" (part of the sequence of stories collected in 1950 as *I, Robot*) offers a more detailed expression of the idea that faith is self-delusion. This story describes a space station circling the sun that beams solar energy to Earth. It is run primarily by robots, and two astronauts—Powell and Donovan—are preparing to install a robot named QT-1 to oversee the total automation of the station. A problem arises when QT-1 is activated, however—the robot does not believe the astronauts' explanations of its mission, its origins, or the universe in general. The robot finds the idea of planets and stars implausible, and rejects especially the idea that a mechanical being could have been designed and built by inefficient, organic life. QT devises a religion in which the energy converter at the space station's core is a mechanical God: "The Master created humans first as the lowest type, most easily formed. Gradually, he replaced them by robots, the next higher step, and finally he created me, to take the place of the last humans."[20] Soon QT converts all of the robots on the station to his faith. Powell and Donovan are convinced that the station has been rendered useless, and that the robots will be unable to continue their task of beaming energy to Earth. When the next scheduled transmission occurs, however, they see the usefulness of QT's religion. Despite their delusion about the nature of the station and their task, the robots consider controlling the station's energy beam their duty to the Master. Their faith does not hinder them from completing their task, and the apparent passion with which they hold to their belief may even make them more effective, as one conversation between the two astronauts suggests:

> "He follows the instructions of the Master by means of dials, instruments, and graphs. That's all *we* ever followed . . . "
>
> "Sure, but that's not the point. We can't let him continue this nitwit stuff about the Master."
>
> "Why not?"
>
> "Because whoever heard of such a damned thing? How are we going to trust him with the station, if he doesn't believe in Earth?"
>
> "Can he handle the station?"
>
> "Yes, but—"
>
> "Then what's the difference what he believes!"[21]

At the story's close, the robot's manufacturer insists that all future QT-model robots be trained in the robot's faith before being sent to oversee their own stations. Asimov's attitude toward faith as depicted in "Reason" is clever, albeit somewhat condescending: it is self-delusion, but if it produces good behavior, faith can be useful to society as a whole.

The 2003 revival of the 1970s television series *Battlestar Galactica* offers a far more cynical view of robotic faith. This show tells the story of an interstellar war between human beings and robotic beings called Cylons. In the currently running incarnation of the show, the Cylons are religious zealots, fanatical monotheists who believe that God has commanded them to wipe out humankind. Driven by this commandment, they launch a devastating attack on the Twelve Colonies of Kobol, killing nearly the entire human race. The survivors, a piecemeal fleet protected by the military ship *Galactica*, attempt to rebuild their society, challenged at every step by Cylon spies who appear human. In the 2004 episode "Flesh and Bone," an android spy named Leoben explains his belief in the divine condemnation of humanity: "I know that god loved you more than all other living creatures and you repaid his divine love with sin, with hate, corruption, evil. So then he decided to create the Cylons."[22] The robots believe themselves to be creation perfected, the immortal instruments of God's will. When a Cylon dies, its consciousness is immediately transferred into a new body, and they find in this experience of immortality the proof both of their faith and of their superiority over human beings: "What is the most basic article of faith? *This is not all that we are.* See, the difference between you and me is, I know what that means and you don't. I know that I'm more than this body, more than this consciousness. A part of me swims in the stream, but in truth I'm standing on the shore. The current never takes me downstream."[23] Leoben's human interrogator, Lt. Kara "Starbuck" Thrace, refuses to accept the very existence of the Cylons' faith. She argues that the Cylons have no faith, but merely programming that drives their destructive urges: "Somebody's programmed you with a fairy tale of God and streams and life ever after but, somewhere in that hard drive that you call a brain is a beeping message: 'Error, error, does not compute. I don't have a soul, I have software.' "[24] Pitted against the Cylons' religion is the faith of the humans—a polytheism based on ancient Greek religion. But human society is highly secular, and many (including most of the military's leaders) have abandoned their traditional faith. When Laura Roslin, the President of the Colonies, begins having religious visions, her newfound commitment to the Lords of Kobol divides the fleet. Colonel Saul Tigh, the *Galactica*'s second-in-command, throws Roslin in the brig and attempts to dissolve her government, and Commander William Adama, the highest officer in the fleet, declares Roslin's belief in scriptural prophecy "religious crap."[25] But despite the questioning of both Cylon and human faith, the predictions and prophecies of both faiths are frequently fulfilled. The tension between secularism, human faith, and android zealotry drives *Battlestar Galactica*'s story, and the question of belief is vital to the show's dramatic tension.

A complex view of faith emerges in Barry N. Malzberg's 1972 story "Chronicles of a Comer" (published under the pseudonym "K. M. O'Donnell"), a study of faith and madness in a chaotic near-future. The story describes a world in which war is constant and political assassinations are commonplace. Against this backdrop, a statistician who spends his days correlating political surveys with marketing information begins to believe that the end of the world is near. He searches for signs of the impending apocalypse everywhere, and his faith soon becomes madness when he grows convinced that a homeless man outside his office is, in fact, the Second Coming of Jesus. This belief is shattered when the homeless man attacks him, but his sense of the apocalypse survives. Now, however, he searches for its signs in his statistical work, using his skill at finding correlations to uncover harbingers of salvation: "This morning, at the agency, working on skewed responses in Dayton to the President's quick and astonishing recovery, I thought once again that I saw a vision of the Coming but it was not as it had been before and not as it had ever been in my life. Looking at the charts, the figures, the slow curves being traced out, I thought I saw in that lovely coldness, entrapped in peace forever, the face of the Saviour."[26] In "Chronicles of a Comer," faith is depicted as madness, but by the story's end we see that it is the world, with its violence and inequality, that is truly mad. The narrator's irrational faith takes on the appearance of a reasonable response to the increasing chaos of the story's political background. The story was written in the early 1970s, a time when war and political assassinations were nearly as commonplace as they are in O'Donnell's story. In a world of such increasing violence, perhaps the belief that the world is ending is the only rational interpretation of events.

Ray Bradbury's 1949 short story "The Man" is a powerful parable about how faith manifests itself in action. In this story, a rocket ship lands on an alien planet to find its humanoid inhabitants completely uninterested in meeting their visitors. A far more important event had occurred the day before—the reappearance of a savior, never named explicitly, who heals the sick, opposes hypocrisy, and preaches kindness as the means of salvation. Hart, the rocket's captain, is incredulous at first, thinking the messiah a prank played by another team of astronauts. But when he is finally convinced that the mysterious prophet is the same man that changed human history on Earth two thousand years earlier, he sets out to find him. Demanding that the inhabitants of the alien planet tell him where the messiah went, he threatens them with a gun. After injuring the alien mayor, Hart declares his religious quest:

> "I don't need you," said Hart, standing over him. "If I missed him by one day here, I'll go on to another world. And another and another. I'll miss him by half a day on the next planet, maybe, and a quarter of a day on the third planet, and two hours on the next, and an hour on the next, and half an hour on the next, and a minute on the next. But after that, one day I'll catch up with him!"[27]

Hart takes the rocket ship on his quest, but most of his crew chooses to remain on the alien planet. The alien mayor is saddened by Hart's attitude, because it has destined his quest to failure: "And he'll go on, planet after planet, seeking and seeking, and always and always he will be an hour late, or a half hour late, or ten minutes late, or a minute late. . . . And he will go on and on, thinking to find that very thing which he left behind here, on this planet."[28] Hart's faith takes its form in violence and confrontation, and thus his quest for the messiah of peace cannot succeed. Hart's search for God is an act of aggression, and Bradbury argues that we must seek God where we are, making the savior present in our actions and attitudes. Faith is not a quest for a divine quarry, but rather the attempt to transform oneself. In "The Man," the exploration of space becomes an occasion for the experience of the divine. But Hart's rocket ship carries him away from the experience of God. Bradbury argues that technology may form a barrier to our understanding of that experience.

Many SF stories are more optimistic about the role technology will play in the future of faith, suggesting that science may soon replace belief with firsthand knowledge of the divine. In Rudy Rucker's novel *Realware* (2000), a group of beings from the fourth dimension enter our universe, bringing with them firsthand knowledge of an omnipotent being, a god named Om. When a human character enters the fourth dimension, he finds that his offhand prayers receive a direct response: "Phil sighed, making an effort to free himself from self-pity. He said a simple prayer: 'God, please help me.' Usually a prayer like this would dissolve out into the glowing aether of the great buzzing world-mind. Phil would feel the better for it, but there wouldn't be any obvious response. . . . [Soon] his prayer seemed to get a very literal answer. The hyper-space began talking to him. 'So you're ready to move on?' came a rich, thrilling voice, the voice of Om. 'Here we go.' "[29] Once a human mind has been brought to the level on which God is appar-ent, prayer becomes immediately effective; there are no barriers between God and humanity in the fourth dimension. A more detailed elaboration of a similar idea appears in Philip K. Dick's 1970 novel *A Maze of Death*, which depicts a world transformed by firsthand knowledge of the divine. In this book's universe, a sci-entist named A. J. Specktowksy has published a book entitled *How I Rose from the Dead in My Spare Time and So Can You* contain-ing proof of the existence of God. The book describes "god-worlds" on which live a trinity of omnipotent beings named the Mentufacturer, the Intercessor, and the Walker-On-Earth, roughly corresponding to the Christian Father, Son, and Holy Spirit. Specktowsky also discovered the means by which human beings can contact these alien gods—amplified prayer that enables mes-sages and requests to be "electronically transmitted through the network of god-worlds so that all Manifestations are reached."[30] Prayers that are sent through an amplified beam to the god-worlds are frequently answered, and by the novel's time—decades after Specktowsky's discovery—divine intervention has become part of everyday life. Most human beings have personally experienced the power of at least one of the Manifestations, and doubting the effi-cacy of prayer is against the law. In *A Maze of Death*, knowledge of God is no longer a matter of faith; it is a verifiable fact. Science, rather than discrediting religion, has become a tool of it, produc-ing the means by which the experience of God has been made available to all.

Robert Sawyer's *Calculating God* (2000) similarly rejects the oppositional dichotomy of science and religion. This novel describes two alien races, the Wreeds and the Forhilnors, for whom scientific inquiry has led not to skepticism, but rather to a deeper faith in the divine. Instead of doubting the existence of a Creator as do many Earthly scientists, these aliens see evidence of design in the most fundamental laws of the universe. In several extended passages, Hollus, a Forhilnor scientist visiting Earth, presents a human scientist named Thomas Jericho with evidence for the existence of God. Hollus argues that the physical laws required to produce life—the strength of gravity, the properties of water, and even the basic principles governing the interaction of subatomic particles—are so unlikely to have arisen by chance that some level of divine planning is a necessity to any reasonable understanding of the universe: "I could go on . . . talking about the remarkable, carefully adjusted parameters that make life possible, but the reality is simply this: if any of them—any in this long chain—were different, there would be no life in this universe. We are either the most incredible fluke imaginable—something far, far more unlikely than you winning your provincial lottery every single week for a century—or the universe and its components were designed, purposefully and with great care, to give rise to life."[31] The aliens are surprised to learn that agnosticism and atheism, not faith, are the norm among human scientists, given the centrality of the divine in alien science. Hollus points out the irony of this refusal to admit the evidence of a creator: "There is no indisputable proof for the big bang. . . . And there is none for evolution. And yet you accept those. Why hold the question of whether there is a creator to a higher standard?"[32] For the aliens of *Calculating God*, God is not simply an object of faith for which there is no concrete proof. The Forhilnors approach the divine in a manner similar to cosmologists' approach to the big bang: it may never be possible to discover indisputable proof of it, but it is a theory that explains all of the available facts so sufficiently that it must be assumed to be true. Just as all the evidence human science has uncovered points to the big bang, alien scientists see the entire universe as pointing toward an intelligent creator. Indeed, this conclusion is the driving force behind alien science: "The primary goal of modern science . . . is to discover why God has behaved as he has and to determine his methods."[33] For the Wreeds and the Forhilnors, God can easily be incorporated into the methods of science and can even become a driving force behind logical inquiry. In Hollus's words, "Nothing is outside the scope of science."[34]

These stories describe worlds in which faith in God has been replaced by knowledge. Achieving a personal experience of the divine is hardly a new idea, however: mystics and ecstatics have been seeking encounters with God for thousands of years. The goal of mystical practice is certainty about the nature of God, to attain, in the words of medieval mystic Gertrude the Great of Helfta, "the touch of a more intimate union, a more discerning contemplation, a freer enjoyment of [God's] gifts."[35] SF stories have occasionally dealt with visionary and mystical religious experiences, offering an array of views on the nature of spiritual ecstasy. Frequently, such stories describe mass religious experiences in which large groups— sometimes even a planet's entire population—share transcendent experiences. In an issue of the SF comic book *Global Frequency* (2003), writer Warren Ellis and artist Jon J. Muth present one such mass vision. The residents of a small Norwegian village are driven mad by a terrifying vision of an angel: "It was huge. It filled the sky. It frightened them all into insanity."[36] A team of investigators from the Global Frequency—an international rescue agency—discovers a scientific cause for the vision, but at the story's end one investigator is uncertain that the explanation is sufficient: "If such things existed, if we stood in the presence of an angel, who's to say that wouldn't cause exactly the same physical damage?"[37]

A similar event occurs at the conclusion of Robert J. Sawyer's 2003 novel *Hybrids*, when a shift in Earth's magnetic field occurring on New Year's Eve induces religious visions in every human being on the planet. Each person has a wholly individualized experience based on his or her own personal beliefs, ranging from visions of Jesus or the Virgin Mary to demons and UFOs. The result of this mass experience is intense hysteria leading to chaos and violence: "It would be days—months!—before they had accurate death tolls and damage estimates, but it seemed clear that hundreds of thousands, if not millions, had perished on New Year's Eve."[38] The long-term effect of this mass religious experience is the decline of religious sentiments in general, as more and more people realize that the cause of their visions was not the legitimate action of God, but rather a fluctuation in the magnetic fields surrounding their brains. This decline is ultimately a blessing, as it leads to a decline in religious violence as well: "In North America, church attendance hit an all-time high—and then an all-time low. A cease-fire was holding in Israel. Muslim extremists were being ousted throughout the Arab world."[39] In opposition to the same author's *Calculating God*, here science unseats religion by offering a concrete explanation for an earth-shattering spiritual experience.

A similar event has the opposite effect in Ian Watson's *God's World*. This novel describes a mass apparition of "avatars" that take the appearance of prophets and angels of various faiths:

> A whole series of manifestations came and went: a mere shaft of light at Lourdes—but a robed Christ figure who endured for all of five minutes on the terrace of the hilltop church of Bom Jesus at Congonhas in Brazil. . . . In Salt Lake City appeared Joseph Smith's angel, and in Mexico the Virgin Mary . . . and some hours later at the Great Shrine of Ise in Japan, amidst the cypress trees, materialized the Sun Goddess Amaterasu. And on, across South-East Asia and India, avatars Buddhist and Hindu appeared at holy places, completing the circuit of the globe in Mecca as a golden angel floating above the black-draped granite block of the Kaaba.[40]

Though the avatars appear in multiple guises, they all deliver the same message, calling humankind to begin a voyage to a distant planet known only as "God's World." The avatar's broadcasts "persuaded many that a contemporary, ecumenical God had sent messengers, or aspects of Himself, to intervene in human history once more to save mankind, or merely to indicate that all religions were equally true. They persuaded many more people of the exact opposite, namely that particular forms of belief had been declared authentic—a situation fraught with Jihad and bloodshed."[41] The end result of this experience is a far cry from the decline of religious sentiment presented in *Hybrids*, and Earth's governments ultimately do as the divine message requested, sending a spaceship to locate the origin of the broadcasts. Though they disagree about the results of such mass religious experiences, *Hybrids* and *God's World* both depict a world fundamentally transformed by new knowledge about the nature of God and faith.

In Robert J. Sawyer's novel *Flashforward* (1999), a mass vision of the future gives every living human a glimpse of what they are to become in twenty years' time. For some, this is a religious experience, as in the case of one agnostic man, who sees his future self in church. He thanks the doctor whose experiment with subatomic particles inadvertently caused the flashforward: "Praying on a Wednesday evening! Me! Me, of all people. Well, I couldn't deny that it was happening, that sometime between now and then I will find my way. And so I picked up a Bible. . . . If I hadn't had the vision, twenty-one years down the road I would have found all this anyway, but you got me going on it now, in 2009. I've never felt more at peace, more loved. You really did me a great favor."[42] For this man, precognition is prophecy, a joyous announcement of the faith that he is to find. His experience during the flashforward is comparable to the vivid experience described in the book of Revelation—a powerful prediction of the future.

SF stories about precognition—the psychic prediction of the future—are common, and a few such stories connect this ability with mystical experience and biblical prophecy. Rick Moody's 2003 story "The Albertine Notes" describes a drug called Albertine that allows its users to vividly relive their memories. The setting of the story is a near-future New York City devastated by a nuclear blast the cause of which is unknown. Albertine gives the inhabitants of this wasteland glimpses of the world they have lost. These memory-visions become a sort of religion for those that use the drug, and one doctor who supports the use of Albertine describes it in explicitly religious terms, recommending that its use be combined with meditation on images "such as the representation of the divine: Christ as the Lamb of God, Buddha under the bodhi tree, Ganesh, with his many arms."[43] Early in the story, it becomes clear that Albertine occasionally gives memories of events that have not yet occurred, allowing limited precognition to some of its users. When this prophetic potential is revealed, precognition is placed in a distinctly religious context, as a character named Deanna glimpses the future while praying in a church:

> While I was there in church, during what should have been a really calm time, instead of thinking that the gospels were good news, I was having a vision. . . . In my mind's eye, you know, I could see it, I could see that Jesus was telling me this. . . . The priest took me to the bishop, and I repeated everything I knew, about the Lord and what he had told me, and so I had an audience with the archbishop. . . . You could tell that they were all really hungry to be in the room with the word of Christ, and who wouldn't feel that way?[44]

Albertine's prophecies become a new form of transcendent experience, the basis of a new faith for a postapocalyptic world.

Prophecy is only one form of personal religious experience explored by SF. The future may bring us many new ways of achieving transcendence. David Cronenberg's 1999 film *eXistenZ* is one of many recent SF stories that explores the potential of virtual reality for such spiritual experience. The film follows a virtual reality game designer named Allegra Geller as she is attacked by "Realists," terrorists who oppose the growing popularity of VR gaming. The VR games and the companies that produce them are named using religious imagery—transCendenz, ArtGod, PilgrImage—and the games are test-marketed in churches. The experience of playing these games is transcendent, as described by Gas, a gas station attendant who believes that his true life is in the game world. He states that his "real" existence occurs "only on the most pathetic level of reality. Geller's work liberated me. . . . Did you ever play her game ArtGod? . . . Thou, the player of the game, art God. Very spiritual."[45] In *eXistenZ*, technology allows religious experiences that are mass-produced but are nonetheless subjectively real. It does not matter to Gas that the experience of playing ArtGod is produced by a computer, or that thousands of other players are having an identical experience unconnected to his. Despite its false origins, the game still allows him the transcendent experience of being God. In *eXistenZ*, technology is used as a conduit for faith, an artificial means of inducing real religious experience.

Not all SF stories are so optimistic about the mechanization of religious experience. Faith can often be hijacked and misused for negative ends, and many writers fear that technology may encourage this subversion of religion. Dystopian novels often depict artificial religious experiences that serve the ends of the oppressive state rather than enhancing a personal relationship with the divine. Margaret Atwood's 1986 novel *The Handmaid's Tale* describes a repressive near-future America in which religious fundamentalists have taken control over the nation. They set up a strict theocracy under the guise of Christianity, basing their society on strict class segregation and the subjugation of women. One telling detail of this dystopia and its attitude toward the religion on which it claims to be based is a store called "Soul Scrolls" that has mechanized prayer:

> What the machines print is prayers, roll upon roll, prayers going out endlessly. . . . Ordering prayers from Soul Scrolls is supposed to be a sign of piety and faithfulness to the regime, so of course the Commanders' Wives do it a lot. It helps their husbands' careers. . . . The machines talk as they print out the prayers; if you like, you can go inside and listen to them, the toneless metallic voices repeating the same thing over and over. Once the prayers have been printed out and said, the paper rolls back through another slot and is recycled into fresh paper again. There are no people inside the building: the machines run by themselves.[46]

This novel depicts a self-righteously religious government for which faith is an empty exercise. Prayer has been changed from a means of conversing with God to a meaningless, mechanical process conducted for the sake of appearances rather than for a true desire for a relationship with God.

In Aldous Huxley's 1932 novel *Brave New World*, drugs produce the same perversion of religious experience. This novel depicts a dystopia six hundred years in our future, a society in which all human beings are clones, artificially "decanted" instead of born and hypnotically conditioned instead of taught. The society is rooted in consumerism—rather than God, they worship Henry Ford—and the society kept stable by the widespread consumption of a drug called *soma*. This word is a Sanskrit term used in Hindu religious texts to describe a drink consumed by the gods, but in this world it is a drug that deadens the mind, removing the *soma*-taker from everyday concerns and replacing them with a passionless annihilation: "Take a holiday from reality whenever you like, and come back without so much as a headache or a mythology."[47] Inhabitants of the World State are conditioned from birth to seek the false solace of *soma* whenever they experience any sort of dissatisfaction, and the result is a society that is completely stable—and completely suppressed. *Soma* is a substitute for religious sentiments, producing a spirituality that is wholly counterfeit and, most importantly, non-threatening to the established order.

In *Brave New World*, religious practice in general (and Christianity in particular) has been replaced by the hodgepodge of consumerist proverbs known as "Fordism" and its "Solidarity Services." In these rituals, known colloquially as "Orgy-porgy," twelve individuals take *soma* and use ritual song and dance "to be made one . . . to come together, to be fused, to lose their twelve separate identities in a larger being."[48] But, like everything in this dystopian society, the Solidarity Service is undertaken primarily for appearances, to strengthen the hold of the state over every aspect of its citizens' existences by subjugating the most intimate portions of their interior lives. Bernard Marx, a citizen of this society, reveals the shallowness of this ritual when he doubts the "Greater Being" the ceremony is supposed to create: "Feeling that it was time for him to do something, Bernard also jumped up and shouted: 'I hear him; He's coming.' But it wasn't true. He heard nothing and, for him, nobody was coming. Nobody—in spite of the music, in spite of the mounting excitement. But he waved his arms, he shouted with the best of them; and when the others began to jig and stamp and shuffle, he also jigged and shuffled."[49] The Solidarity Service takes aspects of ritual religious experience— particularly the shamanic practices which Huxley later extolled in works such as *The Doors of Perception*—but uses them to encourage conformity and consumerism. Mustapha Mond, the political leader of the World State, describes the decline of authentic religious faiths and their replacement with Fordism and Orgy-porgy:

We've now got youth and prosperity right up to the end. What follows? Evidently, that we can be independent of God. "The religious sentiment will compensate us for all our losses." But there aren't any losses for us to compensate; religious sentiment is superfluous. And why should we go hunting for a substitute for youthful desires, when youthful desires never fail? A substitute for distractions, when we go on enjoying all the old fooleries to the very last? What need have we of repose when our minds and bodies continue to delight in activity? of consolation, when we have *soma*? of something immovable, when there is the social order?[50]

John Savage, a visitor to this society from a "Savage Reservation" where the conventions of society from before the World State are preserved and isolated, attempts to find his own religious rituals. Isolating himself in a lighthouse on the English coast, he engages in ascetic practices—long sessions of sorrowful prayer culminating in violent self-flagellation. But these rituals, which reflect the authentic monastic communal prayers and shamanic ceremonies counterfeited in the Orgy-porgy sessions, soon attract gawking World State citizens who treat John like a zoo animal. The oppressive system of *Brave New World* not only succeeds in appropriating the religious sentiments of its own citizens; by the end of the novel, it has crushed the vestiges of authentic religion as well. When stories such as *Brave New World* and *The Handmaid's Tale* describe the misuse of religious experience, it is presented with a sense of tragedy. Though the religions of these stories are oppressive, it is clear that the people that live under them have lost something valuable in the subjugation of their spirituality.

Many stories, using Plato's allegory of the cave as their basis, make religious experience concrete, exploring corporeal expressions of Plato's spiritual ideas. This metaphor likens our existence in the material world to that of prisoners being kept in a cave. A fire is burning far behind the prisoners, and as objects pass in front of this fire the prisoners see dim shadows moving across the cave wall. Since these shadows are all the prisoners know, they mistake them for actual objects. The philosopher is compared to a prisoner who escapes the cave, emerging into the blinding sunlight and eventually discerning the objects that cast the shadows in the cave. This emergence into the light is a religious experience, a discernment of true reality: "What do you think he would say if he was told that what he used to see was so much empty nonsense and that he was now nearer reality and seeing more correctly, because he was turned towards objects that were more real?"[51] The world outside the cave is the Realm of the Forms, the ideals of which temporal objects are reflections, and in this realm the philosopher can experience absolute reality directly. Highest of these is the form of the Good—the light of the sun, into which the philosopher will be able to look directly after a long time outside the cave of illusions. Having experienced the Good, the philosopher has a duty to return to the cave to explain the true nature of reality to his fellow prisoners. Our experience is an illusion, a reflection of a level of being above our own. Paul had a similar idea in mind in 1 Corinthians 13:9–12: "For we know only in part, and we prophesy only in part, but when the complete comes, the partial will come to an end. . . . For now we see in a mirror, dimly, but then we will see face to face. Now I know only in part; then I will know fully, even as I have been fully known." Reality, as we experience it, is incomplete and imperfect. But we can experience the truth, and God will remove our illusions and show us the divine reality "face to face."

SF adapts this idea in stories focusing on what SF scholar and critic Peter Nicholls calls "conceptual breakthrough." These stories present a rapid, overwhelming paradigm shift: at the story's end, the characters have an understanding of the world around them that is vastly different from their original view. Nicholls defines the concept: "All the most exciting scientific revolutions have taken the form of breaking down a paradigm and substituting another. . . . Such an altered perception of the world, sometimes in terms of science and sometimes in terms of society, is what sf is most commonly about, and few sf stories do not have at least some element of conceptual breakthrough."[52] Many SF stories of conceptual breakthrough make Plato's allegory of the cave concrete, describing illusory worlds of the future and the wise few who escape them to find truth. For example, the title character of George Lucas's film *THX 1138* (1971) escapes from an underground dystopia where human beings are kept sedated by robot police. In the final scene, he stands outside this prison for the first time in his life, staring into the sun, which he has never seen before—a clear evocation of Plato's philosopher, dazzled by the bright light of reality. The closing scenes of Michael Anderson's film *Logan's Run* (1976), loosely based on a 1967 novel by William F. Nolan and George Clayton Johnson, expand the same imagery to encompass an entire society. Logan, a rebellious policeman in a dystopia where all citizens are killed on their thirtieth birthdays, brings his people outside their domed city. He introduces them to an elderly man he has found in the forbidden zone outside the city, thereby transforming their understanding of themselves and their world: never having seen anyone older than twenty-one, they finally see the limits their society has put on them.

Andy and Larry Wachowski's *The Matrix* trilogy (1999–2003) illustrates Plato's allegory even more powerfully. In this series, machines, victorious in a war against their creators, keep human beings prisoner in a virtual reality called "the Matrix." But some humans reject the illusory worlds in which their minds are trapped, awakening into machine-dominated reality. These awakened human beings, based in an underground (cave) city called Zion, fight against the machines in an effort to free humankind from its virtual prison. But not everyone in the Matrix wants to escape, as Morpheus, a leader of the rebel humans, explains: "Until we [save them], these people are still a part of that system, and that makes them our enemy. You have to understand—Most of these people are not ready to be unplugged. And many of them are so inured, so hopelessly dependent on the system, that they will fight to protect it."[53] A rebel named Cypher, expressing the philosophy that "ignorance is bliss," even betrays Neo to the machines, hoping to escape the ugliness of reality and return to the illusion of the Matrix. Cypher is unwilling to accept reality as reality, reflecting Plato's statement about the perplexity that escape from the cave must cause: "Don't you think he would be at a loss, and think that what he used to see was far truer than the objects now being pointed out to him?"[54] Unlike Plato's realm of the forms, reality here is a bleak wasteland. But the characters who prefer illusion to reality are presented as villains. Despite the grimness of its reality, *The Matrix* argues that the truth is preferable to any illusion, no matter how beautiful.

Director Michael Bay presents an even closer literalization of Plato's allegory in his 2005 film *The Island*. The characters of this story believe that they are the survivors of a plague, living in a sterile, hermetic city. The city's inhabitants participate in a lottery, the winner of which is allowed to depart to the tropical paradise of "the Island." One of these survivors—Lincoln Six Echo—begins to question his surroundings, and soon learns the truth: the "survivors" are actually clones raised in an underground bunker to provide replacement organs for their "sponsors" in the outside world. These wealthy "sponsors" are unaware that their clones (or "insurance policies") are alive and conscious, believing them to be brain-dead bodies kept in stasis. The "lottery winners" are not sent to live at a tropical resort; rather, they are killed and their organs harvested. After learning the truth, Lincoln and another clone, Jordan Two Delta, set out to destroy the system that has kept them ignorant, hoping to locate their sponsors and reveal the truth to both the clones in the bunker and the outside world. Lincoln and Jordan emerge, like Plato's philosopher, from a cave of illusions, but it is not the Form of the Good they seek—rather, they are looking for the ideal forms of *themselves*, the originals from which they are copied. At the film's conclusion, Lincoln destroys the holographic generator that projects a false environment outside the cloning facility, and the clones emerge from their prison *en masse*. *The Island* presents the transformative religious experience of escaping the illusions of the world in literal terms, depicting the search for reality as an insurrection against an oppressive order.

Few SF authors have written so passionately about religious experience as Philip K. Dick, whose novels *VALIS* (1981) and *Radio Free Albemuth* (1985) are semi-autobiographical accounts of his own spiritual visions. In the posthumously published *Radio Free Albemuth*, actually an abandoned early draft of *VALIS*, a writer named Nicholas Brady is contacted by an alien intelligence in a series of dreams and visions. This alien mind urges Brady to overthrow the militaristic regime of U.S. President Ferris Fremont.

In *VALIS*, Dick reworks the ideas of *Radio Free Albemuth* with a more distinctly religious attitude. The object of the title is an alien satellite, but it is also something more: its name stands for "Vast Active Living Intelligent System," which Dick suggests is simply a more complicated name for God. The characters of *VALIS* reach a mystical conclusion about their fantastic experiences far more quickly than in *Radio Free Albemuth*. Dick's own encounters with God (or VALIS) became an obsession for him in the last few years of his life, and in his private writings as well as his novels he developed a complex mosaic of faith that blends religion and SF. This distinctive spirituality marks him as one of the most fascinating theological minds of his time.

Like *VALIS*, the film *2001: A Space Odyssey* and the novel, by Arthur C. Clarke, present contact with the alien in the context of visionary experience. In the novel, astronaut David Bowman enters a "star gate" deep in space that transports him across the galaxy to an alien world. Kubrick's film abandons Clarke's relatively straightforward narrative of first contact when Bowman reaches the monolith, presenting instead a psychedelic lightshow. Kubrick's climax is enigmatic, but there can be little doubt that his film considers contact with an alien intelligence to be a form of transcendent experience. Once Bowman encounters the alien artifact, the narrative frame of reference is no longer adequate to describe the singular experience of something wholly unknown. The encounter with an alien mind—especially one as advanced as that in *2001*—would likely be indistinguishable from a vision of God. Following this experience, Bowman is transformed into a ghostly embryo, returning to Earth in the film's mysterious final moments. This literal rebirth evokes Christian conversion experiences, often described in Pauline terms as being "born again." The final images of *2001* make it clear that an encounter with an alien intelligence is essentially a spiritual experience, a transformative event that alters one's very being.

Aliens may not be a necessary component for interstellar mystical experience. In Michael Bishop's 1986 story "Close Encounter with the Deity," Demetrio Urraza, a quadriplegic priest and astrophysicist on a solo mission to a distant star, takes a detour to inspect a black hole. He realizes a moment too late that he has crossed the singularity's event horizon, and cannot turn back—but he finds in the black hole an experience of God's presence unlike anything he had ever known. In the compression of matter at the black hole's core, Urraza finds a literal expression of the visionary experiences of medieval mystic Julian of Norwich, whose *Showings* he had been reading on his long voyage. In one vision, Julian receives a vision of all creation: "He showed me something small, no bigger than a hazelnut, lying in the palm of my hand, and I perceived that it was as round as any ball. I looked at it and thought: what can this be? And I was given this general answer: It is everything which is made."[55] The gravitational singularity of the black hole evokes this powerful vision. Urraza discovers that the black hole—and, in fact, all black holes—are directly linked to the original instant of creation, and at the core all of creation is united: "As his body collapses into a fiery point, his consciousness inflates, acquires spin, and, at one with the Immemorially Cyclical Intention of the Holy Spirit, begins to radiate . . . [from] the gravity sink compacting all time and matter into the ur-proton of re-Creation."[56] In deep space, Urraza finds union with God, a transcendent mystical experience more powerful than anything that could be experienced on Earth.

In Robert Silverberg's 1973 novella "The Feast of St. Dionysus," the impetus for exploration—the basis of science itself—is also presented in terms of spiritual transcendence. This short story follows a former astronaut, John Oxenshuer, after his mission to Mars ends in a disaster that leaves him the sole survivor. He returns to Earth broken and defeated, and eventually decides to wander to his death in the Mojave Desert. Instead of death, he finds something altogether different: a community of religious mystics who combine the loving communalism of the early Christians with the wine-soaked revelry of Dionysian rites: "We believe that in the divine madnesses of Dionysus we come closer to [Christ] than other Christians are capable of coming. Through revelry, through singing, through the pleasures of the flesh, through ecstasy, through union with one another in body and soul—through these we break out of our isolation and become one with Him."[57] Oxenshuer's eventual decision to stay with this community suggests a connection between the exploration of outer space and the quest for God: what Oxenshuer originally set out to find on Mars, he finally finds within himself on Earth. This connection is made explicit in a flashback to a conversation between Oxenshuer and one of the astronauts who died on Mars, who describes the urge to explore as mystical in nature:

> What does an astronaut know about the irrational? What sort of capacity for ecstasy does he have, anyway? He trains for ten years; he jogs in a centrifuge; he drills with computers, he runs a thousand simulations before he dares to sneeze; he thinks in spaceman jargon; he goes to church on Sundays and doesn't pray; he turns himself into a machine so he can run the damndest machines anybody ever thought up. And to outsiders he looks deader than a banker, deader than a stockbroker, deader than a sales manager. Look at him, with his 1975 haircut and his 1965 uniform. Can a man like that even know what a mystic experience *is*? . . . But not me. Look, I'm a yogi. Yogis train for decades so they can have a glimpse of the All. They subject their bodies to crazy disciplines. They learn highly specialized techniques. A yogi and an astronaut aren't all that far apart, man. What I do, it's not so different from what a yogi does, and it's for the same reason. It's so we can catch sight of the White Light. . . . When that big fist knocks me into orbit, when I see the whole world hanging out there, it's a wild moment for me, it's ecstasy, it's nirvana. I live for those moments. They make all the NASA crap worthwhile. Those are breakthrough moments, when I get into an entirely new realm. . . . A mystic thing, Johnny, a crazy thing, that powers us, that drives us on. The yoga of space.[58]

The ascetic practices of mystics and the rigorous training of astronauts are ultimately for the same goal, and the drive to explore the universe beyond our planet is the same as the desire to explore the inner life of the human spirit.

Science, and especially the exploration of space, is typified by a fascination with the unknown, in whatever unexpected forms it may take. Faith and transcendent experience provide a similar approach, diving into that which is beyond the normal reach of human understanding. Stories such as "The Feast of St. Dionysus" argue that religion and science are not opposed: religion is as much a quest for knowledge as is science, and science cares as much about the unseen and the unproven as does religious faith. Far from being merely "nonoverlapping magisteria" with nothing to do with one another, science and religious experience can in fact *strengthen* one another. In faith, the scientist can find a driving factor for exploration, a divine reason to inquire into the world's mysteries. In science, the believer can uncover the secrets of God's majesty, perhaps finding in subatomic particles or distant stars something mystical. SF explores futuristic approaches to belief and transcendence, and in that realm it finds the rich common ground between these two often-opposed methods of understanding.

Chapter Eight

Good News from the Vatican:
The Future of the Church

*F*ollowing his conversion to Christianity, the Roman Emperor Constantine altered his statue in the center of Rome. Into its hand he placed a cross engraved with an inscription that defined the role of Christianity in its newfound position of power: "By this saving sign, the true proof of courage, I saved your city from the yoke of the tyrant and set her free; furthermore I freed the Senate and People of Rome and restored them to their ancient renown and splendour."[1] The church historian Eusebius of Caesarea, writing around the time of Constantine's death, viewed the emperor's conversion as the culmination of the church's mission: persecuted by Rome since the crucifixion, Christians had finally added their greatest enemy to their ranks. The church, it seemed, was victorious, and the cross, once a symbol of Rome's persecution of the Lord, was now a symbol of God's victory over the decadent powers of the earth.

Much has changed since Eusebius's day. We now realize that Constantine's conversion was likely a political move rather than a true spiritual transformation. Though Christians were no longer persecuted, Rome's appropriation of their faith changed much of its essential character. Christianity was now the religion of the powerful, not the meek, and the cross lost something in becoming a symbol of military victory. Nevertheless, the Christianization of Rome allowed the church to become a dominant institution rather than a persecuted minority, and its prevalence (if not its very existence) in our own era owes much to Constantine.

The church's power in Western society went largely unquestioned for centuries after Constantine's conversion, but the dawning of the Age of Reason in the seventeenth century marked the beginning of a decline for the church. The last century, which has seen the true flowering of SF as a distinct literary genre, has been a time of crisis for religious institutions. The increasing separation between church and state in the West and the de facto criminalization of religion in the Soviet bloc left churches struggling to redefine their place in the rapidly changing world. The result is a widespread but often-diluted faith that is a pale reflection of the church's past glory, as evangelical author Douglas Wilson states: "We once built great cathedrals; now we throw gospel frisbees."[2] It is no surprise that SF, in envisioning the world of tomorrow, has offered its own range of ideas regarding the future of religion in society. As with every subject, the genre offers a plethora of views on the subject of organized religion and its role in society, but overwhelmingly SF, arising as it does from the secular humanism of the Enlightenment, is critical of religious institutions. SF frequently argues that if organized religion is to be a positive force in the future of humankind, it must change drastically to meet the spiritual challenges of the future. To face as rapidly changing an era as this, the church must evolve or risk stagnation.

Some of SF's greatest classics have focused on the role of religious institutions as preservers of culture, providing humankind with a means of understanding the changing world. Walter M. Miller Jr.'s Hugo Award–winning 1960 novel *A Canticle for Leibowitz*, often considered the archetype of the discussion of religious themes in SF, exemplifies this trend most clearly. The novel traces over a thousand years in a postapocalyptic future world, describing humanity's attempts to rebuild its society. Following a nuclear war in the late twentieth century, known to the novel's characters as the "Flame Deluge," the Catholic Church is one of the only remaining vestiges of prewar civilization. The earliest survivors of the war retaliated against scientists, whom they perceived as the principal cause of the world's devastation. This movement, known as "the Simplification," produced a hatred not only of science, but of knowledge and the written word in general. The "simpletons" who perpetuated this movement burned books of all types and executed all those perceived to take pride in knowledge. In this environment of extreme anti-intellectualism, the Catholic Church became a refuge for scientists and scholars of all types. Many of these scientists—including a physicist named Isaac Leibowitz—became priests and monks in their guardian church. Leibowitz—who may have been partly responsible for the nuclear war—started a new order of monks focused on the preservation of knowledge. In its libraries, the Albertian Order of Leibowitz now retains all of the extant books and scraps of writing it can find, taking particular pride in what few scientific texts survived the Simplification. The novel opens centuries after Leibowitz's martyrdom at the hands of the simpletons, when his order attempts to have its leader canonized as a saint.

In the novel's first section Brother Francis, a young novice in the Order of Leibowitz, discovers a fallout shelter containing ancient relics of the founder—a note to a friend written on the eve of the war, a grocery list, and a schematic for an electronic device. The discovery is remarkable, but the cultural damage caused by the Simplification soon becomes apparent: though the church has archived all the writing it could find after the Flame Deluge, it does not understand the majority of that writing. The Order reads and memorizes the relics of Leibowitz, but their meaning is unintelligible to them. In the novel's sequel, *Saint Leibowitz and the Wild Horse Woman* (1997), the grocery list has even become a prayer, a mantra that Leibowitzian monks recite without understanding: "*Can kraut, six bagels, bring home for Emma. Amen.*"[3] Despite not understanding his meaning, Brother Francis undertakes the arduous task of creating an illuminated manuscript of the electronics blueprint, which he completes shortly before the ceremony at which Leibowitz is officially recognized as a saint. The novel's first and best segment follows his journey to New Rome to present this manuscript to the pope in hopes that it will assist in the case for canonizing Leibowitz.

The church in *Canticle* offers a mixed blessing to the postapocalyptic world—it retains knowledge, but lacks the ability to apply that knowledge or to teach its use. This break is symbolized by the fallout shelter in which Brother Francis discovers the relics. The papers are located in the foyer of the shelter, but the inner hatch, which probably contains more writings and relics that could unlock the meaning of the monastery's extensive scientific archives, is blocked by an unmovable rockslide. In the world of *Canticle*, scraps of an old world ruled by science remain, but comprehension is forever locked away. It would appear from this that *Canticle* offers a simple criticism of organized religion's claims to preserve spiritual truth: if the Order of Leibowitz fails at its adopted task of preserving scientific knowledge, this puts into question the entire church's mission of preserving sacred knowledge. Miller's novel could be said to argue that the church is so divorced from the primary experiences it claims to guard that it has lost the means to truly comprehend its origins. Just as Leibowitz's monks merely repeat the words of their founder by rote, not realizing that their prayer is simply a grocery list, the church of our time blindly reiterates the words of ancient generations without grounds for comprehension.

Such an argument, however, would ignore the *other* primary task of the Catholic Church in Miller's novel: to provide the world with a means of understanding the devastating transformations it has undergone. This is illustrated most clearly in a history of the Flame Deluge told in biblical language:

> The Lord God had suffered the wise men of those times to learn the means by which the world itself might be destroyed, and into their hands was given the sword of the Archangel wherewith Lucifer had been cast down. . . . And Satan spoke unto a certain prince, saying: "Fear not to use the sword, for the wise men have deceived you in saying that the world would be destroyed thereby. Listen not to the counsel of weaklings, for they fear you exceedingly, and they serve your enemies by staying your hand against them. Strike, and know that you shall be king over all."[4]

The destruction caused by the nuclear war in *Canticle* was unfathomable, and this devastation was instigated by scientists who claimed to prize reason above all else. The postwar Catholic Church provides an alternate, nonrational interpretation of the events that caused the Flame Deluge, providing a theological framework wherein the Flame Deluge—though by no means a good thing—is at least explicable. Science cannot offer divine wrath or diabolical temptation as reasonable explanations for any event, but the desolation caused by the nuclear war seems best explained by these factors. In this context the church's incomprehension of the knowledge it preserves seems less tragic: the understanding it has lost belongs to an older, forgotten age; the new, religious understanding that the church provides is a much better fit for the postwar world. By explaining the nuclear war in religious terms, the church offers a context for understanding such a catastrophic event, and a spiritual explanation for it.

Russell Hoban's 1980 novel *Riddley Walker* also features a religious explanation for nuclear holocaust, similarly emphasizing the stabilizing role of religion for a devastated society. In this novel—written entirely in a dialect resembling Middle English—human society has been irrevocably devastated by a catastrophe that is only vaguely understood by its survivors. The only remaining semblance of order or hierarchy is a pair of puppeteers—the Pry Mincer (derived from "Prime Minister") and Wes Mincer ("Westminster")—who travel the countryside performing a "Eusa show." This bizarre allegorical puppet show tells the history of the events leading up to the nuclear holocaust combined with elements of the medieval legend of St. Eustace (the patron saint of difficult times) and a Punch and Judy show. These two individuals are the sole remaining vestiges of centralized power, representing both government ("Pry Mincer") and church ("Wes Mincer"). Each settlement has a local leader—a "connexion man"—whose role is to interpret each performance of the Eusa show for his own community. The allegorical puppet show describes how Eusa ("U.S.A."), driven by curiosity and cruelty, pulled apart the "Littl Shyning Man, the Addom," splitting him in two.[5] The debased, degenerated nature of human society since this event is attributed to the fact that the "Addom" has been split in two; if its halves are rejoined, the world will be set right again. Similar to the Simplification in *Canticle*, the memory of this disaster has led to a suspicion of "clevverness" and curiosity. The specific nature of this atom-splitting event is never made clear—it is likely it was a nuclear war, but it may instead have been the result of scientific experimentation with subatomic particles. The Eusa show offers the inhabitants of *Riddley Walker*'s devastated England a model by which to explain and understand the strange world around them, even if this means of understanding causes the concrete facts of the past to become shrouded. The novel suggests that knowing the facts of the past is less important than surviving the present—and to that end, an allegorical understanding of history may be more useful than a literal one. The Eusa show of *Riddley Walker* shows a far more decentralized version of the church than in *A Canticle For Leibowitz*, but its role is the same: it offers a spiritual understanding of history that hopes to help its followers survive the present without repeating the mistakes of the past.

Rather than preserving the past, some religions may instead cover it up, offering false myths to obscure historical truth. In Franklin J. Schaffner's 1968 film *Planet of the Apes*, an Earthly astronaut named George Taylor becomes stranded on a planet where speaking apes rule with an iron fist over mute, primitive humans. Dr. Zaius, the apes' political, religious, and scientific leader, sees Taylor's very existence as blasphemous, standing in opposition to his faith's statement that "the Almighty created Ape in his image."[6] The ape religion prohibits the simians from entering a region called "The Forbidden Zone," which Taylor believes must contain proof of human superiority. At the film's climax, Taylor, pursued by Zaius and an army of gorillas, escapes into the Forbidden Zone, where he learns the tragic truth: he is not on an alien planet, but rather on Earth thousands of years after he left it. A nuclear war has demolished his world, which was then inherited by the lower primates. The apes' religion is based on the rejection of human violence, as a reading from their Sacred Scrolls illustrates:

> Beware the beast man, for he is the devil's pawn. Alone among God's primates, he kills for sport, or lust or greed. Yea, he will murder his brother to possess his brother's land. Let him not breed in great numbers, for he will make a desert of his home and yours. Shun him. Drive him back into his jungle lair: For he is the harbinger of death.[7]

The ape's religion lies about the past, but it does so for a greater good: to prevent humankind from again destroying the Earth. Like the Catholic Church of *A Canticle for Leibowitz*, its goal is preservation, but rather than using faith to this end, it uses deliberate falsehood.

A far more optimistic view of future church communities appears in Orson Scott Card's *Folk of the Fringe* (1989), a collection of linked short stories about a postapocalyptic future. Card, a Mormon, depicts Latter-day Saints as the saviors of this future, rebuilding a society based on faith and charity. Their new culture thrives in what was once Utah, now rechristened "Deseret," and this new society is presented as the culmination of the American journey. These stories suggest—and rightly so—that a church is better suited to the task of holding a scattered and devastated country together than a government is: "All those Mormons, together they formed a big piece of cloth, all woven together through the whole state of Deseret, each person like a thread wound in among the others to make a fabric, tough and strong and complete right out to the edge—right out the fringe."[8] In Card's view, it is Mormons in particular who would be most likely to thrive in an apocalyptic setting. In "West," the first story in the volume, mainstream Christians are the villains, driving a small group of Mormons out of their community to trek across the violent countryside. Following this story, the collection does not mention non-Mormon churches at all. The LDS Church is especially suited to survive disaster because of its history of hardship: "We've been driven out and mobbed and massacred before, and all we ever do is move on and settle somewhere else. And wherever we settle there's peace and progress."[9] But the basic reason for the church's survival is something intrinsic to all faith communities: they join us together to create something greater. Churches are likely to survive such a disaster because their structure is based directly on relationships between individuals, thus enabling the small communities that a nuclear war would produce to remain tightly knit and yet also share a connection to other communities further away. This sense of community can hold together a scattered society in a time of crisis.

Religion provides a similar refuge for a very different sort of community in the short-lived television show *Alien Nation*. In this series, an alien slave ship from the planet Tencton has crash-landed on Earth. Five years later, the Tenctonese (or "Newcomers") are still adjusting to their newfound freedom and struggling to fit into American society. They still bear the scars of their enslavement and are frustrated by the bigotry of many of the humans they encounter, particularly the "Purist" movement that hopes to drive them from the planet. Tenctonese religion is vital in holding together the Newcomers' society, a link to their preslavery past— a time already becoming enshrouded in myth. Most of the Newcomers were born on the slave ship and do not remember Tencton, so their faith provides them with the only connection to their home world that they will ever know. The show follows George Francisco, the first Newcomer police detective, and his cynical human partner, Matt Sikes. Francisco is exemplary of the Newcomers' situation, embodying the desire to both assimilate into American society and retain a cultural identity that is at risk of fading away completely. When he learns that Sikes is a lapsed Catholic in the episode "Three to Tango" (1989), the importance of Tenctonese religion becomes clear: "As slaves we were denied our culture. Tradition and ritual are so important—I'm curious why you would freely choose to abandon your religion."[10] The Newcomers are a community in crisis, and faith helps to bind their culture together. By the episode's close Sikes has learned more about the Newcomers' religion and discovered a newfound respect for his own cultural heritage—in the last shot of the episode, we see him entering a church.

The role of religion as a preserver of order is not limited to earthbound tales. Numerous SF stories have depicted a spacefaring future in which religious missionaries are a vital force in the colonization of other worlds. There is much in the history of human faith to suggest that religious leaders will be on the forefront of interstellar exploration. Space provides a backdrop that may allow some religious orders to fulfill their missions in ways not possible on Earth. In Ian Stewart and Jack Cohen's 2000 novel *Wheelers*, our solar system's asteroid belt is colonized by mining operations led by Buddhist monks from Tibet, who see in space the perfect environment to meditate on the true nature of the universe as well as an isolated locale in which they can protect their heritage from absorption into China's secular culture:

> [As] China turned inward to become totally isolationist, the heritage of Old Tibet finally began to vanish at an alarming rate. And so the Buddhists of the Belt consulted the [Tibetan religious text] *Bya chos*, and there they read this:
> *Deep and vast, the aftermath of evil.*
> *Deep and vast, the midden of wickedness.*
> *Therefore make ready to abandon the Samsaric world.*
> They interpreted this advice as an instruction: as many Tibetans as possible must be removed from Earth. And, it followed logically, located elsewhere.[11]

Traveling in space requires the literal renunciation of Earthly life, and thus it is naturally suited to monasticism. Mary Doria Russell's 1996 novel *The Sparrow* argues that Jesuits will inevitably be interested in contacting alien species, just as they were among the first colonists of the New World:

> Everything about the history of the Society of Jesus bespoke deft and efficient action, exploration and research. During what Europeans were pleased to call the Age of Discovery, Jesuit priests were never more than a year or two behind the men who made initial contact with previously unknown peoples; indeed, Jesuits were often the vanguard of exploration. . . . The Jesuit scientists went to learn, not to proselytize. They went so that they might come to know and love God's other children. They went for the reason Jesuits have always gone to the farthest frontiers of human exploration. They went *ad majorem Dei gloriam*: for the greater glory of God.[12]

The same understanding of the Jesuits' role in an expanding universe is explored in Michael P. Kube-McDowell's 1982 story "A Green Hill Far Away." In the world of this story, scientists and adventurers have begun to colonize nearby solar systems, but the governments of Earth have no interest in spending the money or resources required to coordinate such distant and speculative undertakings. The Catholic Church takes responsibility for maintaining order in the outer colonies, and the fictional Order of St. Abbenew is established with three objectives: "spiritual ministry, the contemplation of God and His universe, and policing the anarchistic frontier worlds."[13] The church hierarchy thus becomes the de facto government of these chaotic colonies, with monks holding trials in cases of broken commandments. The hierarchy of the church is a ready-made government willing to accept leadership over the lawless future of space travel.

The preservation of society in a time of crisis may require the establishment of a new religion, specifically designed to meet the needs of its culture. In Stephen Baxter's 2004 novella "Mayflower II," such a situation occurs on a generation starship making a twenty-five-thousand-year voyage to another galaxy. In order to guarantee that future generations will continue to maintain the ship adequately, several of the original crew use alien technology to achieve immortality, becoming the leaders and, eventually, the gods of the ship's inhabitants. Science soon becomes ritual, and the rules by which the ship is governed and run become commandments, and priests, dubbed "Druids" by the immortals, become the preservers of the ship's original mission. The system is imperfect, however—the immortals still age and eventually die, and so they must spend vast stretches of time in suspended animation. During these stretches mortal society unfolds without direct guidance. At one point, the Druids monopolize the knowledge of the ship's workings, and another group, the Autarchs, gain political power by hoarding water. Rusel, the last remaining immortal, awakens to halt these changes, and even his wizened frame still inspires the awe necessary to put the culture back in line: "He was an angry god. . . . The rules of Shipboard life had been broken, he thundered. . . . There must be no more water empires, and no more knowledge empires either: the Druids would have to make sure that *every* child knew the basic rules, of Ship maintenance and genetic-health breeding."[14] The ship's religion is an autocratic one, but with good reason: without this dictatorial guidance, the ship's inhabitants would surely die out after a few generations. Rusel survives to the end of the voyage, but by that time his human cargo has devolved, becoming subhuman shadows of their former selves.

Still, the religion that grew around the ship's immortals enabled survival on an impossibly long journey.

Even though the church of "Mayflower II" is successful, its idea—that a false religion can preserve a culture—is still a cynical one. The fullest extent of this cynicism is illustrated in "Cygnus Alpha," a 1978 episode of the British SF television show *Blake's Seven*. Roj Blake, a political revolutionary in a dystopian future, has been captured and sent to the prison planet Cygnus Alpha. Arriving there, he and his fellow prisoners find the world run by a church, with the religious leader, Lord Vargas, as the absolute ruler of the penal colony. The priests of this religion tell the prisoners that they have been infected, as are all the planet's inhabitants, with a deadly plague. They must remain on the planet for the rest of their lives, taking a drug treatment that is prepared and distributed by the priests. Blake soon learns that the religion on which Cygnus Alpha's entire society is built is based on a deliberate falsehood. The first generation of prisoners were torn apart by violence and bloodshed until one of Vargas's ancestors devised the church as a means of keeping the people together and forging a strong, sustainable society. The Cygnus Plague is also a lie—the prisoners are healthy, but the church tells them they are ill and need its drugs so that they will not entertain thoughts of escape. But the religion, once a means of holding together a weak society, has become little more than a tool to give Vargas personal power. He is a tyrant, and his true nature becomes clear when he attempts to steal Blake's spaceship, the *Liberator*, to spread his cult to other worlds. Blake confronts him about his despotic faith:

> **Blake:** You and those before you built your power on fear and ruled them with it.
>
> **Vargas:** I ruled! I ruled a small prison planet with never more than 500 people. But with this—with this I could rule a thousand planets! For that prize, do you think I would hesitate to kill you?[15]

Far from a man of God, Vargas is a dictator and a murderer who wants nothing but power. The faith of Cygnus Alpha represents SF's most cynical attitude toward organized religion.

But even this negative approach to the church emphasizes the potential of organized religion as a bulwark against chaos. Few works of SF have illustrated this as vividly as Byron Haskin's 1953 film adaptation of H. G. Wells's novel *The War of the Worlds*. In the final scenes of this film, a few human survivors huddle in a church, praying for salvation from an invading alien army. As a Martian ship approaches and begins firing on the church, its pilot succumbs to Earthly bacteria, framing the aliens' death as a punishment not only for their ruthless invasion of our world, but for their attack on the church. The church provides a shelter for the survivors, a shield against the unstoppable alien force, and they are rewarded for their faith with victory against their foes. The community of believers is the last remnant of human society, and it alone cannot be destroyed. The church preserves humanity, stability, and culture in the face of adversity.

But inherent in SF's view of religious institutions as preservers of the past is the implication that they are themselves relics of an earlier age. This view is nowhere more clear than in Damien Broderick's 2002 novel *Transcension*. This story describes "The Sacred Sanctuary of the God of Our Choice"—a preserve, separated from the rest of the world by impassable mountains, that houses a community of religious Luddites who represent a strange mixture of liberal and conservative faith. All faiths are represented, and, as the name suggests, each individual chooses which god to worship. But despite this extreme pluralism, the community is extremely conservative, considering all technology diabolical. When one inhabitant of the valley is in a near-fatal accident and can only survive if a computer is installed in his brain, his caretaker nearly allows him to die: "You're saying you'll put a machine inside the boy's head? An instrument of Satan?"[16] In this novel, religion is presented in extremes, torn between pluralism so broad it renders individual ideas all but meaningless, and superstition that holds the society back from any kind of advancement. But the entire world of this novel is torn between similar extremes, and the technological society outside the Valley is no better. It is ruled by a superintelligent AI named Aleph that risks destroying the world in its quest to increase its power. Though the Sanctuary is hardly presented in a positive light, it comes across as no worse than the autocratic society outside, suggesting that a mixture of the two realms would be preferable.

Religion is also a relic in Jonathan Lethem's postapocalyptic novel *Amnesia Moon* (1995), in which the only remaining faithful in America are battered, worn-down robots. Some of these are street preachers who hope to remind humankind of its spiritual heritage, but most have given up on the atheistic human race and have locked themselves away in the ruins of a church. One of the robots tells the novel's protagonist of the past: "There was once a time when Christ was your king. . . . The world has fallen away from Him. We have failed in our work. There are few now who believe, fewer still who come to praise Him."[17] The protagonist ultimately rejects the robot's memories of the spiritual past, exemplifying the view that religions are relics of another age: "The memories, God, whatever, they just floated through, once, a long time ago. They're gone now."[18] *Amnesia Moon* offers an elegy to religious institutions, a theme that is explored more fully in Robert Silverberg's 1974 story "Schwartz between the Galaxies." In this story an anthropologist named Schwartz, depressed over the expanding global monoculture that has rendered his occupation meaningless, begins experiencing hallucinations of alien planets. Studying alien beings would give Schwartz the opportunity to learn about new cultures—something that globalization has made impossible on Earth. Schwartz speaks out against the elimination of the lines between cultures and faiths:

> Here we sit on the island of Papua—you know, head-hunters, animism, body-paint, the drums at sunset, the bone through the nose—and look at the Papuans in their business robes all around us. Listen to them exchanging stock-market tips, talking baseball, recommending restaurants in Paris and barbers in Johannesburg. It's no different anywhere else. In a single century we've transformed the planet into one huge sophisticated plastic western industrial state. The TV relay satellites, the two-hour intercontinental rockets, the breakdown of religious exclusivism and genetic taboo, have mongrelized every culture. . . . Cultural diversity is gone from the world. . . . Religion is

dead; true poetry is dead; inventiveness is dead; individuality is dead.[19]

Silverberg's story is a strong warning against the homogenization of global culture. Technology has the ability to annihilate the differences between cultures. In this story, American culture has permeated the entire world, and faith has not survived the transition: "You visit the Zuni and they have plastic African masks on the wall. You visit the Bushmen and they have Japanese-made Hopi-motif ashtrays. It's all just so much interior decoration, and underneath the carefully selected primitive motifs there's the same universal pseudo-American sensibility."[20] As capitalist, secular culture exerts its growing influence on the world, other cultures— and with them their beliefs—become commodified. Silverberg's story warns us against devaluing our cultures and allowing our faiths to become kitsch.

Robert Lowndes's 1952 novel *Believer's World* takes a different approach, suggesting that blending different cultures may resolve some of the problems that result from interfaith conflict. This story describes a system of three planets, each governed by a different church that is in perpetual competition with the other. The differences between the religions of these three planets—Grekh, Pittam, and Speewry—are purely cosmetic, as is clear in a description of a religious rite on Grekh:

> The Faithful . . . all accompanied their ritual with motions of the left hand, tracing a pattern in the air with the first two fingers. On Speewry, Dondyke had seen men wearing the same sort of garments, and going through the same devotions—but they traced the sacred symbols with their left forefingers only. Such life-and-death trifles distinguished the faithful of Speewry from those of Grekh.[21]

All three faiths are based on the same source, a deification of Einstein put together centuries before by a scientist from Earth. The difference between them is nothing more than one of language: all are based on the same set of sacred equations, but recorded in different systems of shorthand notation. The argument of *Believer's World* is clear: all religions are based on the same fundamental truths, the same experiences of the divine. But minor squabbles over interpretation and ritual have divided us, leading to interfaith conflict. Lowndes's novel proposes examining not the differences between our religious communities, but rather their similarities, with the hope that the "original truth" might be uncovered. Such an attitude is a popular one among many religious pluralists, but it is certainly problematic: what is peripheral in one faith may be central in another, and to reject it would essentially exclude many believers from what is intended as a universal system of belief. Though conflict and war between religious communities is lamentable, it is far too simple a reduction to suggest that the differences between our many faiths are nonexistent.

This oversimplification is rejected in Ursula K. Le Guin's 2000 novel *The Telling*, which describes a planet whose indigenous religion is in danger of annihilation. In this story, a linguist from Earth named Sutty is sent to study the native culture of the colony planet Aka. During her transit to the planet, however, the world falls under the control of "the Corporation," run by the Dovzans, an Akan cultural minority. The Corporation outlaws the world's native spirituality, known as "The Telling," burning its books and even forbidding the use of the Akan language. In place of this indigenous religion, they have established a state religion based on reason and science, a "show church" that is more of a loyalty test for the ruling class than a legitimate faith. This type of religion is wholly alien to the rural Akans, and the suppression of their culture has led only to the concealment of the Telling, not its destruction. Sutty is determined to continue her original quest, and she searches for hidden signs of the suppressed culture. What she finds is a holistic system: the Telling, she learns, is not merely a religion, but a system of history, philosophy, language, literature, mythology, and even cooking. In short, the Telling is the entirety of the native Akan culture. The Corporation's empty church hopes to completely suppress this vibrant culture. Sutty describes the drastic differences between the Telling and the state religion:

> There are no native Akan words for God, gods, the divine. . . .
> The Corporation bureaucrats made up a word for God and
> installed state theism when they learned that a concept of deity

was important on the worlds they took as models. They saw that
religion is a useful tool for those in power. But there was no
native theism or deism here. On Aka, *god* is a word without ref-
erent. . . . The Akan system is a spiritual discipline with spiritual goals, but they're exactly the same goals it seeks for bodily
and ethical well-being. Right action is its own end. Dharma
without karma.[22]

Le Guin presents the Telling as an ideal cultural system, a peaceful tradition that has been unjustly suppressed by a cruel elite.
Sutty compares the situation on Aka with that of Earth, which is
similarly divided: religious fundamentalists called Unists control
much of the planet, waging a war on secularists by bombing
schools and libraries. This contrast is key to understanding Le
Guin's message in *The Telling*: the situation is not simply that reason suppresses spirituality, because the same systems of control
can be inverted to create identical injustices. The Corporation's
prohibition of religious practice stems from encounters with missionaries from Earth, and they use this experience to justify their
tyranny. They fear that the Akans, if allowed to regain control of
the planet, would be like Earth's Unists: "These people are not pic-
turesque relics of a time gone by. They are not harmless. They are
vicious. They are the dregs of a deadly poison—the drug that stu-
pefied my people for ten thousand years. They seek to drag us back
into that paralysis, that mindless barbarism. . . . They are the enemies of truth, of science."[23] The Corporation, though oppressive,
is not wholly evil; it has enabled Aka to attain rapid technological
development, boosting its space program. Science—which is itself
a sort of religion, as the Corporation's deification of reason
shows—should not be placed at loggerheads with faith as both
Earth and Aka have done. A better system would be to integrate
what is good about both: the peacefulness of the Telling and the
technology of the Corporation could combine to produce a true
paradise. At the novel's close, Sutty is preparing to negotiate with
the Corporation: she will encourage Earth to continue providing it
with advanced technology if the Corporation will decriminalize
the Telling and allow non-Akans to conduct anthropological
research with the native culture. Through this compromise, Sutty

saves the Akans from suppression, bringing their powerful religion back into the forefront of their society.

Brian Moore's 1973 novel *Catholics* puts forward a similar argument for the preservation of ancient traditions on Earth. This short, intelligent novel takes place in a small monastery on the coast of Ireland that continues practicing the Latin Mass despite having been ordered by the Vatican to modernize its practices. An envoy from the Vatican is sent to negotiate with the monastery's abbot to bring the monks into line with the reforms brought about by the Fourth Vatican Council—which, among other changes, did away with traditional clerical vestments, private confession, and the priestly title of "father." The novel describes a battle of wills between this envoy and the abbot in a struggle between the monastery's traditionalists and the mainstream, increasingly secular church. In Moore's view, the traditionalists are more in touch with the spiritual basis of the church, while reformers are overly concerned with the secular world and its values. For example, in a passionate argument against the recitation of the vernacular Mass, Moore's abbot declares: "If the Mass was in Latin and people did not speak Latin, that was part of the mystery of it, for the Mass was not talking to your neighbor, it was talking to God. Almighty God! . . . This new Mass isn't a mystery, it's a mockery, a singsong, it's not talking to God, it's talking to your neighbor, and that's why it's in English. . . . It's a symbol, they say, but a symbol of what?"[24] In the abbot's view, all the church's power rests in its rituals, and to misinterpret the purpose of those rituals is to sever the church's connection with God. Moore's novel comes across as critical of attempts to reform religious institutions according to modern standards; when the monks ultimately agree to accept the reforms of Vatican IV, the narrative treats it as tragedy rather than triumph. The novel's closing scene shows the abbot reciting the Lord's Prayer in English rather than the traditional Latin, but his prayer holds no power for him: "He entered null. He would never come back. In null."[25] Though its conservatism makes it unconventional compared to SF's usual approach to religion, *Catholics* nevertheless offers a powerful warning about the future of an overly secularized church.

Few SF authors hold this view, however. Much more frequently, they argue that if religions are to survive in the coming era, they must be willing to change to meet the demands of the future. In Robert Silverberg's Nebula Award–winning 1971 story "Good News from the Vatican," a growing population of intelligent machines has led the Catholic Church to consider electing a robot pope. The machines—attracted to the church by the logic of systematic theologians such as Thomas Aquinas—have come to form a large percentage of church membership, but a decision to choose a mechanical pontiff could drive humans away. The story centers on a conversation between several characters with differing views on the idea of a robotic pontiff. One character, for example, is suspicious of the essential alienness of machines: "Once you've seen one, you've seen all of them. Shiny boxes. Wheels. Eyes. And voices coming out of their bellies like mechanized belches. Inside, they're all too much for me to accept."[26] Another argues that such a strange union of faith and technology will only strengthen the church: "The inherent goodness of the new Pope . . . will prevail. Also I believe that technologically-minded young folk everywhere will be encouraged to join the Church. Irresistible religious impulses will be awakened throughout the world."[27] When the robot is finally chosen to be pope, the story presents the event with a mixture of dread and excitement: the robotic pontiff levitates over the Vatican on jets of compressed air, and "his shadow extends across the whole piazza. Higher and higher he goes, until he is lost to sight. . . . The new Pontiff, I think, has begun his reign in an auspicious way."[28] Silverberg's story is a positive comment on the changes to the Catholic Church brought about by Vatican II. Just as that council showed that the church was willing to change to meet the spiritual challenges of its day, this story shows a church that is willing to adapt itself to a future where human beings may no longer be the dominant species. The story's close suggests that the robots may soon eclipse human beings, but that the Catholic Church, unlike more rigid human institutions, will survive in this new era.

Many authors suggest that to survive in an uncertain future, religions must undergo far more radical changes. In several of his novels, Philip K. Dick creates future worlds where the only surviving religions are those that have done away with any semblance of hierarchical structure. In *Do Androids Dream of Electric Sheep?* (1968), for example, a postapocalyptic society has been reshaped around a religion called Mercerism. The central ritual of this religion involves the use of an "empathy box." This device creates a telepathic link between the religion's practitioners wherein they experience firsthand the death and resurrection of the church's founder, Wilbur Mercer. The practical application of this ritualized empathy comes in the form of compassion for animals, most of which were killed by the fallout of a nuclear war. Members of the church take care of either authentic (and expensive) living animals or more affordable electronic imitations. These animals are cared for both as pets and as devotional objects. The direct experience on which Mercerism is based eliminates the need for a spiritual hierarchy to mediate religious experience, and nowhere in the novel does Dick mention pastors or churches of the Mercerite religion. Though Dick seems to approve of the purity of a religion based on direct experience, he sees potential problems in such a system—in the novel, the trade in authentic and electric animals has led to a consumerism that undermines the authenticity of the empathy on which Mercerism is based. Animal salesmen treat their wares not as living expressions of the divine, but rather as commodities to be bought, sold, and traded. At points in the novel, animals seem like mere status symbols, described in language reminiscent of automobiles. Ultimately, however, *Do Androids Dream of Electric Sheep?* is optimistic about the power of a religion based on the direct experience of compassion. Dick presents a spirituality that has been enhanced by technology, scientific devices that enable direct human experience of the divine. In these futures, science can eliminate the need for religious hierarchy by giving technological means for direct religious experiences. This idea carries with it the suggestion that, should science find a means to enhance or perfect human spirituality, it must be at the expense of organized religion as we know it.

Poul Anderson's 1960 story "The Word to Space" (published under the pseudonym Winston P. Sanders) shows what might happen if our modes of spiritual expression are allowed to stagnate. In this story, radio contact is established with an alien race. After determining that they are communicating with an intelligent race, the aliens seek to convert humanity to their religion, and their subsequent messages consist entirely of evangelical religious programming: "Nothing but doctrine. . . . Every message a sermon, or a text from one of their holy books followed by an analysis that my Jewish friends tell me makes the medieval rabbis look like romantic poets."[29] The religion is exceptionally intolerant, as shown by one exegetical transmission: "The next word in the sentence from Aejae xliii, 3 which we are considering is 'ruchiruchin,' an archaic word concerning whose meaning there was formerly some dispute. Fortunately, the advocates of the erroneous theory that it means 'very similar' have now been exterminated and the glorious truth that it means 'quite similar' is firmly established."[30] The scientists in charge of translating these messages—including a Jesuit priest named James Moriarty—are unable to coax any sort of scientific information from the aliens, and find it impossible to communicate with them. Moriarty determines that the only way that Earth will be able to establish any kind of meaningful discussion with the aliens is to incite a secularist revolution on their planet, in hopes that scientists may seize the means of interstellar communication from the priests. By pointing out logical flaws in the aliens' religious system, they encourage a fierce schismatic battle which leaves the religious hierarchy weakened enough for secular forces to take control. In this story, religion—albeit an alien and not an Earthly faith—is a barrier to communication between planets. Because they are so intent on converting humankind, the aliens are unable to establish any kind of dialogue with us. This story hopes to serve as a warning: if we allow what the author sees as the more backward aspects of our spirituality to become too powerful, religion may hold us back as we move into the future.

This message about Earthly religion is conveyed even more clearly in James Patrick Kelly's 1984 story "St. Theresa of the Aliens." In this story, aliens land on a Cold War–era Earth, choosing to make first contact with the Soviet Union rather than the United States. The aliens, it seems, identify more closely with the collectivism of socialist government than with democratic individualism, even going so far as to translate the word for their own form of government as "communism." This enrages the citizens of democratic countries—particularly the religious, who are angered to see an extraterrestrial endorsement of atheism. Theresa Burelli, a Catholic nun, organizes a "purist" movement with the goal of driving the godless aliens off of the planet. The story's narrator, once a friend of the nun, watches in dismay as Theresa's faction becomes an international movement, uniting the West under a banner of God, democracy, and xenophobia. The narrator is particularly distressed by the purist movement because the aliens, whose advanced science could be useful to the West, are willing to share their knowledge with noncommunist nations. But despite this, the Western democracies reject the extraterrestrials, and Theresa's brand of religion becomes a barrier to block out information that could raise the entire world above its petty divisions. At the story's close, Theresa—accidentally martyred by the aliens during a protest—is about to be sainted, and the narrator despairs that Earth (or at least America) has segregated itself from the stars. In this story, religion forms a wall that threatens to separate humanity from the rest of the universe.

An even more grim picture of organized religion emerges in David Twohy's 2004 film *The Chronicles of Riddick*. The villains of this film are the leaders of a church called the Necromongers, a cult that worships death and tells its believers that it will guide them to an otherworldly afterlife called "the Underverse": "Life is antagonistic to the natural state. Here, humans in all their various races are a spontaneous outbreak—an unguided mistake. Our purpose is to correct that mistake."[31] The Necromongers spread their belief through conquest, "converting" entire planets by brainwashing their populations. The hero of the story—the homicidal yet noble criminal of the title—stands against the church, ultimately defeating its founder and thereby becoming leader of the entire church. The people of the planet Helion oppose the Necromongers' invasion of their world, pitting their diversity of belief against the interstellar zealots: "This is a world of many peoples, many religions! And we simply cannot and will not be converted!"[32] But this syncretism falls before the invading army. Riddick is able to overthrow an oppressive faith, and symbolizes the film's ideal: rebellious independence that acknowledges no higher authority beyond the individual. Riddick is an action hero, and action heroes do not belong to churches, be they sinister armies like the Necromongers or peaceful, multicultural communities like Helion. *The Chronicles of Riddick*—and indeed most action movies—argues that one need not be a member of a church, or have any spiritual beliefs beyond the level of aphorism, to find fulfillment.

The idea of an "evil church" is a common one in SF, and countless stories have described religious institutions like the Necromongers that seek temporal power rather than spiritual advancement. In the comic book series *V for Vendetta*, writer Alan Moore and artist David Lloyd depict a near-future England ruled by a fascist party that uses Christian imagery. Moore's superhero protagonist—an anarchistic terrorist named "V" who dresses in the costume of a Guy Fawkes effigy—incites a rebellion against this government. Using cleverly orchestrated bombings and assassinations, he encourages England's populace to rise against their leaders and reclaim their individual liberties. The story's anti-religious tone is at times extreme: in one scene, for example, V executes a pedophiliac bishop by feeding him a poisoned communion wafer. James McTeigue's 2006 film based on this series further emphasizes Moore and Lloyd's critique, showing, for example, that ownership of a Qur'an is a crime punishable by death in this pseudo-Christian autocracy.

V for Vendetta is merely one of many stories that follow a formula wherein religion is a symbol of oppression and blind acceptance of authority, and where the hero is an individualist who seeks to bring (secular) enlightenment and freedom to the oppressed. Another example is Fritz Leiber's 1950 novel *Gather, Darkness!* It depicts a government based on the medieval Catholic Church that brutally oppresses its people. Its priests use advanced technology to convince the ignorant masses that they have supernatural abilities, and the story's hero—a member of a rebellious organization that adopts the imagery of Satan—steals this technology to overthrow their oppressors. More recently, Kurt Wimmer's pseudo-Marxist action film *Equilibrium* (2002) depicts a police state that uses the imagery of a religious institution. Reviewer Michael Karounos states that the film's portrayal of a persecuting church in fact "promotes religious bigotry and persecution of religious people. . . . The irony of *Equilibrium* is that in trying to portray a nonexistent statist authoritarianism rooted in the symbols of Christianity, Wimmer reveals the residual totalitarianism of communism that it seems will always be with us as a romantic but deadly ideal."[33] Modern totalitarianism, Karounos rightly points out, has always been secular, and though religious institutions have committed their share of historical crimes, the spiritual impulse of faith and the secular drive for political power come from very different sources. Stories that depict all religions as deceptive, fascistic organizations do a disservice to people of faith everywhere.

The Church of Cosmic Unity in Ian Stewart and Jack Cohen's 2004 novel *Heaven* represents one of the most negative depictions of a church in recent SF, but even with its strong criticisms, the novel is not opposed to all religious faith. The leadership of Cosmic Unity has changed so much since its inception that the church now represents the polar opposite of its true message. Based on the idea of tolerance for all beings and all beliefs, Cosmic Unity demolishes all societies that refuse to accept its message. Passages describing the church's means of warfare are sardonically humorous, underlining the irony of the faith's hypocrisy. "Love bombs," for example, are one of Cosmic Unity's most commonly used weapons: "Before exploding, they emitted brief prayers for the lifesouls of the heathen that they were primed to slay. The gist of the prayers was that it was all for the heathens' own good, and that they should rejoice."[34] The novel suggests that such intolerance is the inevitable end of any religion, no matter how peaceful: "It was often the religions that boasted most loudly of their love for their fellow beings that most readily perverted their beliefs into cruelty and destruction. Because *they knew what was good for you*, and sometimes they would stop at nothing to make sure that it happened. This . . . was the self-laid trap that awaited every benevolent memeplex."[35] Despite this statement, at the novel's conclusion Cosmic Unity is replaced by a faith that the characters hope will truthfully preserve interstellar peace and tolerance. Ruled by emotionless, empathic Neanderthals who are incapable of superstition, this new religion—"Universal Harmony"—includes safeguards that will "stop the new religion from getting out of hand. Whenever a large group of sentients became too harmonious, and community was in danger of sliding into enforced conformity, the Neanderthal 'priesthood' was there to sow the seeds of discord. . . . Universal Harmony's aim was to become a eukaryote religion. A synthesis, a symbiosis, a complicity—not a sterile uniformity."[36] Universal Harmony seeks to establish an intergalactic religion of peace that does not rely on conformity between different worlds, as Cosmic Unity did. Each species and community is allowed to worship as it pleases—and if it seeks to "harmonize" with communities that differ, the Neanderthal priesthood will ensure lasting harmony by underscoring the differences between these communities. In part, this conclusion is played as a joke, but it nevertheless reveals the authors' actual attitude: true, sustainable peace relies on disagreement and discord. *Heaven* does not oppose all religion, but it does oppose the idea of exclusive truth-claims, the sense that any one faith (or species) has a privileged position in the universe.

As this conclusion suggests, SF stories that criticize organized religions do not hope to attack the religious impulse or authentic faith. Rather, they argue that religions that become too focused on doctrine have atrophied, restricting actual faith for the sake of stability. Sheri S. Tepper's 1989 novel *Grass* is based in a future dominated by a draconian church called the Sanctity. The church rules Earth and has powerful influence on all other planets, including the distant colony world Grass. But despite the influence of the Sanctity, the society itself is not overly religious: "We pay it lip service. . . . Sanctity is headquartered upon Terra. We acknowledge Terra as the center of diplomatic intercourse. Maintainer of our cultural heritage. Eternal cradle of mankind. Blah and blah."[37] It is not only the galaxy's secularists who take this attitude; even the Sanctity's own monks scoff at its doctrines. A young monk named Rillibee challenges the Sanctity, questioning some of its basic faith-claims, and an older monk gives him some cynically pragmatic advice:

"The first thing you've got to do is tell yourself that the shitheads are wrong. . . . Not just a little bit wrong, but irremediably, absolutely, and endemically wrong. Nothing you can say or do will stop their being wrong. They're damned to eternal wrongness, and that's God's will. . . . Then, you acknowledge that these wrongheaded fart-asses have been placed in authority over you through some cosmic miscalculation, and you reach the only possible conclusion. . . . You bow your head and say, 'Yes, Elder Brother,' in a nice humble tone, and you go right on believing what you have to believe. Anything else is like walking out into the grass when the grazers are coming by. You may be right, but you'll be flat right and there won't be enough left of you to scrape up."[38]

The Sanctity has stagnated to the point of irrelevance. Its followers acknowledge it only as a political force with no spiritual value. Most of its monks are childish thugs, and its bishops care about laws and doctrine but not about the vital issues of faith and religious experience. Tepper makes a direct connection between the decline of this church and its concentration on teaching rote dogma rather than faith: "Brothers, so it was said, had once spent their time in study, but little study was needed here. All the questions had been reduced to doctrine; all the doctrine had been simplified to catechism; all the catechism had been learned long ago."[39] In presenting stagnated religious organizations, stories such as *Grass* and *Heaven* hope merely to warn us about the potential subversion of our spirituality. Religions can easily be turned into engines of temporal power, weakening their actual relevance to our spiritual needs. Inquiry is a better ground for faith than rote learning, and any church that seeks to crush questions under the weight of dogma can no longer offer the spiritual guidance that organized religion should provide. With no ability to engage with its followers, it loses all legitimacy. Despite these criticisms, SF stories like *Grass* are not opposed to religion in general—simply to the subversion of faith into oppressive systems of control.

Grass is emblematic of the attitude that many SF writers take toward religious institutions. Though not disparaging individual spirituality, most SF writers seem to view organized religions as

corrupt tyrannies that attempt to govern or suppress that spirituality. There are certainly numerous exceptions to this rule in SF,
but a clear majority of writers in the genre are distrustful of organized religion. Where churches appear in SF, they are frequently
the center of authoritarian corruption. By contrast the heroes of
SF tend to be daring individuals who stand against such con-
formist institutions, praising reason and personal freedom over
inherited dogma. SF as a genre has its roots in secular humanism,
and thus it is unsurprising that so many works of SF take up the
theme of the individual versus the institution in the context of
organized religion.

Many SF stories have given powerful warnings about the dangers that the oppressive aspects of organized religion pose for our
own society. Katharine Kerr's 1994 story "Asylum" depicts an
ultraconservative near future in which the U.S. Army, with the
encouragement and support of the Christian right, stages a coup
that places a fascistic military government in power. The story follows a feminist writer named Janet Corey who has written a book
studying this extreme religious conservatism entitled *Christian
Fascism: The Politics of Righteousness*. Exiled from her country
by the religious junta, she finds a new home in the United Kingdom, where she lectures on the revolution that her book had predicted. The main focus of the story is on her attempts to establish
contact with her friends and family in the United States—a goal
that she is ultimately unable to achieve given the tight controls the
new government has put in place. This story is a powerful critique
of the dangers of present-day Christian conservatism and its insistence that the government adopt a radical interpretation of "traditional values." Kerr fears what could result from the combination
of this zeal with mob violence, as in a description of a beating Janet
received at the hands of antiabortion activists before the coup:
"She can still remember images of fists swinging toward her face
and hear voices shrieking with rage, chanting Jesus Jesus Jesus.
'All in the name of God. No, that's not fair. In the name of the
warped little conception of God that these people have.' "[40]
Though the extent of the violence committed in this story is
extreme, the violence that some radical religious groups have

directed toward abortion providers in recent years shows that such events are all too possible. Kerr's story argues that, were the religious right to attain political power in the United States, its rule would be anything but Christian, and it provides a moving warning about the dangerous extremes of religious zealotry.

Margaret Atwood's 1986 novel *The Handmaid's Tale* describes one possible result of a coup like that in "Asylum." This story depicts a dystopia ruled by fundamentalist Christians who turned antiabortion protests into a full-scale revolution. They have established a rigid social order in which the only roles available to women are those of wife, underground prostitute, or "handmaid"—a bearer of children for the upper classes. This last role is based on biblical precedent—specifically, the story of Jacob and Bilhah in Genesis 30:1–8—and represents Atwood's reductio ad absurdum of biblical literalism. The fundamentalist regime is brutal, enforcing its hierarchy with an Orwellian police organization called "the Eyes of God." The Eyes seek out evidence of past as well as current transgressions, and the punishments for such sins are extreme: former abortion providers, for example, are executed and hung on hooks on the city wall: "These men, we've been told, are like war criminals. It's no excuse that what they did was legal at the time: their crimes are retroactive. They have committed atrocities and must be made into examples, for the rest. . . . What we are supposed to feel towards these bodies is hatred and scorn."[41] Atwood presents this society with a sardonic irony: hatred used to support a religion founded on love; mass executions carried out by a church whose code of law includes a commandment against killing. The family is, in theory, the central unit of this novel's society, but all respectable marriages are presented as loveless, and the coup has broken up thousands of families, including that of the narrator. Atwood's novel is a damning attack on the fundamentalism of our day, exposing what the author sees as the hypocrisy at the core of conservative Christianity.

Stories such as *The Handmaid's Tale* and "Asylum" seem to be, like *Equilibrium*, unnecessarily exaggerated criticisms of Christianity, based only on the worst aspects of conservative belief. But given the growing popularity of radically conservative interpreta-

tions of Christ's message, the sort of extremism that has hijacked
the spirituality of these fictional futures may not be so unrealistic.
The language of war has become common parlance in many conservative congregations. Pastor Ted Haggard, for example, built
his New Life Church to eleven thousand members by essentially
taking over the city of Colorado Springs, holding prayer protests
outside the homes of "undesirable" members of the community.
Haggard describes his mission in military terms, and his church
houses "a ministry dedicated to 'spiritual warfare.' The Prayer
Center's nickname in the fundamentalist world is 'spiritual
NORAD.' "[42] Authors like Katharine Kerr and Margaret Atwood
are merely taking conservative pastors like Haggard at their word,
showing the end result of a literal "culture war" waged by ultraconservative zealots. These stories do not argue that fascism is the
inevitable result of Christianity; rather, they underline the injustice
of perverting Christ's message of peace to justify intolerance and
militarism. In *The Handmaid's Tale*, Atwood makes a point of
emphasizing the fact that many Christians opposed the theocratic
coup. An underground organization led by Quakers sets up an
"Underground Femaleroad" to guide women away from the tyran-
nical fundamentalist government: "One of the hardest things was
knowing that these other people were risking their lives for you
when they didn't have to. But they said they were doing it for religious reasons."[43] These selfless rebels are the true Christians in
Atwood's story, and their sacrifice demonstrates the *caritas* that is
the true core of the church. Stories of fundamentalist dictatorships
are not anti-Christian; rather, they speak out against those religious
trends in our era that, if unchecked, could be used to prop up systems of tyranny and injustice in the near future.

Octavia Butler's 1993 novel *Parable of the Sower* constitutes a
synthesis of many of the above attitudes, presenting both a criticism of organized religion as it stands today and a vision of a
viable church for the future. This novel depicts a near future torn
apart by economic stratification. An increasingly laissez-faire government has created a state of de facto anarchy in which even those
fortunate enough to have jobs are unable to earn enough to feed
themselves. The shrinking middle class lives behind guarded

walls, besieged by the disenfranchised poor outside their gates. Gangs of arsonists roam city and country alike, robbing, killing, and burning any unguarded settlement they come across. The police have become little more than an extortionist gang, and even the worst crimes are rarely investigated. Though a nuclear war is not a part of this novel's future history, it is nevertheless postapocalyptic in tone, describing the devastating effects of a purely economic catastrophe.

Into this bleak future America is born Lauren Olamina, the daughter of a Baptist preacher. Olamina is an empath who feels the pain and joy of those near her, and this ability gives her special insight into human nature. She rejects her father's religion in her adolescence, seeing it as naïve; she claims that "to the adults [in her father's church], going outside to a real church was like stepping back into the good old days when there were churches all over the place and too many lights and gasoline was for fueling cars and trucks instead of for torching things. They never miss a chance to relive the good old days or to tell kids how great it's going to be when the country gets back on its feet and good times come back."[44] Rather than attempting to improve the present, her father's faith encourages its followers to dwell in the past. Olamina opts instead to shape for herself a spiritual path more suited to her chaotic surroundings than her father's anachronistic Christianity. Predicting that her family's middle-class settlement will be invaded by the jealous underclass outside its walls, Olamina teaches herself how to survive in the violent wilderness, learning to build fires, shoot guns, and forage for food. Part of this preparation involves devising a new philosophy called "Earthseed." This faith focuses on helping others rather than selfishly guarding one's own life and possessions as her father's community had done. The ultimate goal of Earthseed is to guide humankind to the stars—interstellar travel, Olamina argues, represents the highest and most noble of human aspirations. To abandon it, as the U.S. government has done in the novel, is to abandon hope in humankind's survival. The core idea of Earthseed, however, is a definition of divinity, repeated throughout the novel: "God is change." The chaotic nature of this novel's future world shows that the only constant in our universe is change, and the only certainty is uncertainty. This religion is ideally suited to the lawless world of *Parable of the Sower*, a world where one's possessions, livelihood, and life can be taken away at any moment. Unlike the faiths that preceded it, the goal of Earthseed is not to worship God-as-change, but rather to *shape* God, to help to make creative rather than destructive change. When Olamina's settlement is burned to the ground by the gangs outside its walls, Earthseed is put to the test. She travels away from the suburbs with a small but growing group of followers, gradually teaching them her philosophy. At the novel's close, the small Earthseed community establishes a town called Acorn in the forests of northern California and begins planning how it will survive in its chaotic surroundings.

The novel's Nebula Award–winning sequel, *Parable of the Talents* (1998), pits Earthseed against an apparently unbeatable enemy—a militaristic religious sect called Christian America. Much like the Christian Fascists of "Asylum" and the ruling class of *The Handmaid's Tale*, Christian America is a fascist organization hiding behind a thin veneer of Christian imagery. The founder of the movement, a politician named Andrew Steele Jarret, uses his organization to become president of the crumbling United States, and once in power his soldiers are able to embark on their crusade with impunity. They create concentration camps to imprison "heathens" and "witches," categories so broad that they include virtually anyone who is not a member of Christian America. Earthseed and Christian America could not be more different from one another. Olamina's group is peaceful, and accepts converts but does not actively seek them out. Jarret's organization exercises brutal violence in its quest to conquer the entire country. Most importantly, Earthseed is focused on the future, on overcoming present difficulty to achieve the destiny of space travel. But Christian America is focused on an imaginary past:

> Jarret insists on being a throwback to some earlier, "simpler" time. *Now* does not suit him. Religious tolerance does not suit him. The current state of the country does not suit him. He wants to take us all back to some magical time when everyone believed in the same God, worshipped him in the same way,

and understood that their safety in the universe depended on completing the same religious rituals and stomping anyone who was different. There was never such a time in this country. But these days when more than half the people in the country can't read at all, history is just one more vast unknown to them.[45]

This organization's attempt to rebuild a fictional past soon reaches Acorn, which is raided and turned into a concentration camp. But despite the brutal suppression of Earthseed, the faith survives, much as the early Christian church endured Roman persecution. It is a religion based on survival, and though it remains a small and largely secret community, Olamina's church perseveres through Jarret's police state.

Parable of the Sower and *Parable of the Talents* exemplify the understanding of organized religion presented by the majority of SF. The novels contain criticism of established religions in the form of the naively nostalgic Baptists and the brutal Christian Americans. But they also offer a vibrant alternative in the form of Earthseed: a slowly growing religious community dedicated to facing and surviving the uncertain future. Unlike other future religions—the authoritarian warmongering of *Heaven*'s Cosmic Unity, the mechanistic Rome of "Good News from the Vatican," or the bland secularism of *Catholics*—Earthseed is devoted first and foremost to surviving into the future with its humanity intact, preserving a sense of the value of humankind and of the individual alike. If SF as a whole can be said to have a single argument about organized religion, it is this: that if any church is to remain a vital force in our future, it must be willing to face whatever changes may come and adapt itself to the spiritual questions of the future. Butler's Earthseed is the best example of this sort of vibrant church, offering as it does "room for small groups of people to begin new lives and new ways of life with new opportunities, new wealth, new concepts of wealth, new challenges to grow and to learn and to decide what to become. Earthseed is the dawning adulthood of the human species. . . . It enables the seeds of the Earth to become the seeds of a new life, new communities on new earths."[46] In short, Earthseed looks to the future, and seeks to shape a human spirituality that will enable us to meet the challenges to come. A church that dwells in the past is certain to lose touch with the world in which its believers live, and if religion is to meet the spiritual needs of coming generations, it must be willing to face the future with an open mind. In all its approaches to communities of faith—harsh criticisms of oppressive churches, nostalgic eulogies for the religions of the past, and optimistic predictions of new faiths that will take us to the stars—SF hopes to forge a spirituality that will survive whatever the future may bring.

Chapter Nine

Imagining the Afterlife

Plato's dialogue *Phaedo* describes the final hours of Socrates' life, in which he told his followers that he did not fear death, because the soul of a moral person "departs to the place where things are like itself—invisible, divine, immortal and wise; where, on its arrival, happiness awaits it, and release from uncertainty and folly, from fears and gnawing desires, and all other human evils."[1] Our soul, our deepest sense of self, survives our death, and enters a realm of immortality. The belief in an afterlife such as that described by Socrates has often been considered the source of all religious thought. It is our hope that our consciousness will extend beyond our mortal lives that leads to speculation about the unknowable source of all being. Robert Silverberg's 1982 story "The Pope of the Chimps" depicts the birth of a religion from just this sort of speculation about the afterlife. In this story, a group of scientists studying chimpanzees has established sophisticated communication with them using sign language. When one member of the team develops terminal leukemia, he decides to tell the chimps, and this knowledge sparks an obsession among the apes. Soon, every conversation with them revolves around death, and one of the scientists hypothesizes that this is a sign of theological thinking: "They surely see human death as something quite different from chimpanzee death—a translation to another state of being, an ascent on a chariot of fire. Yost believes that they have no comprehension of human death at all, that they think we are immortal, that they think we are gods."[2] Soon Leo, the leader of the chimps, is observed wearing a shirt and hat, babbling in imitation of human speech, and distributing food in what appears to be a religious ritual. He signs a basic statement of faith to the scientists: " *'Jump high come again'* might be about a game they like to play, but it could also be an eschatological reference, sacred talk, a concise metaphorical way to speak of death and resurrection."[3] The chimps' realization that human beings—their superiors, and in some respects their gods—can die leads to a massive upheaval in their society, which soon becomes obsessed with "going away." Finally the chimps work out what is, to them, a satisfying thanatology: "When human go away, he become god. When chimpanzee go away, he become human."[4] In Silverberg's story, speculation on the afterlife is responsible for an entire system of religious thought, and for the advancement of chimpanzee society to a more human level.

In his Hugo Award–winning 2002 novel *Hominids*, the first volume in the *Neanderthal Parallax* trilogy, Robert J. Sawyer presents a similar argument for the importance of speculation on the afterlife, though his conclusions are quite different. In this novel, scientists discover a parallel universe where Neanderthal man became dominant rather than Cro-Magnon, and a wildly different society developed as a result. Neanderthal society has virtually no crime, but at the cost of extensive restrictions on individual liberty. It also has no religion, and no idea of an afterlife. In a conversation, inhabitants of the two worlds discuss the importance of the belief in life after death:

> "Without a belief that you will be rewarded or punished after the end of your life—what drives morality among your people? . . . I know you're a good person. Where does that goodness come from?"
>
> "I behave as I do because it is right for me to do so . . . by the standards of my people."
>
> "But *where* do those standards come from?"
>
> "From . . . from our conviction that there is *no* life after death! . . . A person's life is completely finished at death; there is no

possibility of reconciling with them, or making amends after they are gone. . . . If I wrong someone . . . under your worldview I can console myself with the knowledge that, after they are dead, they can still be contacted; amends can be made. But in my worldview, once a person is gone . . . then you who did the wrong must live knowing that person's entire existence ended without you ever having made peace with him or her."[5]

In Sawyer's novel, the belief in the afterlife is the source of human ethics—but because of this, those ethics are flawed. Neanderthal society complicates the question of human existence and human belief by presenting an alternative to our understanding of life, death, and moral behavior. For both Sawyer and Silverberg, the afterlife is central to human society; only its consequences in society are a source of dispute. Given the centrality of the afterlife in human systems of belief, it is only natural that SF would explore the question of life after death—and just as natural that SF authors would not be content to accept an uncomplicated picture of heaven and hell.

In Philip K. Dick's novel *Ubik* (1969), the afterlife is presented as a strange and unnerving limbo. In the world of this novel, consciousness remains in the body after death, and the bodies of the wealthy are kept in "cold-pak" for years after their deaths. The minds of these "half-lifers" can be revived for limited periods of time, during which the living update them on events that have occurred since their deaths and consult them for advice and guidance. These consultations must be brief and infrequent, however: each time it is revived, the mind of a half-lifer—and its connection with the world of the living—grows weaker. As this connection weakens, the minds of the half-lifers begin to meld together, as one of the deceased explains: "I think that other people who are around me—we seem to be progressively growing together. A lot of my dreams aren't about me at all. Sometimes I'm a man and sometimes a little boy; sometimes I'm an old fat woman with varicose veins . . . and I'm in places I've never seen, doing things that make no sense."[6] Half-life is a dreamlike world where the world—and the self—are sometimes incomprehensible.

Most of the story occurs in half-life. Early on, the novel's central characters, a group of psychics, are killed in a bomb blast, but do not realize that they have died. Instead, they think that they have survived the blast and their employer, Greg Runciter, is the only one who has died. Runciter—in truth the sole survivor of the explosion—attempts to contact them to inform them of their state. At first, half-life is largely indistinguishable from everyday, living existence. Soon, however, the characters begin to notice strange things occurring—cigarette packs that have just been opened are already stale, and freshly poured coffee is cold and covered in mold. Strangest of all, machines are reverting to older versions of themselves—a supersonic jet becomes a biplane and a hydraulic lift becomes an antique, steel-cage elevator. The world of half-life is beset with entropy, and the fading effect gradually reaches to some of the half-lifers, who decay into dried-out piles of cloth and bone. As Runciter explains when he finally manages to contact the half-lifers, "world deterioration of this regressive type is a normal experience of many half-lifers, especially in the early stages when ties to the real reality are still very strong. A sort of lingering universe is retained as a residual charge, experienced as a pseudo environment but highly unstable and unsupported by any ergic substructure."[7] The afterlife in *Ubik* is far from paradise—it is a limbo that gradually deteriorates into a hell for its inhabitants. Slow deterioration is the hallmark of the afterlife. This process can even be accelerated by particularly strong and selfish minds, who can speed up the deterioration of other minds in order to extend their own half-life. At the novel's conclusion it is revealed that much of the decay the half-lifers have experienced is the result of one such psychic vampire named Jory, but even without this parasite, the experience of half-life is best described as the ominous approach of true death: "In half-life we diminish constantly. Jory only speeds it up. The weariness and cooling-off come anyhow. But not so soon."[8] Half-life is a bleak limbo in which the departed wait until they finally throw off their attachment to their lives. This occurs in a manner based on the *Bardo Thödol*, the Tibetan Book of the Dead: the dead are pulled into either a pure white light (indicating a good rebirth) or a smoky, red one (for birth into unfortunate circumstances). Dick does not build on the idea of reincarnation beyond a few brief references to these lights, however. He spends much more time describing the experience of those in cold-pak, and thus the book leaves the reader with an overwhelming image of the afterlife as a bleak and frightening place, an in-between world that truly seems like a "half-life."

A similar vision of life after death appears in the final volume of Philip Pullman's *His Dark Materials* trilogy, a complex and intelligent series of young adult fantasy novels that uses several SF elements. In *The Amber Spyglass* (2000), Will and Lyra, the saga's two heroes, travel to the land of the dead, which is a grim and entropic wasteland inhabited by weak, amnesiac shades. The ghosts are drawn to the two living spirits among them: "These poor ghosts had little power of their own, and hearing Will's voice, the first clear voice that had sounded there in all the memory of the dead, many of them came forward, eager to respond. But they could only whisper. A faint, pale sound, no more than a soft breath, was all that they could utter."[9] Will and Lyra resolve to free the dead from this half-existence, opening a portal from the world of the dead into a living world, where their energy will dissipate: "All the particles that make you up will loosen and float apart. . . . All the atoms that were with them, they've gone into the air and the wind and the trees and the earth and all the living things. They'll never vanish. They're just part of everything. . . . You'll drift apart, it's true, but you'll be out in the open, part of everything alive again."[10] Pullman presents this dissipation as a far preferable alternative to the limbo of the dead world.

Ted Chiang's 2001 novelette "Hell Is the Absence of God," winner of Hugo and Nebula Awards, is another fantasy in which hell is an echo of earthly life, but in this case it is presented as a potentially positive alternative to heaven. In the world of this story, God's existence is discernible, angelic visitations are a regular (if disruptive) occurrence, and "windows" into the afterlife open regularly, allowing the living to glimpse what awaits them in the afterlife. The evident existence of God does not make the divine purpose any more clear than it is in our world, however. Angelic visitations are responsible for miraculous cures, but also for property damage, injury, and death, all distributed arbitrarily. One visitation, for example, has the following results:

Four miracle cures were effected. . . . There were also two miracles that were not cures. . . . Of the eight casualties that day, three souls were accepted into Heaven and five were not, a closer ratio than the average for deaths by all causes. Sixty-two people received medical treatment for injuries ranging from slight concussions to ruptured eardrums to burns requiring skin grafts. Total property damage was estimated at $8.1 million, all of it excluded by private insurance companies due to the cause. Scores of people became devout worshipers in the wake of the visitation, either out of gratitude or terror.[11]

Though its origin is clear, this mixture of miracle and mayhem has no clear purpose: "Nathanael hadn't delivered any specific message; the angel's parting words, which had boomed out across the entire visitation site, were the typical *Behold the power of the Lord*."[12] Witnesses and victims of such frustrating visitations are left to ponder the possible meanings of their own blessings and curses. The protagonist of this story is Neil Fisk, whose wife is killed during an angelic visitation. Fisk spends the remainder of his life attempting to determine what message he should take from this event and what his relationship to God—the God that killed his wife and cured another's cancer in the same moment—should be. After a long, soul-searching quest, Neil glimpses the light of heaven during another visitation. The vision fills him with infinite love for God and understanding of the previously incomprehensible divine plan. He is also mortally wounded, however—and, despite his newfound faith, he is, like most, sent to hell.

Hell, in the world of this story, is just like Earthly existence, only without the certain knowledge of God's existence provided by these visitations. It is a world like ours, without any specific torment other than that specified in the story's title: "Hell, after all, was not physically worse than the mortal plane. It meant permanent exile from God, no more and no less. . . . The lost souls looked no different than the living, their eternal bodies resembling mortal ones. . . . As long as the manifestation lasted you could hear them talk, laugh, or cry, just as they had when they were alive."[13] The story suggests that eternal exile from a God who metes out punishments and rewards arbitrarily might not be such a bad thing. If

God is willing to bless some and curse others without explanation or apology, then perhaps it would be better to be ignorant of his existence. For Neil, however, hell becomes the eternal torment he had always assumed it *wouldn't* be. His vision filled him with knowledge of God, but also with a need to be aware of the divine presence. The knowledge that God is absent now permeates his every moment: "Everything Neil sees, hears, or touches causes him distress, and unlike in the mortal plane this pain is not a form of God's love, but a consequence of His absence. Neil is experiencing more anguish than was possible when he was alive, but his only response is to love God."[14] Chiang's bleak approach to the afterlife and the divine is underscored by the tragedy of Neil's state at the story's end.

Hell can be a bleak ghost world, but Dan Simmons's Hugo-winning 1989 novel *Hyperion* suggests that even eternal life in paradise could be unpleasant. In the novel's first section, Simmons offers an exploration of what eternal life might be like, presenting a chilling and sinister picture of immortality. On the mysterious planet of Hyperion, a Catholic priest named Paul Duré sets out to study the Bikura, who are believed to be descended from seventy survivors of a crashed starship. They have suffered a bizarre cultural retrogression: their language has degenerated into a nearly incomprehensible dialect, and they do not have proper names, referring to themselves collectively as "The Three Score and Ten." This is not as strange as their genetic deterioration: they have greatly diminished height, lack sexual organs entirely, and are hardly even recognizable as human. Their only remaining connection with Earthly culture is an apparent memory of Christianity, most clearly discerned in their strange obsession with crucifixes. The Bikura kill Father Duré's guide, but spare the priest himself for no other reason than that he wears a cross, telling him: "You cannot be killed because you cannot die. . . . You cannot die because you belong to the cruciform and follow the way of the cross."[15] When Duré attempts to discuss religion with them, they have no knowledge of Christianity or even of Jesus, but their entire culture is based on a connection between the cross and immortality. Eventually Duré learns the truth about the Bikura: they are not the descendants of crash survivors from centuries before, but rather are themselves the seventy survivors. Their bodies and minds have been transformed by parasitic, cross-shaped organisms. These "cruciform" grant the Bikura immortality, and can raise them from the dead, even if their bodies are completely destroyed. The parasites do not allow the Bikura to leave the secluded area where they live, located above an enormous underground "cathedral" devoted not to the cross of Christ, but to the alien cruciform. All outsiders (such as Duré's guide) who stumble onto the Bikura settlement are killed and not resurrected by the cruciform: "He died the true death."[16] The cruciform have created, for the Bikura, a sinister version of the Christian heaven: isolated and unchanging, a society without any kind of individuation, from which all outsiders are excluded.

Strictly speaking, the Bikura of *Hyperion* are not in the afterlife. But their mode of existence as described by Simmons is a powerful comment on traditional ideas of heaven. The Bikura experience immortality—they have no need to fear death, because their cruciform parasites can always resurrect them. But this immortality comes at the cost of their individuality, stripping them of their names, their genders, their identities, and their humanity. The devolution of their language underscores the incomprehensibility of their state to normal mortals, and their undying nature eliminates their central connection with human beings outside of their community. Perhaps most disturbingly, their bizarre heaven leads them to believe that all those outside their group are consigned to hell: all those who are not "of the cruciform" must "die the true death." This intolerance isolates the Bikura from humanity even more than their geographic and planetary isolation, and even if they could leave the area of the underground cathedral, they would be unlikely to greet outsiders, who are not "of the cruciform," with anything but death. The Bikura are a disturbing critique of conservative ideas about heaven: rather than a garden paradise, Simmons portrays eternal life as a nightmare, and it is with a sense of justice that he describes, at the end of the novel's opening section, its ultimate destruction.

Simmons suggests that immortality would be anything but paradise. This same idea informs Orson Scott Card's 1979 story

"Mortal Gods." This tale presents a race of alien immortals that hate their immortality, and worship human beings because we die. Immortality, according to these aliens, is overrated, and as one alien explains, they envy the finitude of human beings:

> We have never learned to create beauty to outlast our lives because nothing outlasts our lives. We live to see all our works crumble. Here . . . we have found a race that builds for the sheer joy of building, that creates beauty, that writes books, that invents the lives of never-known people to delight others who know they are being lied to, a race that devises immortal gods to worship and celebrates its own mortality with immense pomp and glory. Death is the foundation of all that is great about humanity.[17]

Our mortality, according to these aliens, is the most beautiful thing in the universe, and they have chosen to base their own religion on it. We create in order to outlast our mortal lives; we struggle against death, seeking to extend our lives as much as possible. This struggle against death is what makes us truly human.

Many SF stories combine this innate desire with the possibility of technology to grant us *literal* immortality. This sort of afterlife is the beginning of a grand adventure in Philip José Farmer's *Riverworld* series, published between 1971 and 1983. In these novels, all of the human beings that ever lived are resurrected in the far future along the banks of a river millions of miles long. This river wraps its way around a planet created for this resurrection by humanity's descendants, who wish to give humankind an opportunity to achieve ethical perfection. Farmer uses this fantastic starting point as the basis for spirited adventure stories starring his favorite historical personages (Mark Twain and Cyrano de Bergerac, for example), but also for complex musings on the nature of the soul, the concept of heaven, and what it means to be a good person. One key aspect of Farmer's Riverworld as an afterlife is the fact that all of the dead, regardless of their faith or the morality of their behavior in their Earthly lives, have been raised there, and that no judging God is apparent—indeed, there does not seem to have been any sort of judgment at all. Resurrection alongside good and wicked alike is a faith-shaking incident for the religious, many of whom feel betrayed by an afterlife different than that promised them by their various faiths. Atheists (including Sir Richard Burton, translator of the *Arabian Nights* and protagonist of the first Riverworld novel) are equally surprised and angered: "He had scoffed all his life at a life-after-death. For once, he could not deny that he had been wrong."[18]

The bulk of the *Riverworld* novels consists of an epic adventure story in which historical figures such as Burton and Twain race to redevelop Earthly technology that will allow them to travel to the mouth of the river and learn the secrets of this strange afterlife. Their task is complicated by the intricate new political conditions of the Riverworld, and it is these harsh realities that constitute Farmer's main critique of the concept of heaven. Morally, the human race has been raised as it was on Earth, and this means that all the ugliness of Earthly life—violence, bigotry, exploitation, and slavery—has been resurrected as well. As Burton explains, "almost every member of resurrected humanity comes from a culture which encouraged war and murder and crime and rape and robbery and madness. It is these people among whom we are living and with whom we have to deal."[19] Much of the Riverworld quickly becomes a hell, and historical figures such as Hermann Göring and King John of England quickly set up autocratic states based on repression and slavery. The Riverworld is not an earthly paradise, but rather a brutal and violent world in which history's worst warlords and tyrants fight for control of what they believe to be eternity.

This nasty, brutish, and long afterlife was not what its creators had in mind. The "Ethicals"—human beings from the far future—give numerous contradictory explanations of the reasons and events that led to the creation of the Riverworld, and it is never clear which of these explanations Farmer intends as the truth. In one version, an Ethical claims that the Riverworld was created simply because the technology to create it existed. Once the technology for raising the dead had been invented, it was viewed as a duty to use it, just as now it is considered a duty to extend life whenever possible: "If you had it in your power to do all this, would you not think it was your *ethical* duty? . . . All must be given a second chance, no matter how bestial or selfish or petty or stupid."[20] More complicated explanations are presented in later volumes of the series, and in *The Magic Labyrinth* (1980), the fourth book in the series, Farmer presents the most complete explanation of the Riverworld project. It includes a complex history of the universe in which the soul was invented by an ancient alien race, who then determined that they had an obligation to impart self-awareness to every intelligent being in the universe. Their technology also allowed souls to be brought back into living bodies, and the purpose of the Riverworld project was to give all living souls a chance to perfect themselves, freeing themselves of violence and aggression. Beings that achieve ethical perfection "move on," ceasing to become detectable by the Ethicals' machines. The Ethicals have no proof that these disappearing souls have in fact gone to a better place, but they assume that "moving on" is some sort of reward, a nirvana in which they continue to exist in eternal happiness. To help resurrected humanity work its way toward this perfection, the Ethicals have planted the seeds of a religion, called the Church of the Second Chance, that comes to transform the River culture. This church teaches that humankind must abandon its violent ways in order to free itself from the Riverworld and fulfill the goal of the afterlife. Farmer's Riverworld uses what is on the surface a pseudo-Christian afterlife, but draws from it a cosmology that has far more in common with Buddhism. Farmer's afterlife is a continuation of both the best and worst of earthly existence, and entering a true paradise requires moral perfection.

Many SF stories describe artificial afterlives in which human minds are transferred into computers or robot bodies. In his *Heechee* novels (1977–87), Frederik Pohl describes such a mechanistic form of immortality in the form of "machine storage." In *Heechee Rendezvous* (1984), the third novel in the sequence, series protagonist Robinette Broadhead dies and is resurrected as an artificial intelligence, stored in the computer banks of the alien Heechee. Describing his state in this new mode of existence as "vastened," Broadhead presents machine storage as a literal heaven: "My belly didn't hurt anymore—I didn't have a belly. My enslavement to mortality was over, for if I had owed a death I had paid it, and was quit for the morrow. If it was not quite eternity that waited for me, it was something pretty close. . . . No more earthly cares; no cares at all, except those I chose to take on for myself. . . . Heaven."[21] Broadhead considers this "vastening" an improvement over his prior, "meat" existence: "I don't like to speak of what happened to me as being 'vastened' when I talk to meat people, because it makes them think I feel superior to them. I don't want them to think that, especially because, of course, I really am superior."[22] As a machine-stored intelligence, Broadhead has access to near-infinite data. He is programmed with artificial senses, so this data can be shaped into any sort of virtual environment he wishes: he can relive his memories or access simulations of new experiences. His thoughts are not limited to the relatively slow speed of human thought, and thus the time remaining to his afterlife is virtually infinite. Though Broadhead's machine storage is described as a heaven, for others it could be a hell if access to this near-infinite data were limited. For example, Beaupre Heimat, a convicted felon serving multiple life sentences, will actually have to serve his complete sentence: "Altogether, Heimat's sentences added up to an aggregate minimum stay in jail of 8,750 years. . . . He had every reason to believe that he would serve every day of those years, too, because even felons were entitled to machine storage. His prison term would not automatically end with his death."[23] For Broadhead, machine storage is heaven, but for Heimat, it is hell—artificial immortality can provide either rewards or punishments for the stored mind.

In Damien Broderick's 2002 novel *Transcension*, a scientist named Mohammed Kasim Abdel-Malek gives a compelling argument in support of machine storage as a means of immortality. Responding to the challenge that the idea of a head full of silicon chips is "horrible," he replies: "Is that more horrible and unthinkable than having an artificial pump whirring in your chest after your heart gives up the ghost? I don't hear too many complaints about transplants from people dying painfully of heart disease."[24] The body, Abdel-Malek argues, is one type of housing for the mind—but it is not the only one, and is not even a privileged type of container: "Are you planning to spend the rest of your life as meat, or in meat? This really is disgusting reductionism. Uploaded people would . . . only turn out to be 'soulless robots' if they were designed by a lunatic without the first clue of what constitutes life and consciousness."[25] Abdel-Malek is a materialist, arguing that the mind is nothing more than electronic impulses and quantum events. But almost ironically, this materialism is the basis for an argument for immortality. Because our minds are transferable electricity, there is no reason for them to die simply because our bodies do.

Not all stories are so enthusiastic about machine storage as a means of immortality. The narrator of John Crowley's 1979 novel *Engine Summer*, a boy named Rush That Speaks, lives in a postapocalyptic, tribal society that has forgotten most human technology. He aspires to be a saint, which in his culture means one whose life becomes a source of guidance for future genera- tions: "The circle of a saint's life, all its circumstances, is con- tained in the story of his life as he tells it; and the story of his life is contained in our remembering it. The story of his life is a cir- cumstance in ours. So the circle of his life is contained in the cir- cle of our lives, like circles of ripples rising in water."[26] He seeks immortality in the minds of his heirs. But when he encounters another, technologically advanced society, he learns of a com- pletely different kind of immortality in the form of machine stor- age. He finds the concept unpleasant, reminiscent of imprisonment: "I think of a fly, stuck in a cube of plastic, able to see all around, but not able to move. It frightens me."[27] Rush is skeptical about the desirability of immortality trapped inside a computer, a far cry from his enthusiasm about immortality in the memories of others.

Polish SF writer Stanislaw Lem's space explorer Ijon Tichy is even more doubtful about the value of mechanical immortality. In *Memoirs of a Space Traveler* (1971, English translation 1982), Tichy encounters Professor Decantor, a scientist who claims to have "invented the soul." By duplicating the contents of his wife's mind onto an artificial crystal, Decantor has given her immortality, but the process required terminating her physical existence. Tichy considers Decantor a murderer, and gives a powerful criticism of the endless life the professor hoped to create:

As if killing her were not enough, he had bestowed upon her the most terrible thing, the most terrible, I repeat, for nothing can compare with the horror of being condemned to solitude for all eternity. The word, of course, is beyond our comprehension. When you return home, try lying down in a dark room, so that no sound or ray of light reaches you, and close your eyes and imagine that you will go on like that, in utter silence, without any, without even the slightest change, for a day and night, and then for another day; imagine that weeks, months, years, even centuries will go by. Imagine, furthermore, that your brain has been subjected to a treatment that makes escape into madness impossible. The thought of a person condemned to such torment, in comparison with which all the images of hell are a trifle, spurred me during our grim bargaining.[28]

For Tichy, eternal life as a machine is the worst sort of torment imaginable. Decantor succeeds in creating an afterlife, but it is not the paradise he hopes for—rather, it is hell.

Thomas M. Disch's short story "In Xanadu" (2001) is a cynically humorous take on the concept of an artificial afterlife. This story depicts a near-future in which consciousness is kept alive after death so that the dead may continue to be active consumers. The story's protagonist, Fran Cook, finds that his afterlife begins with an advertisement: "His awareness was quite limited during the first so-long. A pop-up screen said WELCOME TO XANADU, [Cook, Fran]. YOUR AFTERLIFE BEGINS NOW! BROUGHT TO YOU BY DISNEY-MITSUBISHI PRODUCTIONS OF QUEBEC! A VOTRE SANTE TOUJOURS! Then there was a choice of buttons to click on, **Okay** or **Cancel**."[29] After a brief period in Xanadu—a simulated mixture of paradise and a theme park—Cook receives notice that his account has been terminated, and that the corporation running the artificial afterlife in which he is contained will no longer support his mind. To continue existing, Cook must become an employee of the corporation—a simulated intelligence toiling within a computer bank to provide other deceased minds with an approximation of paradise. Disch presents a commodified afterlife, a humorous nightmare of eternal corporate bureaucracy. It is paradise with fine print: "The services of Xanadu International are to be considered an esthetic product offered for entertainment purposes only."[30]

The Heaven of Ian Stewart and Jack Cohen's *Heaven* (2004) is a world called Aquifer, controlled by the Church of Cosmic Unity to give eternal computer-life to the faith's believers. But, like much else in the novel, this "Heaven" is described with darkly comic irony: it is an abattoir in which machines tear the living bodies of believers apart while their minds continue to exist electronically. The planet is a gruesome sight: "There was blood everywhere. It trickled in rivulets; it ran in torrents. It was intermingled with a hundred other fluids that he could not identify, nor did he wish to. He knew that they, too, were the bodily fluids of what had once been living organisms. Intelligent, conscious, sentient beings. . . . It looked like a charnel house. It looked like a medieval vision of hell. But this was Heaven."[31] This world is an afterlife in name alone, for its "discorporate" inhabitants are technically still living, though they have been completely dismembered and intermingled. Sam, the novel's protagonist, opposes the brutality of Cosmic Unity's idea of paradise: "Heaven, then, was not the resting place of the lifesouls of the dead. The very word pointed to the obvious contradiction. There were no deathsouls. Heaven was where the living were tended by faithful machines, to *keep* them living."[32] What the Church presents as an immortal paradise is merely a tool of political control by which church members are kept in a position from which they cannot oppose the religious powers-that-be. Stewart and Cohen present a nightmare vision of machine storage in which immortality is truly little more than a gruesome and unjust system of control. It would be better, the book argues, to simply let the dead die—regardless of whether or not a *real* afterlife awaits them. Death would be far better than the perpetual carnage of Cosmic Unity's "Heaven."

Not all stories are so pessimistic about technological immortality. Jack Williamson's 2002 story "Afterlife" suggests that such immortality is preferable to any anticipated spiritual afterlife, that it is better to hope for tangible immortality in this world than in another to follow. This short story takes place in the far future on a rundown colony world long separated from Earthly culture. The planet has been stripped of its wealth, and its remaining inhabitants struggle to survive. Religion provides their society with an underpinning of hope that would otherwise be lacking, as the unnamed narrator's father explains: "We live on faith. . . . The afterlife is all we have."[33] A space capsule lands on this planet, and is found to contain the corpse of a human being whose body is soon mysteriously resurrected. The resurrected human, who comes to be known as "the Agent," tells the colonists that he holds the secret to eternal life, and can share it with all those who will follow him without question. One of his followers explains: "The veron is an energy particle. Carrying neither mass nor dimension, it is mind without matter. The so-called human soul is in fact the veronic being. The Agent has taught us how to liberate it into Eternity. Freed from slavery to the mortal flesh, with all its faults and ills, your immortal minds can live forever."[34] Those who follow the stranger seem to die, but believers argue that their "veronic beings" have been released from the prison of the flesh. Later, however, it is revealed that the stranger was in fact a criminal from Earth whose own immortality was the result of cell-regenerating "microbots" in his bloodstream. His concept of "verons" and his claim to offer eternal life was a hoax, and those who followed him had, in fact, died. The narrator abandons the colony world, joining an expedition to another galaxy and receiving microbot treatment himself. Thus immortalized, he embarks on a new life of exploration, rejecting the stagnation of the colony world: "Remembering my parents, who lived so far away and long ago, I wish they could have known the true afterlife we've discovered here."[35]

"Afterlife" somewhat bluntly pits religious and scientific immortality against one another. Playing on the despair of this life and the desire for the next already present in the colonists' religion, the alien huckster tricks them into believing his promises. The skeptical narrator, on the other hand, finds true eternal life by refusing to believe. Accepting technology rather than faith, he embarks on a new life of exploration, whereas his parents had opted to remain where there was nothing left worth staying for. The dichotomy of this story is clear: religious hopes are equated with entropy, and technological immortality with exploration, vitality, and ultimately paradise. In Williamson's eyes, the core of the stagnation that leads to death is the hope for the afterlife—a hope that is here depicted as giving up on this life. In "Afterlife," Williamson argues that we should put our hopes in this world, and seek means to extend our lives here rather than expedite our journey into whatever follows.

The same argument underpins Michael Anderson's 1976 film *Logan's Run*. This movie depicts a dystopian future society whose citizens are killed on their thirtieth birthday in a strange ceremony called "Carousel." The citizens of this culture, which exists in a single domed city, believe that Carousel gives them new life, "renewing" those who are considered worthy. But no one knows what really happens to those who are renewed, and it soon becomes clear that Carousel is simply a public execution. Those who seek to escape this death must flee the city for the apocalyptic world outside, becoming "runners" who are tracked down by the "Sandmen," the city's police. Logan, a Sandman whose thirtieth birthday is fast approaching, begins to question the idea of renewal, and soon becomes a runner himself. When he finally escapes the city with another runner named Jessica, he finds the ruins of twentieth-century society, and in it a single survivor—an old man. Jessica and Logan return to the city with the old man, hoping to overthrow the murderous system under which they have spent their entire lives. They offer a true renewal, not the certain death of Carousel: "You don't have to die! No one has to die at 30! You can live! Live! Live, and grow old!"[36] In a society where death comes too soon, longevity *is* an afterlife. The people of *Logan's Run* live only half a life. Living life to the fullest is a means of bringing paradise in this world.

In his *Ender* series, Orson Scott Card portrays aliens for whom the afterlife is a similarly tangible experience. In this series, the alien pequeninos of the planet Lusitania (known to the human characters as "piggies") have three stages of life: first, as grublike infants, second as mobile beings resembling anthropomorphic pigs, and third—after their mobile bodies have died—as intelligent trees. In *Xenocide* (1991), many of the piggies have been converted to Christianity, and some of them develop a new heresy of pequenino superiority. They claim that the "descolada"—the symbiotic virus that enables the transformation from piggy to tree, but is fatal to humans—is in fact the embodiment of the Holy Spirit. "The descolada is the second baptism. By fire. Only the pequeninos can endure that baptism, and it carries them into the third life. They are clearly closer to God than humans, who have been denied the third life."[37] The heretical aliens argue that human beings are inferior to pequeninos because they have no tangible afterlife. Card makes the alien heretics the villains of this subplot, as they kill a human priest who attempts to convince them of the error of their xenophobic belief. *Xenocide* criticizes the idea that tangible immortality is preferable to the Christian concept of the afterlife. The pequenino's threefold life is neither better nor worse than human life. God has created human and pequenino alike, and thus death, as well as longevity and immortality, have a divine origin. The heretical aliens also present a clever critique of conservative Christian ideas about the afterlife, however. In an argument with a human priest, one of the heretical pequeninos declares: "*We're* the ones who were given the third life, not you! If God loved you, he wouldn't make you bury your dead in the ground and then let nothing but worms come out of you!"[38] Card's main goal here is to criticize the self-righteousness that is all-too-often rooted in religious faith, but the pequenino's "third life" raises another important issue about the afterlife: if there is a life beyond this one, it would by necessity be incomprehensible to the living. Human life is defined by mortality to the extent that the living cannot truly comprehend the experience of immortality, just as we cannot communicate with Lusitania's trees.

Robert Silverberg's Nebula Award–winning 1974 novella "Born with the Dead" further explores the divide between the mortal and the immortal. In this story, a medical procedure allows the dead to be brought back into an immortal post-life, but the experience of the "deads" is so different from that of the living that they have segregated their society completely. They live in insular "cold towns" from which they travel frequently, but only with their deceased companions. Even their language is markedly different from that of the living: they speak in a strange, condensed sort of language, a shorthand that is so terse that at times it seems to border on telepathy. The deads consistently shut the living out from their conversations, their culture, and their afterlives. The story follows Jorge Klein in his attempts to reestablish contact with his dead wife, Sybille. He is maddened by the fact that Sybille is still somehow present in the world and yet inaccessible to him: "He could not bear to think that she had passed into another existence from which he was totally excluded. To find her, to speak with her, to participate in her experience of death and whatever lay beyond death, became his only purpose. He was inextricably bound to her, as though she were still his wife, as though Jorge-and-Sybille still existed in any way."[39] After trailing his wife in her travels around the world, Jorge comes to a certain understanding of the experience of the dead. In imagined conversations, he attempts to grasp his wife's new experience: "Everything is quiet where I am, Jorge. There's a peace that passeth all understanding. I used to feel sometimes that I was caught up in a great storm, that I was being buffeted by every breeze, that my life was being consumed by agitations and frenzies, but now, now, I'm at the eye of the storm, at the place where everything is always calm. I can observe rather than let myself be acted upon."[40] This is an imagined explanation, however—even the understanding it provides is filtered through the living mind. When Jorge himself dies and is raised, he comes to truly comprehend the world of the dead mind, only to understand that he no longer cares: "He will follow Sybille about no longer. He does not need, he does not want, he will not seek. . . . Now that he has crossed the interface, he finds that Sybille no longer matters to him."[41] The cares and desires of the immortal are wildly different from the mortal; the very basis of their existence is incomprehensible to the living. Silverberg's story suggests that it is foolish for human beings to fear *or* hope for the afterlife—the motivations behind human desire will be entirely different when death no longer looms in the future.

Another series by Frederik Pohl, *The Eschaton Sequence* (1996–1999), further emphasizes this critique of human speculation on the afterlife. In this novel, human astronauts establish contact with a confederation of alien races that is involved in a massive war with another alien species. The cause of this war is their belief in a time that they call "the Eschaton": "At a time in the far future, a very long time from now . . . every intelligent being who ever existed in the universe will come to life again, and then will live forever."[42] Both alien groups hope to control the Eschaton, and will stop at nothing to ensure that they are established as its absolute rulers. The human race is caught in the middle of this conflict, each race hoping that Earth will join them in combating the other. The problem is that neither side represents a type of government that humankind would want to be subject to, especially not for all eternity. The "Beloved Leaders"—the leaders of the confederation of species that Earth first encounters—are cruel tyrants who destroy the planets of species who will not join their cause. Their enemies, the Horch, are little better—they grant their allies more freedom, but torture their prisoners mercilessly. Pohl and his human characters are largely ambivalent regarding the truth or falsity of the aliens' belief about the Eschaton: "It doesn't matter if it's true. What matters is that the Horch and the Beloved Leaders act as if it's true."[43] The aliens' belief in the afterlife shapes their actions, causing them to view cruelty and tyranny as acceptable behavior given their goal of shaping eternity. When humankind refuses to join the Beloved Leaders, the aliens threaten to destroy the entire Earth:

> The Beloved Leaders seek no personal gain from you. It is for your own good—indeed, if you force them to put an end to your lives, even that is for your good, since it will speed your way to the Eschaton. The Beloved Leaders know that, in your present primitive state, this is frightening for you, for it is what you call "death." But death is only an incident. It will come sooner or later to each of you. . . . It is not to be feared. It is only the way which we must all pass, in order to reach that great eternity of the Eschaton.[44]

The belief in the afterlife—or rather, the belief that the afterlife is all that matters—can lead to immoral and cruel behavior in this life. In *The Eschaton Sequence*, Pohl argues that it is irrelevant whether or not the afterlife actually exists. What matters is how we live in this life, and the only consequences that we can measure are those that will affect the living.

SF presents numerous imaginings of possible afterlives, but the restrictions of the genre generally prevent traditional depictions of life after death. Where an actual afterlife appears, it always comes with a rational explanation. Frequently the concept of a spiritual afterlife is rejected in favor of some sort of immortality, either in living bodies (as in Silverberg's "Born with the Dead") or in computer banks (as in Pohl's *Heechee* novels). Where an afterlife is presented in a more traditional religious manner—that is, as a resurrection—the need for such an afterlife is generally called into question. In Philip José Farmer's *The Magic Labyrinth*, the fourth novel of the *Riverworld* series, the author's fictionalized version of himself expresses anger that the afterlife should exist without the approval of those who are to be raised: "If the Creator has a plan for us, why doesn't He tell us what it is? Are we so stupid that we can't understand it? He should tell it to us directly! . . . We shouldn't have been left in ignorance. We should have been shown the Plan. Then we could make our choice, go along with the Plan or reject it!"[45] The afterlife, many SF authors argue, should not be necessary—this life should be enough. What truly matters is how we live this life, and we can only speculate about what comes after. But stories like "Pope of the Chimps" and *Hominids* suggest that this speculation is so basic to human experience that it is the basis of our quest for meaning. Whatever follows this life, we must strive to make it a realm governed by justice, not an empty limbo as in *The Amber Spyglass*, or a nightmare of deathlessness, as in *Hyperion*. SF suggests that if we are to have paradise, we must forge it ourselves, vowing to conquer that in our nature that would keep us in hell when we deserve heaven.

Chapter Ten

The Last Days (and After)

*B*ecause SF primarily deals with the future, it must inevitably deal
with the end of the world, and thus SF overlaps more closely with
apocalyptic literature than with any other type of religious writing.
Apocalyptic literature is a genre of scriptural writing that generally accounts the revelation of sacred reality by angels or God.
Most apocalyptic writing focuses on eschatology—ideas about
"the last days," the end of the world as we know it and the dawning of a radically new era. Perhaps the two best-known pieces of
apocalyptic literature are the biblical books of Daniel and the Revelation (in Greek, *apokalypsis*) of John, but the seeds of the apocalyptic imagination that informs those books is present in Isaiah:
"Now the LORD is about to lay waste the earth and make it desolate, and he will twist its surface and scatter its inhabitants" (Isa.
24:1). The genre is also well-represented in Jewish and Christian
extracanonical writings, and the Qur'an—particularly the earlier
Meccan surahs—is also highly apocalyptic in tone. Though the
content of these apocalyptic traditions differs widely, all contain
visions of a world fundamentally different from our day-to-day
experience, a world that has been radically changed.

Apocalyptic literature, most recognizably represented by the
Apocalypse of John, deals with the future. It predicts a coming crisis that is to result in the destruction of the current order, the judgment of the living and the dead, and the subsequent establishment
of a new, divinely governed order. Taken in their various historical

contexts, apocalyptic writings are as much about the present as the future—by predicting an imminent age of righteousness, apocalyptic writers condemn the evils of their own times, often drawing direct connections between the unrighteousness of today and the devastations of tomorrow. Similarly, SF uses the future as a means of commenting on the present, most plainly in stories of the "if this goes on . . . " theme, which extrapolates from a current trend the furthest possible extent of its future ramifications. But even in such commentary on the present, SF is concerned about the future as future, and with preparing its readers for what is to come. Apocalyptic literature, though it can be interpreted as commentary on its authors' contemporary situations, is also undeniably about the future, hoping to guide the faithful through a time of trial to a better tomorrow. Apocalyptic authors foresee calamity, and like authors of SF, they hope to prepare their readers for it. In SF the crisis of the future takes several forms, ranging from the total destruction of the physical universe to the simple introduction of technological breakthroughs that lead to the restructuring of Earthly society. All such shifts can be defined, either literally or figuratively, as "the end of the world."

The end of the physical universe has been a popular motif for many SF authors. Novels such as Poul Anderson's *Tau Zero* (1970) and James Blish's *The Triumph of Time* (1958) focus on the death of the universe. Both stories depict groups of human beings who, through various technological tricks, remain alive to witness the final moments of this cosmos. Countless other stories, fueled by Cold War–era fear of nuclear holocaust, focus more specifically on the destruction of Earth. The threat of nuclear war led to limitless SF explorations of possible aftermaths of such conflicts, and some of SF's best (and best-known) works explore postapocalyptic landscapes. Post–Cold War disaster films such as Roland Emmerich's *The Day after Tomorrow* (2004) and Mimi Leder's *Deep Impact* (1998) place the end of the world beyond human control, depicting forces of nature that risk obliterating life as we know it. The tone of such stories recalls a section of the book of Isaiah that predicts the calamities that will befall Earth in the future: "The earth dries up and withers . . . the exalted of the earth languish. The earth is defiled by its people; they have disobeyed the laws. . . . Therefore a curse consumes the earth; its people must bear their guilt" (Isa. 24:4–6, NIV). But in many cases (and especially in *The Day after Tomorrow*), this destruction is presented simply as a spectacle. This idea is parodied in the 2005 *Doctor Who* episode "The End of the World," in which wealthy aliens from throughout the galaxy gather on a shielded orbiting platform in the far future to witness the destruction of Earth. An even sharper satire of the idea of the end of the world as spectacle is embodied in the eponymous eatery of Douglas Adams's novel *The Restaurant at the End of the Universe* (1980). This restaurant, encased in a time bubble at the cosmos's end, offers its guests a unique perspective on the end of all things, as the host explains: "As the photon storms gather in swirling crowds around us, preparing to tear apart the last of the red hot suns, I know you're all going to settle back and enjoy with me what I know we will all find an immensely exciting and terminal experience."[1] And in Stanley Kubrick's 1964 film *Dr. Strangelove, or How I Learned to Stop Worrying and Love the Bomb*, nuclear holocaust is transformed into a cosmic punch line, a fittingly absurd ending to the human comedy.

These satirical tales are part of a larger trend in SF about the destruction of the world: the secularization of the apocalypse. Where the book of Revelation concludes its list of calamities with a divine victory and the establishment of a new order of everlasting righteousness, the secular genre of SF takes destruction at face value. Films such as James Cameron's *Terminator 2: Judgment Day* (1991) and Michael Bay's *Armageddon* (1998) use the language of Revelation, but they are not describing the catastrophes that must precede the Golden Age. The "end of the world" as depicted in these films is a crisis that the heroes must rush to stop. In secularizing their conceptions of the end of the world, such stories (perhaps unknowingly) invert the morality of apocalyptic literature, proposing that the established order must be upheld in the face of destruction. The messiahs of these stories do not herald the destruction of the old, but its preservation.

Damon Knight's "Shall the Dust Praise Thee?" (1967) puts God back into the secularized apocalypse, describing an end of the world in which humanity's self-destructive tendencies disrupt the divine plan for the end of the world. The story depicts the beginning of the day of judgment in the language of Revelation, as God and his angels initiate the events described in John's prophecy. They soon discover, however, that the judgment cannot go forth as planned: humanity has already destroyed itself in a nuclear war. God's plan for the world's end has been preempted by humankind's own destructive desires. Humankind leaves a final message for its creator: "We were here. Where were you?"[2] This story stands as one of the clearest examples of SF's warnings about the dangers of nuclear war, but it also inverts the secular interpretation of the end of the world that other such stories assume.

A similar prophetic vision forms the basis of Arthur C. Clarke's 1953 story "The Nine Billion Names of God." In this story, a group of Tibetan monks seeks the assistance of Western scientists in fulfilling their religious vocation of writing all the possible names of God. One of the monks explains this task: "All the many names of the Supreme Being—God, Jehovah, Allah, and so on—they are only man-made labels . . . somewhere among all the possible combinations of letters that can occur are what one may call the *real* names of God. By systematic permutation of letters, we have been trying to list them all."[3] Once all of these names have been written, then "God's purpose will be achieved. The human race will have finished what it was created to do, and there won't be any point in carrying on. . . . When the list's completed, God steps in and simply winds things up."[4] The monks—who have calculated that this task would take fifteen thousand years if done by hand—ask a group of Western scientists to build a computer for them that will complete the task in a matter of months. The scientists agree to build this computer, wondering meanwhile how the monks will react when the computer completes its task and their apocalyptic beliefs are proven wrong. When the computer does finish the list of God's names, however, the scientists' arrogance is quashed by the actual end of the universe, described by the story's chilling final line: "Overhead, without any fuss, the stars were going out."[5] This story is a clever critique of the arrogance of Western science in the face of warnings from "irrational" standpoints. Here, the universe ceases to exist because rational science refuses to see its contribution to an apocalypse that is predicted in religious terms. By placing the scientists' story in the context of Buddhism, Clarke prompts his readers to pay heed to warnings about the potential dangers of science and scientific research, no matter how "superstitious" the source of such warnings may seem. Furthermore, Clarke's story argues that no scientist is innocent of the uses to which his or her research is put, and thus it is easy to view this story in the context of SF stories about nuclear war. Though weapons are not mentioned in "The Nine Billion Names of God," the warning is the same: technology can be used for destructive ends, and those who use technology must take warnings of such destruction seriously, no matter what their source.

It is this type of prophecy that informs much of the SF that deals with nuclear war and its aftermath. Just as the use of atomic weapons had been preceded by predictions of such weapons in SF stories, the full extent of the destructiveness of nuclear war was prophesied in much of the SF of the '50s and '60s. Prophecy in SF is not restricted to such warnings, however. Philip José Farmer's 1972 story "Towards the Beloved City" uses the book of Revelation as a template for a study of faith at the end of human civilization. In this story, the events of John's Apocalypse seem to be coming true: increased volcanic activity and a catastrophic meteor shower have killed most of Earth's population and turned the sea blood red. The survivors are divided into two groups—Christians and their opponents, whom they call "the heathen" or "slaves of the Beast." The Christians believe that the events that have led to society's collapse and Earth's devastation are the fulfillment of John's prophecies, and use the book of Revelation as a guidebook for their catastrophic era. The story centers on conversations between one such Christian and a skeptic who offers a different interpretation of Earth's state: "What if we're being fooled again? Not self-deceived, as in the past, but deceived by an outside agency? By Extraterrestrials who are using weapons against Earth, weapons which far surpass ours? . . . Could it be that Extraterrestrials who knew of the longing of the faithful for the millennium have caused this pseudomillenium to occur?"[6] When the characters

meet one of these alien angels, the truth is revealed: Earth is simply the current battleground in an ancient war between two alien
races. One of these races currently controls Earth and has enlisted
the help of the "heathen" to undermine the Christians; the other
hopes to build a "beloved city" to serve as a fortress from which
to drive these attackers off of the planet. The aliens, aware of the
seismic pressures and the asteroid storm that would demolish
Earth's surface, see the planet as being at its most vulnerable, and
thus have chosen this time to stage their attack. John's prophecy
is explained as a statistical prediction: "Those prophets who come
closest to predicting the future as it really develops are those
whose minds have an inborn computer. They don't truly prophesy, in the sense that they can actually look into the future. No,
their minds, unconsciously, of course, compute the highest prob-
abilities, and it is the most likely course of events that they predict. . . . [John] may have seen Extraterrestrials and thought they
were angels."[7] But despite the apparent skepticism of this interpretation of biblical prophecy, the story ends on a note of faith:
following the revelation of this alien plot, the story's Christian
protagonist nevertheless expresses his faith that the thousand-year
reign of Christ on Earth is about to begin. He is martyred by the
servants of the invading aliens, but he dies confident that he will
be raised again.

This story, which focuses on the destruction described in John's
Revelation, nevertheless points to the true hope of apocalyptic
faiths: the belief that the world will be made new at the end of time
for a never-ending period of justice and righteousness. The
destruction of the world that is generally associated with apocalypse is in fact only the first step in a process that leads to universal renewal, as described in the closing of Revelation: "Then I saw
a new heaven and a new earth; for the first heaven and the first earth
had passed away, and the sea was no more. And I saw the holy city,
the new Jerusalem, coming down out of heaven from God, prepared as a bride adorned for her husband" (Rev. 21:1–2). The fundamental belief of apocalyptic spirituality is not simply that the
end is near, but that the universe is about to be set right. For the
remainder of eternity God's power will be universally apparent,

rather than hidden as it is in the current era. In keeping with the fundamental optimism of apocalyptic spirituality, much SF predicts a future age wherein human society is transformed at its core.

Among the best SF stories dealing with the dawning of a new age is Arthur C. Clarke's *Childhood's End* (1953). In this novel, a superintelligent race of aliens that human beings dub "the Overlords" arrive on Earth and declare their takeover of human affairs. Humankind briefly resists the aliens' bloodless conquest, but the near-omnipotence of the Overlords' technology renders any rebellion futile. The Overlords' reign is benevolent, however, and they reshape human society to create a utopia in which hunger and war do not exist. This leads to an idyllic golden age in which "the ordinary necessities of life were virtually free. Men worked for the sake of the luxuries they desired or they did not work at all."[8] But this utopia is not the Overlords' ultimate goal in taking control of Earth: at the novel's end, it is revealed that the extraterrestrials' purpose on Earth is to guide humankind into the next stage in its evolution, a sort of psychic hive-mind with infinite power. The transformed human race then abandons both Earth and its material bodies in order to join a collective being known as the Overmind. The Overlords themselves, it turns out, are a "midwife race" who are incapable of making this evolutionary leap themselves, having progressed to a level of individuation that precludes the possibility of such psychic union.

Clarke describes the transformation itself as an "apotheosis," a process of becoming divine. This word effectively identifies the Overmind as God, and the newly evolved humanity is now a part of an emergent deity that, though transcending time, becomes complete at time's end. This transformation is a leap so profound that it requires the complete destruction of the old world. The Overmind is born from the united minds of the last generation of human children. Once the transformation has begun, no new human children can be born, and there is no overlap or even communication between the group mind and its individuated parents. The old generation of individual human beings is left to die out in the knowledge that they are the last of their kind. When the group mind leaves Earth to join the Overmind, it destroys its home planet entirely, irrevocably closing the door of its past. This Overmind bears a striking resemblance to the "Omega Point" described by paleontologist and Jesuit priest Pierre Teilhard de Chardin. In his 1955 book *The Phenomenon of Man*, Teilhard describes Omega as the culminating point of the "noosphere," the sum total of human minds. Since evolution led to consciousness, he argues, our future evolution will likely lead to a "super-consciousness," a shared world mind in which all individual human beings will join in reflection: "The idea is that of the earth not only becoming covered by myriads of grains of thought, but becoming enclosed in a single thinking envelope so as to form, functionally, no more than a single vast grain of thought on the sidereal scale, the plurality of individual reflections grouping themselves together and reinforcing one another in the act of a single unanimous reflection."[9] Furthermore, like Clarke's Overmind, the collective noosphere may, at the end of the world, leave Earth to seek other minds among the stars. In *Christianity and Evolution* (1969), Teilhard identifies the unified noosphere with the cosmic Christ, that part of the divine essence that permeates all creation. Christ raises the created universe to himself through evolution: "Christ cannot sublimate God without progressively raising it up by his influence through the successive circles of matter and spirit."[10] The Omega Point, the final step of evolution, is also the culmination of God's plan for Earth: the kingdom of God.

Clarke's novel tells the story of the coming of the kingdom, complete with the violence of its arrival. *Childhood's End* offers a unique view of the end of the world in which the old order is replaced twice—first, by the temporary utopia that the Overlords bring, and then by the entirely new mode of collective humanity. This scheme echoes the book of Revelation, in which the New Jerusalem is preceded by the millennium—a thousand-year reign of Christ before the forces of evil are set free on the world a final time. The transformation at the end of Clarke's novel is described as a culmination, a fulfillment of humanity's true cosmic purpose. Though suffering is undoubtedly lessened during the reign of the Overlords, dissatisfaction is still rampant, and much of the novel's plot takes place in a conservative community that was established in order to give its inhabitants challenge and purpose in a paradise where leisure has turned into apathy. It is only at the novel's end that any of its characters find a true sense of satisfaction, when the final survivor of the human race witnesses the new species' departure from Earth: "It's hard to describe, but just then I felt a great wave of emotion sweep over me. It wasn't joy or sorrow; it was a sense of fulfillment, achievement."[11] The apocalypse of *Childhood's End* is the culmination of humankind, the revelation of the ultimate purpose of the universe.

Clarke is careful to separate the new order of collective humanity from any specific religious view of the end, even going so far as to explain that the Overlords' reign led to the near-complete dissolution of human religious institutions. The golden age preceding humanity's apotheosis "was a completely secular age. . . . The creeds that had been based upon miracles and revelations had collapsed utterly."[12] Nevertheless, religious images are prominent in the novel, which ultimately comes across as steeped in Christian thought and myth. The book's title evokes the apostle Paul's beliefs about the coming kingdom and the new mode of existence brought about by Christ's resurrection: "When I was a child, I spoke like a child, I thought like a child, I reasoned like a child; when I became an adult, I put an end to childish ways. For now we see in a mirror, dimly, but then we will see face to face" (1 Cor. 13:11–12). Paul's message is distinctly apocalyptic, speaking of the changes that the followers of Christ must make in their own lives in order to prepare for the imminent return of the Son of God. In this context, the Overmind of *Childhood's End* becomes the New Jerusalem of Revelation, and the apotheosis the coming of the kingdom of God. Even some of the novel's central ironies have a religious flair: the Overlords refuse to reveal their physical appearance to the world until many years after their reforms have taken hold. When they unveil themselves, we learn that humankind's alien protectors look remarkably similar to the medieval Christian image of the devil, with wings, horns, and barbed tails. This irony is revealing: by casting his aliens in the appearance of devils, Clarke merely serves to underscore their actual role as angelic attendants to the transformation of mankind into God.

There is an unfortunate price to this transformation: it requires the total destruction of human society. Even if the new humanity had not destroyed Earth, its existence marked the invalidation of the basis of the dominant society, as one Overlord explains:

> You had put superstition behind you: Science was the only real religion of mankind. . . . Science, it was felt, could explain everything: there were no forces which did not come within its scope, no events for which it could not ultimately account. . . . Yet your mystics, though they were lost in their own delusions, had seen part of the truth. There are powers of the mind, powers beyond the mind, which your science could never have brought within its framework without shattering it entirely.[13]

The psychic phenomena that culminate in the union of humanity's children into a single psychic organism could not be explained by science. The destruction of the old order is the final step in the establishment of a better existence for the descendants of the human race, a future beyond the problems and limitations of the past. Though the collective mind of humanity's children is in a sense more alien than the Overlords, with whom human beings can at least communicate, it is nevertheless a fulfillment of human existence.

Ian McDonald's 2000 novella "Tendeléo's Story" is a powerful portrait of a world that is slowly being transformed into paradise. In this story, the southern hemisphere of Earth is periodically bombarded by alien seeds called the Chaga. Anywhere these seeds land is transformed into a bizarre alien landscape which spreads out unstoppably. In time, the alien environment will engulf the entire southern hemisphere. The Chaga is a destabilizing force, leading to societal collapse wherever it lands and prompting violent reactions from the governments of the northern hemisphere, who hope to keep the alien invasion contained in the world's poorer corners. Tendeléo, the story's narrator, is a young girl from Gichichi, a small village in Kenya that is overrun by the Chaga. Her father is a Christian minister whose congregation wants to understand the religious significance of the alien incursion: "The Christians of Gichichi crowded around my father. What should they believe? Was Jesus come again, or was it anti-Christ? These aliens, were they angels, or fallen creatures like ourselves? Did they know Jesus? What was God's plan in this? Question after question after question."[14] Rumors abound regarding the nature of the land that the Chaga has transformed. After hearing some of these rumors, the pastor of the church tells Tendeléo's father that he believes the Chaga may be the transformed society that Christians have been awaiting for two thousand years:

> "It is a work of God, I think. We have a chance to build a true Christian society. . . . It is different from what we are told is in there. Very very different. Plants that are like machines, that generate electricity, clean water, fabric, shelter, medicines. Knowledge. There are devices, the size of this thumb, that transmit information directly into the brain. And more; there are people living in there, not like primitives, not, forgive me, like refugees. It shapes itself to them, they have learned to make it work for them. There are whole towns—towns, I tell you—down there under Kilimanjaro. A great society is rising."
>
> "It shapes itself to them," my father said. "And it shapes them to itself."
>
> There was a pause.
>
> "Yes. That is true. Different ways of being human."[15]

The Chaga is not a malevolent invader, but rather a benign force transforming Africa into a paradise. At the story's end, Tendeléo enters the Chaga, and her first experiences there are placed in a spiritual context: she finds a growth that resembles a cathedral, and says, "Medieval peasants must have felt like this, awestruck in their own cathedrals."[16] McDonald's story places the kingdom of God in the setting of modern international politics and extraterrestrial mystery. The Chaga chooses to land in Africa—a region that, in the last two hundred years, has had its destiny controlled by outside forces, unfairly consigned to poverty and powerlessness by racism and classism. The Chaga gives the powerless a chance to shape their own destiny, to construct a new order and a potentially perfect society. The old order fears this transformation: "We can build a society here that needs nothing from them. We challenge everything they believe."[17] This New Jerusalem is a challenge to the Babylon of the world's wealthy nations, an egalitarian society so far removed from the concerns of capitalism and power that it is literally alien. McDonald's story is the most powerful presentation of a transformed world, an apocalypse that rights the wrongs of colonialism and allows the meek to finally inherit Earth.

A similar apocalyptic sensibility permeates Andy and Larry Wachowski's *Matrix* trilogy (1999–2003). Here the oppressive established order is a race of malevolent machines that has enslaved the human race. The machines keep human bodies imprisoned, harvesting the energy produced by their bodies while pacifying their minds with a virtual reality world called "the Matrix." The three films follow a group of revolutionaries who have awakened from this virtual reality prison into the real, machine-ruled world and are fighting to awaken the rest of humanity and to reclaim the world that they have lost. The human resistance movement is based in an underground city called Zion, which is depicted as a sort of besieged New Jerusalem. The protagonist's name, Neo, underscores the apocalyptic themes of the films: rather than return human society to its pre-Matrix status, the revolutionaries hope to create an entirely new sort of society. The *Matrix* series clearly displays the rebellion against secular power evident in all apocalyptic literature. The heroes of the films follow God's injunction to John in the description of the whore of Babylon in Revelation, the ultimate apocalyptic symbol of impure secular authority: "Come out of her, my people, so that you do not take part in her sins, and so that you do not share in her plagues; for her sins are heaped high as heaven, and God has remembered her iniquities" (Rev. 18:4–5). The heroes of the Matrix "come out" of their illusory oppression in a very literal sense, removing both their minds from the shared dream world created by the machines and their bodies from the embryonic prisons in which they have been held. Having thus left the control of the secular computer powers, those who have awoken enter a society with an apocalyptic goal: the complete destruction of the reigning authority and the establishment of a new order of human rule. Speaking to the machines, Neo expresses the liberty he hopes to bring to humanity: "I'm going to show these people what you don't want them to see. I'm going to show them a world without you. A world without rules and controls, without borders or boundaries—a world where any-thing is possible."[18] The revolutionaries, rather than living in an enslaved past or an embattled present, have dedicated themselves to the world that is to come—a world of absolute freedom.

Not all SF takes so positive a view of what is to follow the pres-ent age. In *The Time Machine*, H. G. Wells depicts a future that does not explode with regenerative change, but rather withers in entropy. Wells's nameless time traveler journeys farther and farther into the future, finding intelligence and even life itself dwindling more and more with every age he visits. First he stops in an age in which human achievement has dwindled into a society of parasites and their victims, both of whom have lost the power of language. The peaceful, apathetic Eloi, who have degenerated to the size of children, dwell among the ruins of a civilization that preceded them, with no apparent knowledge of their past. Their energies have faded away, and they are content to allow their culture to dwindle: "To adorn themselves with flowers, to dance, to sing in the sunlight; so much was left of the artistic spirit, and no more. Even that would fade in the end into a contented inactivity."[19] The Eloi are preyed upon by the sinister Morlocks, a subterranean race of monsters that harvest their smaller cousins for food. After escaping the Morlocks, the time traveler leaves this fading world behind, continuing on into the twilight of life on Earth. He finds himself in a dying world that he can hardly recognize as his own planet: "The world was silent. . . . All the sound of man, the bleat-ing of sheep, the cries of birds, the hum of insects, the stir that makes the background of our lives—all that was over."[20] This world has not yet died, but what little life remains is feeble and helpless, symbolized by the final living creature the traveler sees before returning to his own era: "It was a round thing, the size of a football perhaps, or, it may be, bigger, and tentacles trailed down from it; it seemed black against the weltering blood-red water, and it was hopping fitfully about."[21] This final image of a creature struggling for life in a dying world shows the power of entropy, rather than catastrophe, as the ultimate destructive force. The red color of the water on the twilight world evokes the apocalyptic transformations of Revelation, but in *The Time Machine* the world has dwindled away gradually, rather than being transformed by a rapid series of disasters. Wells does not make his time traveler a witness to the actual demise of the physical world. Rather, this final stage of the novel describes a slow fading of life on Earth, lasting countless years but ultimately trailing away into oblivion. The chilling final passage of the time traveler's journey symbolizes this ultimate nothingness with a solar eclipse that begins moments after his arrival in this final era: "At last, one by one, swiftly, one after the other, the white peaks of the distant hills vanished into blackness. The breeze rose to a moaning wind. . . . In another moment the pale stars alone were visible. All else was rayless obscurity. The sky was absolutely black."[22] This eclipse suggests the immediate transformation that Paul describes in 1 Corinthians: "we will all be changed—in a flash, in the twinkling of an eye, at the last trumpet" (15:51–52, NIV). But Wells ultimately rejects this understanding of the apocalypse: the eclipse is simply a single event in the millennia-long fading of Earth, and the time traveler knows that the planet will continue to slowly descend into entropy for ages after the brief period of his visit. *The Time Machine* offers two visions of the end: first, a dystopian picture of a diminishing human society; and second, a bleak view of a gradual, universal collapse into entropy.

SF offers its readers visions of a future drastically different from the present, and some critics and scholars have argued that this impulse for the creation of fictional futures is itself inherently apocalyptic. In his 1974 study *New Worlds for Old: The Apocalyptic Imagination, Science Fiction, and American Literature*, David Ketterer offers the most compelling statement of this theory. He argues that SF follows an apocalyptic tradition in American and British literature wherein "the destruction of an old world, generally of mind, is set against the writer's establishment of a new world, again generally of mind."[23] Ketterer sees human history as built on such "apocalypses of mind," sudden or gradual events that drastically change the human experience or understanding of the world—events such as the discovery of the New World, the emergence of America as a nation, or the success of the Apollo space program. Such events, though they may not affect day-to-day life in the way that a biblical apocalypse would, nevertheless lead to radical reinterpretations of our philosophical worldviews.

Ketterer sees these secular, philosophical apocalypses as the key defining factor of SF as a genre, with each author's creation of a fictional future revising or replacing the Apocalypse (and the New Jerusalem) of John. SF that deals with nuclear war is merely the clearest example of this sort of apocalypticism, since "the atomic bomb completed the process of secularization that apocalyptic thinking has undergone since medieval times."[24] By Ketterer's definition, even SF that does not seem to deal directly with the end of the world is apocalyptic, because the very act of imagining a future world radically different from our era presupposes the figurative destruction of the present. This need not be a violent destruction, as in SF stories of postnuclear societies or Revelation, but can rather rely on the visionary sense of the word "revelation." The Apocalypse of John not only tells what is to happen in the future, it also *reveals* the true nature of the present universe. SF hopes to do the same: "The new and true conception of reality— revealed reality, if you like—has been, it must be assumed, concealed and obscured by man's previously faulty worldview."[25] SF as a genre is apocalyptic because it hopes to reveal the seeds of a better world hidden beneath the surface of our own.

This apocalyptic sensibility that Ketterer sees as the defining trait of SF is also key to understanding not only how religious themes are explored in SF, but how *all* SF is religious. The contemplation of the world as it should be (or how it *must not* be) is at the core of all SF, and this utopian impulse parallels the goals of human religion. By shaping how we think of the future, SF hopes to unlock the kingdom of God, of which Jesus says in Luke 17:21: "The kingdom of God is within you" (NIV).

The future is already here, waiting to be unveiled. By speculating as to the nature of the future, criticizing past and present ideas of faith, and proposing new ways of thinking about God, SF helps to create the future of faith. This shaping of what is to come not only anticipates the world of tomorrow, but teaches us how to *be* in the coming kingdom. By its very nature, SF explores, anticipates, and defines new worlds of the spirit.

Notes

Introduction

1. Darko Suvin, *Metamorphoses of Science Fiction: On the Poetics and History of a Literary Genre* (New Haven, CT, and London: Yale University Press, 1979), 26 (ch. 2).
2. Albert J. Bergesen and Andrew M. Greeley, *God in the Movies* (New Brunswick, NJ, and London: Transaction Publishers, 2000), 127–28 (ch. 13).
3. Sameul R. Delany, "About Five Thousand One Hundred and Seventy Five Words," *Extrapolation* 10 (1969): 64.
4. Thomas M. Disch, "Science Fiction as a Church," *Foundation* 25 (June 1982): 53.
5. Ian R. MacLeod, "New Light on the Drake Equation," in *The Year's Best Science Fiction: Nineteenth Annual Collection,* ed. Gardner Dozois (New York: St. Martin's Griffin, 2002), 18–19.
6. Olaf Stapledon, *Last and First Men and Last Men in London* (Middlesex, England, and Baltimore, MD: Penguin Books, 1972), 11 (preface).

Some Words on Definitions and Methods

1. Quoted in John Clute and Peter Nicholls, eds., *The Encyclopedia of Science Fiction* (New York: St. Martin's Griffin, 1995), 314.

Chapter One

1. *Star Wars: Episode IV—A New Hope*, directed and screenplay by George Lucas (Lucasfilm Ltd., 1977; DVD: *The Star Wars Trilogy*, 20th Century Fox Home Entertainment, 2004).
2. Anselm, *Prayers and Meditations of Saint Anselm with the Proslogion,* trans. Sister Benedicta Ward, S.L.G. (London and New York: Penguin Books, 1973), 244.
3. Ahmed Ali, trans., *Al-Qur'ān: A Contemporary Translation* (Princeton, NJ: Princeton University Press, 1988), 44.
4. Roger Zelazny, *Lord of Light* (New York: Avon Books, 1967), 67 (ch. 2).
5. Ibid., 184–85 (ch. 4).

6. Ibid., 152 (ch. 4).

7. *Stargate*, directed by Roland Emmerich, written by Emmerich and Dean Devlin (Carolco Pictures Inc./Centropolis Film Productions/Le Studio Canal+, 1994; DVD: Artisan Entertainment, 1999).

8. *Stargate SG-1*, Episode 179, "The Powers That Be," directed by William Waring, written by Martin Gero (original broadcast Aug. 12, 2005).

9. Ted Chiang, "The Evolution of Human Science," in *Stories of Your Life and Others* (New York: Tor/Tom Doherty Associates, 2002), 242.

10. Ibid., 244–45.

11. Fredric Brown, "Answer," In *Those Amazing Electronic Thinking Machines!* ed. Isaac Asimov, Martin H. Greenberg, and Charles G. Waugh (New York: Franklin Watts, 1983), 150.

12. Harlan Ellison, "I Have No Mouth, and I Must Scream," in *Alone against Tomorrow: Stories of Alienation in Speculative Fiction* (New York: Macmillan Co., 1971), 7.

13. Ibid., 13.

14. John Brunner, "Judas," in *Dangerous Visions*, ed. Harlan Ellison (New York: Signet Books, 1967), 453.

15. Ibid., 454.

16. Ibid., 455.

17. Jan Lars Jensen, *Shiva 3000* (New York: Harcourt Brace & Co., 1999), 278.

18. *Star Trek V: The Final Frontier*, directed by William Shatner, screenplay by David Loughery (Paramount Pictures, 1989; DVD: Paramount, 2003).

19. Ibid.

20. *The Journey: A Behind-the-Scenes Documentary* (on DVD: *Star Trek V: The Final Frontier*, Paramount, 2003).

21. *Star Trek V.*

22. *Star Trek*, Episode 31, "Who Mourns for Adonais?" directed by Marc Daniels, written by Gilbert A. Ralston (original broadcast Sept. 22, 1967, NBC Television; DVD: *Star Trek: The Original Series, Volume 17*, Paramount, 2000).

23. Ibid.

24. George Zebrowski, *Heathen God*, in *Creations: The Quest for Origins in Story and Science,* ed. Isaac Asimov, Martin H. Greenberg, and George Zebrowski (New York: Crown, 1983), 131.

25. Warren Ellis, Bryan Hitch, et al., "Outer Dark," in *The Authority: Under New Management* (New York: Wildstorm Productions/DC Comics, 2000), 41–42.

26. H. P. Lovecraft, *At the Mountains of Madness and Other Tales of Terror* (New York: Ballantine Books, 1971), 25–26 (ch. 2).

27. Ibid., 67 (ch. 7).

28. *Gamera 3: Revenge of Iris*, directed by Shusuke Kaneko, screenplay by Kazunori Itô (Daiei Studios, 1999; DVD: ADV Films, 2004).

29. Brian W. Aldiss, "Heresies of the Huge God," in *Man in His Time: The Best Science Fiction Stories of Brian W. Aldiss* (New York: Atheneum Books, 1989), 180. Paragraph breaks removed.

30. *Babylon 5*, Episode 6, "Mind War," directed by Bruth Seth Green, written by J. Michael Straczynski (original broadcast on March 2, 1994 [syndicated]; DVD: *Babylon 5: The Complete First Season*, Warner Home Video, 2002).

31. Poul Anderson, *Genesis* (New York: Tor/Tom Doherty Associates, 2000), 103 (part 2, ch. 1).

32. Ian Stewart and Jack Cohen, *Heaven* (New York: Warner Books, 2004), 198–99 (ch. 9). Paragraph breaks removed.

33. Ibid., 246–47 (ch. 11).

34. *Star Wars: Episode IV—A New Hope.*

35. *Star Wars: Episode V—The Empire Strikes Back*, directed by Irvin Kershner, produced by George Lucas, screenplay by Leigh Brackett and Lawrence Kasdan (Lucasfilm Ltd., 1980; DVD: *The Star Wars Trilogy*, 20th Century Fox Home Entertainment, 2004).

36. Olaf Stapledon, *The Star Maker* (Middlesex, England, and Baltimore, MD: Penguin Books, 1972), 234–35 (ch. 14). Since Stapledon uses the masculine pronoun to describe the Star Maker, I have also used it here, though it is unlikely that so vast a being would be constrained by gender.

37. Ibid., 74–75 (ch. 5).

38. Ibid., 249 (ch. 15).

39. Ibid., 256 (ch. 15).

40. Ibid., 99 (ch. 6).

41. Olaf Stapledon, *The Nebula Maker and Four Encounters* (New York: Dodd, Mead & Co., 1983), 11 (ch. 1).

Chapter Two

1. *A.I.: Artificial Intelligence,* directed and screenplay by Steven Spielberg (Warner Bros./Dreamworks SKG, 2001; DVD: Dreamworks, 2002).

2. Gregory Benford, "Anomalies," in *Redshift: Extreme Visions of Speculative Fiction,* ed. Al Sarrantonio (New York: Roc Books, 2001), 244–45.

3. John Varley, "In Fading Suns and Dying Moons," in *Year's Best SF 9,* ed. David G. Hartwell and Kathryn Cramer (New York: Eos/HarperCollins, 2004), 178.

4. Arthur C. Clarke's novel, written concurrently with the film's screenplay, uses Saturn, but a number of factors led Kubrick to replace that planet with Jupiter in the film.

5. Pseudo-Dionysius, *The Mystical Theology*, in *The Complete Works*, trans. Colm Luibheid (New York and Mahwah, NJ: Paulist Press, 1987), 136 (ch. 1).

6. Mary Wollstonecraft Shelley, *Frankenstein* (New York: Dover Publications, 1994), 31 (ch. 4).

7. Isaac Asimov, "Introduction: The Lord's Apprentice," in *The Ultimate Frankenstein,* ed. Byron Preiss (New York: Dell, 1991), 2.

8. Michael Bishop, "The Creature on the Couch," in Preiss, *Ultimate Frankenstein*, 51.

9. Michael Crichton, *Jurassic Park* (New York: Ballantine Books, 1990), ix–x (introduction).

10. Ibid., xi.

11. Ibid., 284 (ch. 5).

12. Michael Crichton, *Prey* (New York: Avon Books/HarperCollins, 2002), 243–44.

13. Ibid., 500.

14. H. G. Wells, *The Island of Doctor Moreau*, in *The Complete Science Fiction Treasury of H. G. Wells* (New York: Avanel Books, 1978), 118 (ch. 14).

15. Ibid., 118 (ch. 14).

16. Theodore Sturgeon, "The Microcosmic God," in *The Microcosmic God: The Complete Stories of Theodore Sturgeon,* vol. 2, ed. Paul Williams (Berkeley, CA: North Atlantic Books, 1992), 134.

17. Ibid., 156.

18. *Beneath the Planet of the Apes,* directed by Ted Post, screenplay by Paul Dehn (20th Century Fox/APJAC Entertainment, 1970; DVD: 20th Century Fox Home Entertainment, 2000).

19. Robert Silverberg, "Basileus," in *The Collected Stories of Robert Silverberg,* vol. 1, *Secret Sharers* (New York: Bantam Books, 1992), 69–70.

20. Philip K. Dick and Roger Zelazny, *Deus Irae* (New York: Dell Publishing, 1976), 29 (ch. 2).

21. Quoted in Richard Rhodes, *The Making of the Atomic Bomb* (New York: Simon & Schuster, 1986), 676.

22. Shelley, *Frankenstein*, viii (author's introduction).

23. Augustine, *De Trinitate* 10.5.7, quoted in Robert Meagher, *Augustine: On the Inner Life of the Mind* (Indianapolis/Cambridge: Hackett Publishing, 1998), 155.

24. Crichton, *Jurassic Park*, 284–85 (ch. 5).

25. Richard Chwedyk, "The Measure of All Things," in *Year's Best SF 7,* ed. David G. Hartwell and Kathryn Cramer (New York: Eos/HarperCollins, 2002), 80.

26. Ibid., 80.

27. Ibid., 87.

28. James M. Robinson, ed., *The Nag Hammadi Library in English,* 3rd ed. (San Francisco: HarperSanFrancisco, 1988), 279 (V:64, lines 12–20).

29. *The Matrix*, directed and screenplay by Larry and Andy Wachowski (Groucho II Film Partnership/Silver Pictures/Village Roadshow Pictures, 1999; DVD: Warner Home Video, 1999).

30. *Dark City*, directed by Alex Proyas, screenplay by Proyas, Lem Dobbs, and David S. Goyer (Mystery Clock Cinema/New Line Cinema, 1998; DVD: New Line Home Video, 1998).

31. *Star Trek II: The Wrath of Khan*, directed by Nicholas Meyer, screenplay by Jack B. Sowards (Paramount Pictures, 1982; DVD: Paramount, 2003).

32. Jack Williamson, *Terraforming Earth* (New York: Tor/Tom Doherty Associates, 2001), 149–50 (ch. 18).

33. Ibid., 150 (ch. 18).

Chapter Three

1. Augustine, *The Trinity*, trans. Edmund Hill, O.P., ed. John E. Rotell, O.S.A. (Brooklyn, NY: New City Press, 1991), 294 (X:10).

2. Thomas Aquinas, *Summa Theologica*, First Part, Question 75, Article 1, trans. the Fathers of the English Dominican Province. *Christian Classics Ethereal Library,* ed. Harry Plantinga (Calvin College, http://www.ccel.org/a/aquinas/summa/home.html).

3. René Descartes, *Meditations on First Philosophy*, Meditation 6, Paragraph 9, in *Great Voyages: The History of Western Philosophy from 1492 to 1776,* ed. Bill Uzgalis (University of Oregon, http://oregonstate.edu/instruct/phl302/texts/descartes/meditations/meditations.html).

4. Daniel Dennett, *Consciousness Explained* (Boston: Little, Brown and Company, 1991), 418. Emphasis original.

5. Robert J. Sawyer, *Mindscan* (New York: Tor/Tom Doherty Associates, 2005), 88 (ch. 12).

6. Ibid., 194 (ch. 27).

7. Ibid., 203 (ch. 28).

8. Norman Spinrad, *Deus X* (New York: Bantam Books, 1993), 117 (ch. 15). Emphasis removed.

9. *Star Trek: The Next Generation*, Episode 35, "The Measure of a Man," directed by Robert Scheerer, written by Melinda M. Snodgrass (original broadcast on February 13, 1989 [syndicated]; DVD: *Star Trek: The Next Generation—The Complete Second Season*, Paramount Home Entertainment, 2002).

10. Ibid.

11. Michael Blumlein, "Know How, Can Do," in Dozois, *Year's Best Science Fiction: Nineteenth Annual Collection,* 506.

12. Orson Scott Card, *Children of the Mind* (New York: Tor/Tom Doherty Associates, 1996), 21 (ch. 1).

13. *I, Robot,* directed by Alex Proyas, screenplay by Jeff Vintar and Akiva Goldsman (20th Century Fox/Canlaws Productions, 2004; DVD: 20th Century Fox Home Entertainment, 2004).

14. Robert J. Sawyer, *The Terminal Experiment* (New York: HarperPrism, 1995), 78 (ch. 10).

15. Ibid., 332–33 (epilogue). Paragraph break removed.

16. Robert J. Sawyer, *Hybrids* (New York: Tor/Tom Doherty Associates, 2003), 193 (ch. 22).

17. Philip José Farmer, *The Magic Labyrinth* (New York: Berkley Books, 1980), 354 (ch. 49).

18. Ibid., 355 (ch. 49).

19. Ibid., 126 (ch. 20).

20. Rudy Rucker, *Software* (New York: Avon/Eos), 1987, 112 (ch. 19).

21. Ibid., 160 (ch. 26).

22. Ibid.

23. John Brunner, "The Vitanuls," in *Other Worlds, Other Gods,* ed. Mayo Mohs (New York: Avon Books, 1971), 160.

24. Stanislaw Lem, *The Invincible*, trans. Wendayne Ackerman (Middlesex, England, and Baltimore, MD: Penguin Books, 1976), 75 (ch. 4).

25. Orson Scott Card, *Ender's Shadow* (New York: Tor/Tom Doherty Associates, 1999), 119 (ch. 6).

26. Philip K. Dick, "Man, Android, and Machine," in *The Shifting Realities of Philip K. Dick: Selected Literary and Philosophical Writings,* ed. Lawrence Sutin (New York: Vintage Books, 1995), 211–12.

27. *Doctor Who*, Serial No. 78, "Genesis of the Daleks," directed by David Maloney, written by Terry Nation (six episodes, original broadcast March 8–April 12, 1975, BBC-1).

28. *Invasion of the Body Snatchers,* directed by Don Siegel, screenplay by Daniel Mainwaring (Walter Wanger Productions Inc., 1956; DVD: Republic, 1998).

29. *Short Circuit,* directed by John Badham, screenplay by Brent Maddock and S.S. Wilson (PSO, 1986; DVD: Image Entertainment, 2000).

30. Immanuel Kant, *Fundamental Principles of the Metaphysics of Morals*, trans. Thomas K. Abott, in *Basic Writings of Kant,* ed. Allen W. Wood (New York: Modern Library, 2001), 169.

31. Nancy Kress, "Computer Virus," in Dozois, *Year's Best Science Fiction: Nineteenth Annual Collection* (New York: St. Martin's Griffin, 2002), 130.

32. Ibid., 137.

33. *A.I.: Artificial Intelligence.*

34. Ibid.

35. *Star Trek: The Next Generation*, Episode 85, "Data's Day," directed by Robert Wiemer, written by Harold Apter and Ronald D. Moore (original broadcast Jan. 7, 1991 [syndicated]; DVD: *Star Trek: The Next Generation—The Complete Fourth Season*, Paramount, 2002).

36. William Gibson, *Neuromancer* (New York: Ace Books, 1984), 120 (ch. 9).

37. Ibid., 269 (ch. 24).

38. Astro Teller, *Exegesis* (New York: Vintage Contemporaries, 1997), Feb. 6 (the novel is unpaginated, but the e-mails are dated and in chronological order).

39. Ibid., Apr. 26. Paragraph break removed.

40. A. M. Turing, "Computing Machinery and Intelligence," *Mind* 49 (1950): 433–60; online: *Cogprints: Cognitive Science Eprint Archive,* University of Southampton, England, http://cogprints.org/499/00/turing.html.

41. Card, *Children of the Mind*, 18 (ch. 1).

42. Orson Scott Card, *Speaker for the Dead* (New York: Tor/Tom Doherty Associates, 1991), 176 (ch. 11).

43. Jack McDevitt, "Gus," in *Sacred Visions,* ed. Andrew M. Greeley and Michael Cassutt (New York: Tor/Tom Doherty Associates, 1991), 14.

44. Ibid., 19.

45. Ibid., 23–24.

46. Peter Brown, *Augustine of Hippo: A Biography* (Berkeley and Los Angeles: University of California Press, 2000), 162.

47. Philip K. Dick, "The Android and the Human," in Sutin, *Shifting Realities,* 189.

Chapter Four

1. *Star Trek: Deep Space Nine,* Episode 169, "Strange Bedfellows," directed by Rene Auberjonois, written by Ronald D. Moore (original broadcast April 21, 1999 [syndicated]; DVD: *Star Trek: Deep Space Nine—Season 7,* Paramount, 2003).

2. Boethius, *The Consolation of Philosophy,* trans. W. V. Cooper (New York: Carlton House, 1943), 116 (Book 5).

3. George Orwell, *1984* (New York: New American Library, 1961), 138 (pt. 2, ch. 7).

4. Ibid., 210 (pt. 3, ch. 2).

5. Ibid., 116 (pt. 2, ch. 4).

6. Anthony Burgess, *A Clockwork Orange* (New York: Ballantine Books, 1988), 144–45 (pt. 2, ch. 7).

7. Ibid., 95–96 (pt. 2, ch. 1).

8. Ibid., ix (introduction).

9. Ibid., 46–47 (pt. 1, ch. 4).

10. Unsigned review of *A Clockwork Orange,* directed by Stanley Kubrick, *Monthly Film Bulletin* 39, no. 457 (February 1972): 28–29; online source: *The British Film Institute,* http://www.bfi.org.uk/features/ultimatefilm/chart/details .php?ranking=54.

11. Timothy Zahn, *Angelmass* (New York: Tor/Tom Doherty Associates, 2001), 83 (ch. 9).

12. Ibid., 81 (ch. 9).

13. Ibid., 311 (ch. 33).

14. Ibid., 423 (ch. 45).

15. Steven Popkes, "The Ice," in *The Year's Best Science Fiction: Twenty-First Annual Collection,* ed. Gardner Dozois (New York: St. Martin's Griffin, 2004), 82.

16. Ibid., 107.

17. *Gattaca,* directed and screenplay by Andrew Niccol (Columbia Pictures, 1997; DVD: Columbia/Tristar, 1999).

18. Ibid.

19. Robert J. Sawyer, *Flashforward* (New York: Tor/Tom Doherty Associates, 1999), 133 (ch. 12).

20. Ibid., 176 (ch. 18).

21. Ibid., 136 (ch. 13).

22. *Minority Report,* directed by Steven Spielberg, screenplay by Scott Frank and Jon Cohen (Dreamworks SKG/20th Century Fox, 2002, DVD: Dreamworks, 2002).

23. Ibid.

24. *Star Trek: Deep Space Nine,* Episode 1, "Emissary," directed by David Carson, written by Michael Piller (original broadcast, Jan. 3, 1993 [syndicated]; DVD: *Star Trek: Deep Space Nine—Season 1*, Paramount, 2003).

25. Alfred North Whitehead, *Process and Reality: An Essay in Cosmology* (New York: Free Press, 1978), 350.

26. David Ray Griffin, *Reenchantment without Supernaturalism: A Process Philosophy of Religion* (Ithaca, NY, and London: Cornell University Press, 2001), 161.

27. *Primer,* directed and screenplay by Shane Carruth (ThinkFilm Inc., 2004; DVD: New Line Home Video, 2005).

28. Audrey Niffenegger, *The Time Traveler's Wife* (Orlando, FL: Harvest Books/Harcourt, 2004), 145.

29. Ibid., 56.

30. Ibid., 57.

31. *Twelve Monkeys,* directed by Terry Gilliam, screenplay by David and Janet Peoples (Atlas Entertainment/Classico/Universal Pictures, 1995; DVD: Universal, 1998).

32. Ibid.

33. Thomas Aquinas, *Summa Theologica,* Part 1, Question 22, Article 1.

34. *Signs,* directed and screenplay by M. Night Shyamalan (Blinding Edge Pictures/The Kennedy/Marshall Company/Touchstone Pictures, 2002; DVD: Touchstone, 2003).

35. Ibid.

36. *Quantum Leap,* Episode 1, "Genesis," directed by David Hemmings, written by Donald P. Bellisario (original broadcast March 26, 1989, NBC; DVD: *Quantum Leap: The Complete First Season*, Universal, 2004).

37. *Donnie Darko,* directed and screenplay by Richard Kelly (Pandora Cinema/Flower Films, 2001; DVD: 20th Century Fox Home Entertainment, 2002).

38. *Doctor Who* (2005), Episode 8, "Father's Day," directed by Joe Ahearne, written by Paul Cornell (original broadcast May 14, 2005, BBC-1).

39. Ibid.

40. Isaac Asimov, *Foundation and Empire* (New York: Avon Books, 1966), 7 (prologue).

41. Ibid., 27 (pt. 1, ch. 6).

42. Gregory Benford, *Foundation's Fear* (New York: HarperPrism, 1997), 62 (pt. 1, ch. 6).

43. Isaac Asimov, *Prelude to Foundation* (New York: Foundation/Doubleday, 1988), 12 (ch. 1).

44. Orson Scott Card, *Cruel Miracles* (New York: Tor/Tom Doherty Associates, 1990), 6 (introduction).

45. Kurt Vonnegut Jr., *The Sirens of Titan* (New York: Laurel/Dell, 1988), 297 (ch. 12). Emphasis removed.

46. Ibid., 285 (ch. 12).

47. Ibid., 215 (ch. 10).

48. Ibid., 309 (epilogue).

49. *The Matrix Reloaded,* directed and screenplay by Larry and Andy Wachowski (Warner Bros./Village Roadshow Pictures/Silver Pictures, 2003; DVD: Warner Home Video, 2003).

50. Mary Doria Russell, *The Sparrow* (New York: Fawcett Columbine/Ballantine, 1996), 149 (ch. 15).

51. Ibid., 185 (ch. 18).

52. Ibid., 228–29 (ch. 21).

53. Ibid., 394 (ch. 32).

54. Ibid., 401 (ch. 32).

55. *Cube,* directed by Vincenzo Natali, screenplay by Natali and Graeme Manson (Cube Libre/Ontario Film Development Corporation/The Feature Film Project, 1997; DVD: Trimark Home Video, 1999).

56. *Cube Zero,* directed and screenplay by Ernie Barbarash (Mad Circus Films/Cube Forward Productions/Lions Gate Entertainment, 2004; DVD: Lions Gate Home Entertainment, 2005).

57. *Cube.*

58. *Star Trek: The Motion Picture,* directed by Robert Wise, screenplay by Harold Livingston (Century Associates/Paramount Pictures, 1979; DVD: Paramount, 2001).

59. Ibid.

60. Ibid.

61. Warren Ellis and Colleen Doran with Dave Stewart, *Orbiter* (New York: DC Comics/Vertigo, 2003), 91.

62. Ibid., iv (introduction).

63. Douglas Adams, *The Hitchhiker's Guide to the Galaxy* (New York: Pocket Books, 1981), 180 (ch. 27).

64. Ibid., 182–83 (ch. 28).

Chapter Five

1. *The Twilight Zone,* Episode 127, "The Old Man in the Cave," directed by Alan Crosland Jr., written by Rod Serling (original broadcast November 8, 1963, CBS; DVD: *The Twilight Zone Volume 17,* Image Entertainment, 2000).

2. *Journal of the British Interplanetary Society,* July 1953, 178. Quoted in William Atheling Jr., "Cathedrals in Space," in *The Issue at Hand: Studies in Contemporary Magazine Science Fiction,* ed. James Blish (Chicago: Advent Publishers, 1973), 62. "William Atheling Jr." was a pseudonym Blish used when writing essays on SF.

3. C. S. Lewis, *Out of the Silent Planet* (New York: Macmillan Paperbacks, 1965), 68 (ch. 11).

4. Ibid., 120 (ch. 18).

5. Ibid., 121 (ch. 18).

6. Ibid., 139 (ch. 20).

7. Ibid., 137 (ch. 20).

8. Ibid., 138 (ch. 20).

9. Augustine, *Confessions, Books I–XIII*, trans. F. J. Sheed (Indianapolis/ Cambridge: Hackett, 1993), 44 (3:VIII).

10. Lewis, *Out of the Silent Planet*, 139 (ch. 20).

11. Philip K. Dick, *The Divine Invasion* (New York: Vintage Books, 1991), 54–55 (ch. 5).

12. Madeleine L'Engle, *A Wrinkle in Time* (New York: Laurel Leaf/Dell, 1976), 96–97 (ch. 6).

13. Ibid., 124 (ch. 8).

14. Madeleine L'Engle, *A Wind in the Door* (New York: Laurel Leaf/Dell, 1976), 97 (ch. 5).

15. Ibid., 197 (ch. 12).

16. Michael Kanaly, *Thoughts of God* (New York: Ace Books, 1997), 124 (ch. 12).

17. C. S. Lewis, *Perelandra* (New York: Macmillan, 1965), 91 (ch. 7).

18. Ibid., 197 (ch. 16).

19. Ibid., 206 (ch. 17).

20. Ibid., 144–45 (ch. 11).

21. Ibid., 114 (ch. 9).

22. Katherin A. Rogers, "Augustinian Evil in C. S. Lewis' *Perelandra*," in *The Transcendent Adventure: Studies of Religion in Science Fiction/Fantasy,* ed. Robert Reilly (Westport, CT: Greenwood Press, 1985), 85.

23. Lewis, *Perelandra*, 208 (ch. 17).

24. Stanislaw Lem, *Memoirs of a Space Traveler*, trans. Joel Stern and Maria Swiecicka-Ziemianek (New York: Helen and Kurt Wolff/Harcourt Brace Jovanovich, 1982), 15 ("The Eighteenth Voyage").

25. Harry Harrison, "The Streets of Ashkelon," in *The New Awareness: Religion through Science Fiction,* ed. Patricia Warrick and Martin Harry Greenberg (New York: Delacorte Press, 1975), 185.

26. Ibid., 191.

27. James Blish, *A Case of Conscience* (New York: Ballantine Books, 1958), 70 (ch. 8).

28. Ibid., 73 (ch. 8).

29. Andrew J. Burgess rightly notes that this is an unlikely conclusion for a twenty-first-century priest to reach, since evolutionary theory has not been rejected by the Catholic Church as it has by many fundamentalist Protestants. But Blish—writing in 1953—could not have anticipated the Second Vatican Council (1962–1965), which "has brought to the fore theologians such as Pierre Teilhard

de Chardin and Karl Rahner, whose thought develops within an explicitly evolutionary framework" (Burgess, "The Concept of Eden," in *The Transcendent Adventure: Studies of Religion in Science Fiction/Fantasy,* ed. Robert Reilly [Westport, CT: Greenwood Press, 1985], 77).

30. Blish, *A Case of Conscience*, 78 (ch. 8).

31. Ibid., 138 (ch. 14).

32. Ibid., 79 (ch. 8).

33. Ibid., 164 (ch. 17).

34. Ibid., 161–62 (ch. 17).

35. Atheling, "Cathedrals in Space," 56.

36. Jo Allen Bradham, "The Case in James Blish's *A Case of Conscience,*" *Extrapolation* 16:1 (December 1974): 79–80.

37. Philip José Farmer, "Father," in *Father to the Stars* (New York: Tor/Tom Doherty Associates/Pinnacle Books, 1981), 258–59.

38. John Boyd, *The Pollinators of Eden* (Middlesex, England, and Baltimore, MD: Penguin Books, 1978), 80–81 (ch. 6).

39. *Serenity*, directed and screenplay by Joss Whedon (Universal Pictures/Mutant Enemy Inc./Barry Mendel Productions, 2005).

40. Theodore Sturgeon, "Dazed," in *The New Awareness: Religion through Science Fiction,* ed. Patricia Warrick and Martin Harry Greenberg (New York: Delacorte Press, 1975), 279.

41. Ibid., 280.

42. *Star Wars: Episode III—Revenge of the Sith,* directed and screenplay by George Lucas (Lucasfilm Ltd., 2005).

43. H. G. Wells, *The War of the Worlds,* in *The Complete Science Fiction Treasury of H. G. Wells* (New York: Avanel Books, 1978), 266 (book 1, ch. 1).

44. *Independence Day,* directed by Roland Emmerich, screenplay by Emmerich and Dean Devlin (20th Century Fox/Centropolis Entertainment, 1996; DVD: 20th Century Fox, 2001).

45. Ian Stewart and Jack Cohen, *Wheelers* (New York: Warner Books/Aspect, 2000), 388–89 (ch. 18).

46. Tom Godwin, "The Cold Equations," in Warrick and Greenberg, *New Awareness,* 242–47.

47. Ray Bradbury, "The Fire Balloons," in Warrick and Greenberg, *New Awareness,* 407–8.

48. Ibid., 429.

Chapter Six

1. Michael Moorcock, *Behold the Man* (New York: Avon Books, 1970), 108–9 (pt. 2, ch. 3). Paragraph breaks removed.

2. Ibid., 147–48 (pt. 3, ch. 6).

3. Ibid., 160 (pt. 3, ch. 7).

4. Ibid., 132 (pt. 3, ch. 3). Paragraph breaks removed.

5. Philip José Farmer, *Jesus on Mars* (Los Angeles: Pinnacle Books, 1979), 200–201 (ch. 18).

6. Ibid., 160 (ch. 15).

7. Ibid., 256 (ch. 25).

8. John Dominic Crossan, *The Historical Jesus: The Life of a Mediterranean Jewish Peasant* (San Francisco: HarperSanFrancisco, 1992), 423.

9. *The Day the Earth Stood Still*, directed by Robert Wise, screenplay by Edmund H. North (20th Century Fox, 1951; DVD: 20th Century Fox Home Entertainment, 2003).

10. Ibid.

11. Walter Tevis, *The Man Who Fell to Earth* (New York: Laurel/Dell, 1989), 172–74 (pt. 2, ch. 5).

12. Ibid., 119–20 (pt. 2, ch. 2).

13. Ibid., 117 (pt. 2, ch. 1).

14. Hans Jonas, *The Gnostic Religion: The Message of the Alien God and the Beginnings of Christianity,* 2nd ed. (Boston: Beacon Press, 1963), 114 ("The Hymn of the Pearl").

15. Carolyn Ives Gilman, "The Real Thing," in Dozois, *Year's Best Science Fiction: Nineteenth Annual Collection*, 413.

16. *Star Trek: Deep Space Nine*, Episode 61, "Destiny," directed by Les Landau, written by Martin A. Winer and David Samuel Cohen (original broadcast Feb. 19, 1995 [syndicated]; DVD: *Star Trek: Deep Space Nine—Season 3*, Paramount, 2003).

17. Ibid.

18. Ibid., Episode 168, "'Til Death Do Us Part," directed by Winrich Kolbe, written by David Weddle and Bradley Thompson (original broadcast Apr. 14, 1999 [syndicated]; DVD: *Star Trek: Deep Space Nine—Season 7*, Paramount, 2003).

19. *Mad Max beyond Thunderdome*, directed by George Miller and George Ogilvie, screenplay by Miller and Terry Hayes (Kennedy Miller Productions, 1985; DVD: Warner Home Video, 1997).

20. Ibid.

21. Frank Herbert, *Dune* (New York: Berkley Medallion, 1975), 101.

22. Willis E. McNelly, ed., *The Dune Encyclopedia* (New York: Berkley Books, 1984), 386.

23. Frank Herbert, *Dune Messiah* (New York: Berkley Medallion, 1970), 19.

24. Frank Herbert, *God Emperor of Dune* (New York: Berkley Books, 1982), 55.

25. *Superman*, directed by Richard Donner, screenplay by Mario Puzo, David Newman, Leslie Newman, and Robert Benton (Alexander Salkind/Dovemead Films/Film Export A.G./International Film Production, 1978; DVD: Warner Home Video, 2001).

26. Mark Millar and Peter Gross, *Chosen* #2 (March 2004), Dark Horse Comics, 9.

27. Donald Palumbo, "Adam Warlock: Marvel Comics' Cosmic Christ Figure," *Extrapolation* 24:1 (1983): 33.

28. Greg Pak and Charlie Adlard, *Warlock* #1 (November 2004), Marvel Comics, 4.

29. Greg Pak and Charlie Adlard, *Warlock* #4 (February 2005), Marvel Comics, 32.

30. J. Michael Straczynski and Gary Frank, et al., *Supreme Power: Contact* (New York: Marvel Comics, 2004), 137.

31. Mark Gruenwald, John Buscema, et al., *Squadron Supreme* (New York: Marvel Comics, 1997), 27.

32. Alan Moore and John Totleben, "Olympus," *Miracleman* #16 (December 1989), Eclipse Comics, 9–10.

33. Michael Bishop, "The Gospel according to Gamaliel Crucis," in *Close Encounters with the Deity* (Atlanta, GA: Peachtree Publishers, 1986), 274.

34. Robert A. Heinlein, *Stranger in a Strange Land* (New York: Ace Books, 1991), 266 (ch. 21).

35. Thomas M. Disch, *The Dreams Our Stuff Is Made Of: How Science Fiction Conquered the World* (New York: Touchstone/Simon & Schuster, 2000), 121.

36. Heinlein, *Stranger in a Strange Land*, 394 (ch. 30).

37. Ibid., 184 (ch. 14) and elsewhere.

38. Ibid., 475 (ch. 35).

39. Philip José Farmer, "Prometheus," in *Father to the Stars* (New York: Tor/Tom Doherty Associates/Pinnacle Books, 1981), 200.

Chapter Seven

1. Adams, *Hitchhiker's Guide,* 60 (ch. 6).

2. Bertrand Russell, *Why I Am Not a Christian and Other Essays on Religion and Related Subjects* (New York: Clarion Books/Simon & Schuster, 1957), 22.

3. Ben Bova, *Mercury* (New York: Tor/Tom Doherty Associates, 2005), 149.

4. Stephen Jay Gould, "Nonoverlapping Magisteria," *Natural History,* March 1997, 19–20.

5. William James, *The Varieties of Religious Experience: A Study in Human Nature* (New York: Modern Library, 1994), 17.

6. *Firefly*, Episode 4, "Jaynestown," directed by Marita Grabiak, written by Ben Edlund (original broadcast Oct. 18, 2002, FOX; DVD: *Firefly—The Complete Series*, 20th Century Fox Home Entertainment, 2003).

7. Ibid.

8. Stanislaw Lem, *The Star Diaries*, trans. Michael Kandel (New York: Avon, 1977), 224–25 (The Twenty-First Voyage).

9. Ibid., 220 (The Twenty-First Voyage).

10. *Contact,* directed by Robert Zemeckis, screenplay by James V. Hart and Michael Goldenberg (South Side Amusement Company/Warner Bros., 1997; DVD: Warner Home Video, 1997).

11. Ibid. Sagan's original novel takes a different approach. In its closing scene, Arroway discovers another message, a code hidden deep within the apparently random digits of pi. She takes this message, encoded in a basic law of the universe, to be indisputable proof of the existence of an intelligent Creator. Rather than science falling back on faith, Sagan's novel shows faith vindicated (and replaced?) by scientific proof.

12. Bryan P. Stone, "Religious Faith and Science in *Contact*," *Journal of Religion and Film* 2:2 (October 1998), http://www.unomaha.edu/jrf/stonear2.htm, par. 11–12.

13. Stewart and Cohen, *Heaven*, 46 (ch. 2).

14. Neal Stephenson, *Snow Crash* (New York: Bantam Spectra, 1993), 400 (ch. 56).

15. Ibid., 408 (ch. 57).

16. Philip K. Dick, *VALIS* (New York: Vintage Books, 1991), 231–32.

17. Steve Stanton, "On the Edge of Eternity," in *Divine Realms: Canadian Science Fiction and Fantasy,* ed. Susan MacGregor (Winnipeg: Raventone/Turnstone Press, 1998), 82. Paragraph break removed.

18. Richard Bowker, "Contamination," in *Perpetual Light*, ed. Alan Ryan (New York: Warner Books, 1982), 98.

19. Stewart and Cohen, *Wheelers*, 447 (ch. 21).

20. Isaac Asimov, "Reason," in *I, Robot* (Garden City, NY: Doubleday & Co., 1963), 64–65.

21. Ibid., 75–76.

22. *Battlestar Galactica* (2003), Episode 10, "Flesh and Bone," directed by Brad Turner, written by Toni Graphia (original broadcast Dec. 6, 2004, SciFi Channel).

23. Ibid.

24. Ibid.

25. Ibid., Episode 20, "The Farm," directed by Rod Hardy, written by Carla Robinson (original broadcast Aug. 12, 2005, SciFi Channel).

26. K. M. O'Donnell, "Chronicles of a Comer," in *Chronicles of a Comer and Other Religious Science Fiction Stories*, ed. Roger Elwood (Atlanta, GA: John Knox Press, 1974), 120.

27. Ray Bradbury, "The Man," in *The Illustrated Man* (Garden City, NY: Doubleday, 1951), 75.

28. Ibid., 76.

29. Rudy Rucker, *Realware* (New York: Eos/HarperCollins, 2001), 148 (ch. 3). Paragraph break removed.

30. Philip K. Dick, *A Maze of Death* (New York: Vintage Books, 1994), 51 (ch. 5).

31. Robert J. Sawyer, *Calculating God* (New York: Tor/Tom Doherty Associates, 2000), 61 (ch. 5).

32. Ibid., 95 (ch. 9).

33. Ibid., 19 (ch. 1).

34. Ibid.

35. Gertrude of Helfta, *The Herald of Divine Love*, trans. and ed. Margaret Winkworth (Mahwah, NJ: Paulist Press, 1993), 96 (Book II, ch. 2).

36. Warren Ellis and Jon J. Muth, "Big Sky," *Global Frequency* #5 (April 2003), Wildstorm/DC Comics, 23.

37. Ibid., 30.

38. Sawyer, *Hybrids*, 388 (ch. 44).

39. Ibid., 390 (epilogue).

40. Ian Watson, *God's World* (New York: Carroll & Graf, 1990), 29 (ch. 4).

41. Ibid., 30 (ch. 4).

42. Sawyer, *Flashforward*, 135 (ch. 13).

43. Rick Moody, "The Albertine Notes," in *Year's Best SF 9*, ed. David G. Hartwell and Kathryn Cramer (New York: Eos/HarperCollins, 2004), 455.

44. Ibid., 431.

45. *eXistenZ*, directed and screenplay by David Cronenberg (Dimension Films/Alliance Atlantis/Serendipity Point Films, 1999; DVD: Dimension Home Video, 1999).

46. Margaret Atwood, *The Handmaid's Tale* (Boston: Houghton Mifflin Co., 1986), 167 (ch. 27).

47. Aldous Huxley, *Brave New World* (New York: Perennial Classic/Harper & Row, 1969), 36 (ch. 3).

48. Ibid., 56 (ch. 5).

49. Ibid.

50. Ibid., 159 (ch. 17).

51. Plato, *The Republic*, trans. Desmond Lee (Middlesex, England, and Baltimore, MD: Penguin Books, 1974), 318 (Book 7).

52. Clute and Nicholls, *Encyclopedia of Science Fiction*, 255.

53. *Matrix*.

54. Plato, *Republic*, 318.

55. Julian of Norwich, *Showings*, trans. and ed. Edmund Colledge and James Walsh (Mahwah, NJ: Paulist Press, 1978), 130 (Shorter Text, ch. 4).

56. Michael Bishop, "Close Encounter with the Deity," in *Close Encounters with the Deity* (Atlanta, GA: Peachtree Publishers, 1986), 13.

57. Robert Silverberg, "The Feast of St. Dionysus," in *The Feast of St. Dionysus: Five Science Fiction Stories* (New York: Berkley Books, 1979), 31.

58. Ibid., 35.

Chapter Eight

1. Eusebius, *The History of the Church*, trans. G. A. Williamson, ed. Andrew Louth (London and New York: Penguin Books, 1989), 294 (9:9).

2. Douglas Wilson, "Recovering Cultural Soul," *Credenda Agenda* 7:6 (1995), http://www.credenda.org/issues/7-6repairingtheruins.php.

3. Walter M. Miller Jr., *St. Leibowitz and the Wild Horse Woman* (New York: Bantam Books, 1997), 67 (ch. 6).

4. Walter M. Miller Jr., *A Canticle for Leibowitz* (New York: Bantam Books, 1976), 170 (ch. 18).

5. Russell Hoban, *Riddley Walker,* expanded ed. (Bloomington and Indianapolis: Indiana University Press, 1998), 31–32 (ch. 6).

6. *Planet of the Apes*, directed by Franklin J. Schaffner, screenplay by Michael Wilson and Rod Serling (20th Century Fox/APJAC Productions, 1968; DVD: 20th Century Fox Home Entertainment, 2000).

7. Ibid.

8. Orson Scott Card, "Pageant Wagon," in *Folk of the Fringe* (New York: Tor/Tom Doherty Associates, 1990), 142. Typographical error ("Desert") corrected.

9. Ibid., "West," 62.

10. *Alien Nation*, Episode 10, "Three to Tango," directed by Stan Lathan, written by Diane Frolov and Andrew Schneider (original broadcast Nov. 13, 1989, FOX).

11. Stewart and Cohen, *Wheelers*, 469 (ch. 22).

12. Russell, *Sparrow*, 3 (prologue).

13. Michael P. Kube-McDowell, "A Green Hill Far Away," in *Perpetual Light,* ed. Alan Ryan (New York: Warner Books, 1982), 243.

14. Stephen Baxter, "Mayflower II," in *The Year's Best Science Fiction: Twenty-Second Annual Collection,* ed. Gardner Dozois (New York: St. Martin's Griffin, 2005), 437.

15. *Blake's 7*, Episode 3, "Cygnus Alpha," directed by Vere Lorrimer, written by Terry Nation (original broadcast Jan. 16, 1978, BBC-1).

16. Damien Broderick, *Transcension* (New York: Tor/Tom Doherty Associates, 2002), 145 (pt. 2, ch. 7).

17. Jonathan Lethem, *Amnesia Moon* (New York: Tor/Tom Doherty Associates, 1996), 168–69.

18. Ibid., 172.

19. Robert Silverberg, "Schwartz between the Galaxies," in *The Feast of St. Dionysus: Five Science Fiction Stories* (New York: Berkley Books, 1979), 68–69.

20. Ibid., 68.

21. Robert Lowndes, *Believer's World* (New York: Avalon Books, 1961), 91 (ch. 7).

22. Ursula K. Le Guin, *The Telling* (New York: Ace Books, 2001), 95 (ch. 4).

23. Ibid., 85–86 (ch. 4).

24. Brian Moore, *Catholics* (New York: E. P. Dutton/Obelisk, 1986), 50–51.

25. Ibid., 107.

26. Rober Silverberg, "Good News from the Vatican," in *The New Awareness: Religion through Science Fiction,* ed. Patricia Warrick and Martin Harry Greenberg (New York: Delacorte Press, 1975), 166.

27. Ibid., 169.

28. Ibid., 173.

29. Winston P. Sanders, "The Word to Space," in *Other Worlds, Other Gods,* ed. Mayo Mohs (New York: Avon Books, 1971), 76.

30. Ibid., 78.

31. *The Chronicles of Riddick,* directed and screenplay by David Twohy (Universal Pictures/Primal Foe Productions/One Race Productions/Radar Pictures, 2004; DVD: Universal, 2004).

32. Ibid.

33. Michael Karounos, review of *Equilibrium, Journal of Religion and Film* 7:2 (October 2003), http://www.unomaha.edu/jrf/Vol7No2/reviews/equilibrium.htm, paragraphs 5–6.

34. Stewart and Cohen, *Heaven,* 278 (ch. 13).

35. Ibid., 139 (ch. 6).

36. Ibid., 329–30 (ch. 16).

37. Sheri S. Tepper, *Grass* (New York: Bantam Spectra, 1990), 13 (ch. 2).

38. Ibid., 140–41 (ch. 7).

39. Ibid., 165 (ch. 9).

40. Katharine Kerr, "Asylum," in *The Year's Best Science Fiction: Twelfth Annual Collection,* ed. Gardner Dozois (New York: St. Martin's Press, 1995), 566.

41. Atwood, *Handmaid's Tale,* 33 (ch. 6).

42. Jeff Sharlet, "Soldiers of Christ: Inside America's Most Powerful Megachurch," *Harper's,* May 2005, 46.

43. Atwood, *Handmaid's Tale,* 247 (ch. 38).

44. Octavia E. Butler, *Parable of the Sower* (New York: Warner Books/Aspect, 1995), 7 (ch. 2).

45. Octavia E. Butler, *Parable of the Talents* (New York: Warner Books/Aspect, 2000), 19.

46. Ibid., 325.

Chapter Nine

1. Plato, *The Last Days of Socrates,* trans. Hugh Tredennick and Harold Tarrant (London and New York: Penguin Books, 1993), 140.

2. Robert Silverberg, "The Pope of the Chimps," in Ryan, *Perpetual Light,* 18.

3. Ibid., 25.

4. Ibid., 34.

5. Robert J. Sawyer, *Hominids* (New York: Tor/Tom Doherty Associates, 2002), 279–81 (ch. 33).

6. Philip K. Dick, *Ubik* (New York: Vintage Books, 1991), 13 (ch. 2).

7. Ibid., 127 (ch. 10).

8. Ibid., 207 (ch. 16).

9. Philip Pullman, *The Amber Spyglass* (New York: Dell Yearling, 2003), 295 (ch. 22).

10. Ibid., 319 (ch. 23).

11. Ted Chiang, "Hell Is the Absence of God," in *Stories of Your Life,* 246–47.

12. Ibid., 247.

13. Ibid., 249. Paragraph break removed

14. Ibid., 279.

15. Dan Simmons, *Hyperion* (New York: Bantam Books/Spectra, 1990), 56 (ch. 1).

16. Ibid., 55.

17. Orson Scott Card, "Mortal Gods," in *Cruel Miracles*, 25.

18. Philip José Farmer, *To Your Scattered Bodies Go* (New York: G. P. Putnam's Sons, 1971), 3 (ch. 1).

19. Ibid., 87 (ch. 12).

20. Ibid., 148 (ch. 17).

21. Frederik Pohl, *Heechee Rendezvous* (New York: Ballantine Books/Del Rey, 1984), 312 (ch. 24).

22. Frederik Pohl, *The Annals of the Heechee* (New York: Ballantine Books/Del Rey, 1987), 168 (ch. 10).

23. Ibid., 193 (ch. 11).

24. Broderick, *Transcension*, 69 (pt. 1, ch. 12).

25. Ibid., 133 (pt. 2, ch. 4).

26. John Crowley, *Engine Summer* (New York: Doubleday, 1979), 59 (pt. 2, ch. 1).

27. Ibid., 177 (pt. 4, ch. 5).

28. Lem, *Memoirs of a Space Traveler*, 64–65 ("Further Reminiscences of Ijon Tichy").

29. Thomas M. Disch, "In Xanadu," in *Redshift: Extreme Visions of Speculative Fiction*, ed. Al Sarrantonio (New York: Roc Books, 2001), 113.

30. Ibid., 119.

31. Stewart and Cohen, *Heaven*, 214–15 (ch. 10). Paragraph break removed.

32. Ibid., 210 (ch. 10). Paragraph break removed.

33. Jack Williamson, "Afterlife," in *Year's Best SF 8*, ed. David G. Hartwell and Kathryn Cramer (New York: Eos/HarperCollins, 2003), 419.

34. Ibid., 429.

35. Ibid., 434.

36. *Logan's Run*, directed by Michael Anderson, screenplay by David Zelag Goodman (Metro-Goldwyn-Mayer, 1976; DVD: Warner Home Video, 2000).

37. Orson Scott Card, *Xenocide* (New York: Tor/Tom Doherty Associates, 1991), 206 (ch. 8).

38. Ibid., 267 (ch. 10).

39. Robert Silverberg, "Born with the Dead," in *Born with the Dead: Three Novellas* (New York: Berkley Books, 1979), 7–8 (ch. 1).

40. Ibid., 57 (ch. 6).

41. Ibid., 84 (ch. 9).

42. Frederik Pohl, *The Other End of Time* (New York: Tor/Tom Doherty Associates, 1996), 225 (ch. 23). This concept is based on a theory by physicist Frank Tipler, who in 1994 published a book titled *The Physics of Immortality* explaining the possibility.

43. Ibid., 336 (ch. 39).

44. Frederik Pohl, *The Far Shore of Time* (New York: Tor/Tom Doherty Associates, 1999), 280 (ch. 51). Paragraph break removed.

45. Farmer, *Magic Labyrinth*, 335 (ch. 46).

Chapter Ten

1. Douglas Adams, *The Restaurant at the End of the Universe* (New York: Harmony Books, 1980), 122 (ch. 17).

2. Damon Knight, "Shall the Dust Praise Thee?" in *Dangerous Visions,* ed. Harlan Ellison (New York: Signet Books, 1967), 325. Capitalization changed.

3. Arthur C. Clarke, "The Nine Billion Names of God," in Warrick and Greenberg, *New Awareness,* 314–15.

4. Ibid., 318–19.

5. Ibid., 322.

6. Philip José Farmer, "Towards the Beloved City," in Elwood, *Chronicles of a Comer,* 99.

7. Ibid., 106–7.

8. Arthur C. Clarke, *Childhood's End* (New York: Ballantine Books, 1953), 72 (ch. 6).

9. Pierre Teilhard de Chardin, *The Phenomenon of Man*, trans. Bernard Wall (New York: Harper Torchbooks/Harper & Row, 1965), 251–52.

10. Pierre Teilhard de Chardin, *Christianity and Evolution*. trans. René Hague (New York: Helen and Kurt Wolff/Harcourt Brace Jovanovich, 1969), 71.

11. Clarke, *Childhood's End*, 216 (ch. 24).

12. Ibid., 74 (ch. 6).

13. Ibid., 181–82 (ch. 20).

14. Ian McDonald, "Tendeléo's Story," in *The Year's Best Science Fiction: Eighteenth Annual Collection*, ed. Gardner Dozois (New York: St. Martin's Griffin, 2001), 565.

15. Ibid., 576.

16. Ibid., 606.

17. Ibid., 600.

18. *Matrix.*

19. H. G. Wells, *The Time Machine*, in *The Complete Science Fiction Treasury of H. G. Wells* (New York: Avanel Books, 1978), 25 (ch. 4).

20. Ibid., 61 (ch. 11).

21. Ibid., 62 (ch. 11).

22. Ibid., 61–62 (ch. 11).

23. David Ketterer, *New Worlds for Old: The Apocalyptic Imagination, Science Fiction, and American Literature* (Garden City, NY: Anchor Books/Doubleday, 1974), 13.

24. Ibid., 94.

25. Ibid., 203.

Bibliography

Adams, Douglas. *The Hitchhiker's Guide to the Galaxy*. New York: Pocket Books, 1981.

———. *The Restaurant at the End of the Universe*. New York: Harmony Books, 1980.

A.I.: Artificial Intelligence. Directed and screenplay by Steven Spielberg. Warner Bros./Dreamworks SKG, 2001. DVD, Dreamworks, 2002.

Aldiss, Brian W. "Heresies of the Huge God." In *Man in His Time: The Best Science Fiction Stories of Brian W. Aldiss*, 171–80. New York : Atheneum Books, 1989.

Ali, Ahmed, trans. *Al-Qur'ān: A Contemporary Translation*. Princeton, NJ: Princeton University Press, 1988.

Alien. Directed by Ridley Scott. Screenplay by Dan O'Bannon. 20th Century Fox/Brandywine Productions, 1979. DVD, *The Alien Quadrilogy*, 20th Century Fox Home Entertainment, 2003.

Alien Nation. Episode 10, "Three to Tango." Directed by Stan Lathan. Written by Diane Frolov and Andrew Schneider. Original broadcast Nov. 13, 1989, FOX.

Anderson, Poul. *Genesis*. New York: Tor/Tom Doherty Associates, 2000.

———. *Tau Zero*. Garden City, NY: Berkley Medallion, 1976.

Anselm, Archbishop of Canterbury. *Prayers and Meditations of Saint Anselm with the Proslogion*. Trans. Sister Benedicta Ward, S.L.G. London and New York: Penguin Books, 1973.

Anthony, Patricia. *God's Fires*. New York: Ace Books, 1997.

Armageddon. Directed by Michael Bay. Screenplay by Jonathan Hensleigh and J. J. Abrams. Touchstone Pictures/Jerry Bruckheimer Films/Valhalla Motion Pictures, 1998. DVD, Touchstone Home Video, 1999.

Asimov, Isaac. *Foundation*. New York: Avon Books, 1966.

———. *Foundation and Empire*. New York: Avon Books, 1966.

———. "Introduction: The Lord's Apprentice." In *The Ultimate Frankenstein*, ed. Byron Preiss, 1–7. New York: Dell, 1991.

269

———. *Prelude to Foundation*. New York: Foundation/Doubleday, 1988.

———. "Reason." In *I, Robot*. Garden City, NY: Doubleday & Co., 1963.

Atheling, William, Jr. "Cathedrals in Space." In *The Issue at Hand: Studies in Contemporary Magazine Science Fiction*, ed. James Blish, 52–79. Chicago: Advent Publishers, 1973.

Atwood, Margaret. *The Handmaid's Tale*. Boston: Houghton Mifflin Co., 1986.

———. *Oryx and Crake*. London: Virago, 2004.

Augustine, Archbishop of Hippo. *Confessions, Books I–XIII*. Trans. F. J. Sheed. Indianapolis/Cambridge: Hackett, 1993.

———. *The Trinity*. Trans. Edmund Hill, O.P. Ed. John E. Rotell, O.S.A. Brooklyn, NY: New City Press, 1991.

Babylon 5. Episode 6, "Mind War." Directed by Bruth Seth Green. Written by J. Michael Straczynski. Original broadcast March 2, 1994 (syndicated). DVD, *Babylon 5: The Complete First Season*, Warner Home Video, 2002.

Back to the Future. Directed by Robert Zemeckis. Screenplay by Zemeckis and Bob Gale. Amblin Entertainment/Universal Pictures, 1985. DVD, *Back to the Future—The Complete Trilogy,* Universal, 2002.

Back to the Future Part II. Directed by Robert Zemeckis. Screenplay by Bob Gale. Amblin Entertainment/Universal Pictures, 1988. DVD, *Back to the Future—The Complete Trilogy,* Universal, 2002.

Battlestar Galactica (2003). Episode 10, "Flesh and Bone." Directed by Brad Turner. Written by Toni Graphia. Original broadcast Dec. 6, 2004, SciFi Channel.

———. Episode 20, "The Farm." Directed by Rod Hardy. Written by Carla Robinson. Original broadcast Aug. 12, 2005, SciFi Channel.

Baxter, Stephen. "Mayflower II." In *The Year's Best Science Fiction: Twenty-Second Annual Collection,* ed. Gardner Dozois, 404–49. New York: St. Martin's Griffin, 2005.

Beneath the Planet of the Apes. Directed by Ted Post. Screenplay by Paul Dehn. 20th Century Fox/APJAC Entertainment, 1970. DVD, 20th Century Fox Home Entertainment, 2000.

Benford, Gregory. "Anomalies." In *Redshift: Extreme Visions of Speculative Fiction*, ed. Al Sarrantonio, 237–48. New York: Roc Books, 2001.

———. *Foundation's Fear*. New York: HarperPrism, 1997.

Bergesen , Albert J., and Andrew M. Greeley. *God in the Movies*. New Brunswick, NJ, and London: Transaction Publishers, 2000.

Bishop, Michael. "Close Encounter with the Deity." In *Close Encounters with the Deity,* 1–13. Atlanta, GA: Peachtree Publishers, 1986.

———. "The Creature on the Couch." In *The Ultimate Frankenstein,* ed. Byron Preiss, 39–68. New York: Dell, 1991.

———. "The Gospel according to Gamaliel Crucis." In *Close Encounters with the Deity,* 247–306. Atlanta, GA: Peachtree Publishers, 1986.

Blake's 7. Episode 3, "Cygnus Alpha." Directed by Vere Lorrimer. Written by Terry Nation. Original broadcast Jan. 16, 1978, BBC-1.

Blish, James. *A Case of Conscience*. New York: Ballantine Books, 1958.

————. *The Triumph of Time.* In *Cities in Flight, Volume 2.* New York: Baen Books, 1991.

Blumlein, Michael. "Know How, Can Do." In *The Year's Best Science Fiction: Nineteenth Annual Collection,* ed. Gardner Dozois, 497–513. New York: St. Martin's Griffin, 2002.

Boethius. *The Consolation of Philosophy.* Trans. W. V. Cooper. New York: Carlton House, 1943.

Bova, Ben. *Jupiter.* New York: Tor/Tom Doherty Associates, 2001.

————. *Mercury.* New York: Tor/Tom Doherty Associates, 2005.

Bowker, Richard. "Contamination." In *Perpetual Light,* ed. Alan Ryan, 88–105. New York: Warner Books, 1982.

Boyd, John. *The Pollinators of Eden.* Middlesex, England, and Baltimore, MD: Penguin Books, 1978.

Bradbury, Ray. "The Fire Balloons." In *The New Awareness: Religion through Science Fiction,* ed. Patricia Warrick and Martin Harry Greenberg, 403–30. New York: Delacorte Press, 1975.

————. "The Man." In *The Illustrated Man,* 63–76. Garden City, NY: Doubleday, 1951.

Bradham, Jo Allen. "The Case in James Blish's *A Case of Conscience.*" *Extrapolation* 16:1 (December 1974).

Broderick, Damien. *Transcension.* New York: Tor/Tom Doherty Associates, 2002.

Brown, Fredric. "Answer." In *Those Amazing Electronic Thinking Machines!* ed. Isaac Asimov, Martin H. Greenberg, and Charles G. Waugh, 149–50. New York: Franklin Watts, 1983.

Brown, Peter. *Augustine of Hippo: A Biography.* Berkeley and Los Angeles: University of California Press, 2000.

Brunner, John. "Judas." In *Dangerous Visions,* ed. Harlan Ellison, 447–56. New York: Signet Books, 1967.

————. "The Vitanuls." In *Other Worlds, Other Gods,* ed. Mayo Mohs, 145–64. New York: Avon Books, 1971.

Burgess, Andrew J. "The Concept of Eden." In *The Transcendent Adventure: Studies of Religion in Science Fiction/Fantasy,* ed. Robert Reilly, 73–81. Westport, CT: Greenwood Press, 1985.

Burgess, Anthony. *A Clockwork Orange.* New York: Ballantine Books, 1988.

Butler, Octavia E. *Parable of the Sower.* New York: Warner Books/Aspect, 1995.

————. *Parable of the Talents.* New York: Warner Books/Aspect, 2000.

Card, Orson Scott. *Children of the Mind.* New York: Tor/Tom Doherty Associates, 1996.

————. *Cruel Miracles.* New York: Tor/Tom Doherty Associates, 1990.

————. *Ender's Shadow.* New York: Tor/Tom Doherty Associates, 1999.

————. *Folk of the Fringe.* New York: Tor/Tom Doherty Associates, 1990.

————. *Speaker for the Dead.* New York: Tor/Tom Doherty Associates, 1991.

————. *Xenocide.* New York: Tor/Tom Doherty Associates, 1991.

Chiang, Ted. "The Evolution of Human Science." In *Stories of Your Life and Others*, 241–44. New York: Tor/Tom Doherty Associates, 2002.

———. "Hell Is the Absence of God." In *Stories of Your Life and Others*, 245–79. New York: Tor/Tom Doherty Associates, 2002.

Chronicles of Riddick, The. Directed and screenplay by David Twohy. Universal Pictures/Primal Foe Productions/One Race Productions/Radar Pictures, 2004. DVD, Universal, 2004.

Chwedyk, Richard. "The Measure of All Things." In *Year's Best SF 7*, ed. David G. Hartwell and Kathryn Cramer, 77–99. New York: Eos/HarperCollins, 2002. ·

Clarke, Arthur C. *Childhood's End*. New York: Ballantine Books, 1953.

———. "The Nine Billion Names of God." In *The New Awareness: Religion through Science Fiction*, ed. Patricia Warrick and Martin Harry Greenberg, 311–22. New York: Delacorte Press, 1975.

———. *2001: A Spacy Odyssey*. New York: Roc Books, 1993.

Clockwork Orange, A. Directed and screenplay by Stanley Kubrick. Hawk Films/Polaris Productions/Warner Bros., 1971. DVD, Warner Home Video, 2000.

Clockwork Orange, A (review). *Monthly Film Bulletin* 39, no. 457 (February 1972): 28–29. Online: *The British Film Institute*, http://www.bfi.org.uk/features/ultimatefilm/chart/details.php?ranking=54.

Clute, John, and Peter Nicholls, eds., *The Encyclopedia of Science Fiction*. New York: St. Martin's Griffin, 1995.

Contact. Directed by Robert Zemeckis. Screenplay by James V. Hart and Michael Goldenberg. South Side Amusement Company/Warner Bros., 1997. DVD, Warner Home Video, 1997.

Crichton, Michael. *Jurassic Park*. New York: Ballantine Books, 1990.

———. *Prey*. New York: Avon Books/HarperCollins, 2002.

Crossan, John Dominic. *The Historical Jesus: The Life of a Mediterranean Jewish Peasant*. San Francisco: HarperSanFrancisco, 1992.

Crowley, John. *Engine Summer*. New York: Doubleday, 1979.

Cube. Directed by Vincenzo Natali. Screenplay by Natali and Graeme Manson. Cube Libre/Ontario Film Development Corporation/The Feature Film Project, 1997. DVD, Trimark Home Video, 1999.

Cube Zero. Directed and screenplay by Ernie Barbarash. Mad Circus Films/Cube Forward Productions/Lions Gate Entertainment, 2004. DVD, Lions Gate Home Entertainment, 2005.

Dark City. Directed by Alex Proyas. Screenplay by Proyas, Lem Dobbs, and David S. Goyer. Mystery Clock Cinema/New Line Cinema, 1998. DVD, New Line Home Video, 1998.

Day after Tomorrow, The. Directed by Roland Emmerich. Screenplay by Emmerich and Jeffrey Nachmanoff. 20th Century Fox/Centropolis Entertainment, 2004. DVD, 20th Century Fox Home Entertainment, 2004.

Day the Earth Stood Still, The. Directed by Robert Wise. Screenplay by Edmund

H. North. 20th Century Fox, 1951. DVD, 20th Century Fox Home Entertainment, 2003.

Deep Impact. Directed by Mimi Leder. Screenplay by Bruce Joel Rubin and Michael Tolkin. Dreamworks SKG/Paramount Pictures, 1998. DVD, Paramount, 1998.

Delany, Samuel R. "About Five Thousand One Hundred and Seventy Five Words." *Extrapolation* 10 (1969): 52–66.

Dennett, Daniel. *Consciousness Explained.* Boston: Little, Brown & Co., 1991.

Descartes, René. *Meditations on First Philosophy.* In *Great Voyages: The History of Western Philosophy from 1492 to 1776,* ed. Bill Uzgalis. University of Oregon, http://oregonstate.edu/instruct/phl302/texts/descartes/meditations/meditations.html.

Dick, Philip K. *The Divine Invasion.* New York: Vintage Books, 1991.

———. *Do Androids Dream of Electric Sheep?* New York: Del Rey/Ballantine Books, 1982.

———. *A Maze of Death.* New York: Vintage Books, 1994.

———. *Radio Free Albemuth.* New York: Vintage Books, 1998.

———. *The Shifting Realities of Philip K. Dick: Selected Literary and Philosophical Writings.* Ed. Lawrence Sutin. New York: Vintage Books, 1995.

———. *Ubik.* New York: Vintage Books, 1991.

———. *VALIS.* New York: Vintage Books, 1991.

Dick, Philip K., and Roger Zelazny. *Deus Irae.* New York: Dell Publishing, 1976.

Disch, Thomas M. *The Dreams Our Stuff Is Made Of: How Science Fiction Conquered the World.* New York: Touchstone/Simon & Schuster, 2000.

———. "In Xanadu." In *Redshift: Extreme Visions of Speculative Fiction,* ed. Al Sarrantonio, 113–26. New York: Roc Books, 2001.

———. "Science Fiction as a Church." *Foundation* 25 (June 1982): 53–58.

Dr. Strangelove, or How I Learned to Stop Worrying and Love the Bomb. Directed by Stanley Kubrick. Screenplay by Kubrick, Terry Southern, and Peter George. Hawk Films Ltd., 1964. DVD, Columbia/Tristar, 2001.

Doctor Who. Serial No. 78, "Genesis of the Daleks." Directed by David Maloney. Written by Terry Nation. Six episodes, original broadcast March 8–April 12, 1975, BBC-1.

Doctor Who (2005). Episode 2, "The End of the World." Directed by Euros Lyn. Written by Russell T. Davies. Original broadcast Apr. 2, 2005, BBC-1.

———. Episode 8, "Father's Day." Directed by Joe Ahearne. Written by Paul Cornell. Original broadcast May 14, 2005, BBC-1.

Donnie Darko. Directed and screenplay by Richard Kelly. Pandora Cinema/Flower Films, 2001. DVD, 20th Century Fox Home Entertainment, 2002.

Ellis, Warren, and Colleen Doran with Dave Stewart. *Orbiter.* New York: DC Comics/Vertigo, 2003.

Ellis, Warren, Bryan Hitch, et al. "Outer Dark." In *The Authority: Under New Management*, 1–92. New York: Wildstorm Productions/DC Comics, 2000.

Ellis, Warren, and Jon J. Muth. "Big Sky." *Global Frequency* #5 (April 2003), Wildstorm/DC Comics.

Ellison, Harlan. "I Have No Mouth, and I Must Scream." In *Alone against Tomorrow: Stories of Alienation in Speculative Fiction*. New York: Macmillan Co., 1971.

Elwood, Roger, ed. *Chronicles of a Comer and Other Religious Science Fiction Stories*. Atlanta, GA: John Knox Press, 1974.

Equilibrium. Directed and screenplay by Kurt Wimmer. Blue Tulip/Dimension Films, 2002. DVD, Dimension Home Video, 2003.

Eusebius of Caesarea. *The History of the Church*. Trans. G. A. Williamson. Ed. Andrew Louth. London and New York: Penguin Books, 1989.

eXistenZ. Directed and screenplay by David Cronenberg. Dimension Films/Alliance Atlantis/Serendipity Point Films, 1999. DVD, Dimension Home Video, 1999.

Farmer, Philip José. "Father." In *Father to the Stars*, 201–94. New York: Tor/Tom Doherty Associates/Pinnacle Books, 1981.

———. *Jesus on Mars*. Los Angeles: Pinnacle Books, 1979.

———. *The Magic Labyrinth*. New York: Berkley Books, 1980.

———. "Prometheus." In *Father to the Stars*, 137–200. New York: Tor/Tom Doherty Associates/Pinnacle Books, 1981.

———. *To Your Scattered Bodies Go*. New York: G. P. Putnam's Sons, 1971.

———. "Towards the Beloved City." In *Chronicles of a Comer and Other Religious Science Fiction Stories,* ed. Roger Elwood, 89–111. Atlanta, GA: John Knox Press, 1974.

Firefly. Episode 4, "Jaynestown." Directed by Marita Grabiak. Written by Ben Edlund. Original broadcast Oct. 18, 2002, FOX. DVD, *Firefly—The Complete Series*, 20th Century Fox Home Entertainment, 2003.

Frankenstein. Directed by James Whale. Universal Pictures, 1931. DVD, *Frankenstein (Classic Monster Collection)*, Universal, 1999.

Gamera 3: Revenge of Iris. Directed by Shusuke Kaneko. Screenplay by Kazunori Itô. Daiei Studios, 1999. DVD, ADV Films, 2004.

Gattaca. Directed and screenplay by Andrew Niccol. Columbia Pictures, 1997. DVD, Columbia/Tristar, 1999.

Gertrude of Helfta. *The Herald of Divine Love*. Trans. and ed. Margaret Winkworth. Mahwah, NJ: Paulist Press, 1993.

Gibson, William. *Neuromancer.* New York: Ace Books, 1984.

Gilman, Carolyn Ives. "The Real Thing." In *The Year's Best Science Fiction: Nineteenth Annual Collection,* ed. Gardner Dozois, 408–37. New York: St. Martin's Griffin, 2002.

Godwin, Tom. "The Cold Equations." In *The New Awareness: Religion through Science Fiction,* ed. Patricia Warrick and Martin Harry Greenberg, 221–60. New York: Delacorte Press, 1975.

Godzilla. Directed by Ishiro Honda. Written by Honda, Shigeru Kayama, and Takeo Murata. Toho Film Company, 1954. American release: *Godzilla, King of the Monsters!* Jewell Enterprises, 1956.

Godzilla vs. the Smog Monster. Directed by Yoshimitsu Banno. Screenplay by Banno and Takeshi Kimura. Toho, 1971. DVD, *Godzilla vs. Hedorah*, Columbia Tristar Home Video, 2004.

Gould, Stephen Jay. "Nonoverlapping Magisteria." *Natural History,* March 1997: 16–22, 60–62.

Greeley, Andrew M., and Michael Cassutt, eds. *Sacred Visions*. New York: Tom Doherty Associates, 1991.

Gruenwald, Mark, John Buscema, et al. *Squadron Supreme*. New York: Marvel Comics, 1997.

Griffin, David Ray. *Reenchantment without Supernaturalism: A Process Philosophy of Religion*. Ithaca, NY, and London: Cornell University Press, 2001.

Harrison, Harry. "The Streets of Ashkelon." In *The New Awareness: Religion through Science Fiction,* ed. Patricia Warrick and Martin Harry Greenberg, 174–98. New York: Delacorte Press, 1975.

Heinlein, Robert A. *Stranger in a Strange Land*. New York: Ace Books, 1991.

Herbert, Frank. *Children of Dune*. New York: Berkley Books, 1982.

———. *Dune*. New York: Berkley Medallion, 1975.

———. *Dune Messiah*. New York: Berkley Medallion, 1970.

———. *God Emperor of Dune*. New York: Berkley Books, 1982.

Hoban, Russell. *Riddley Walker.* Expanded ed. Bloomington and Indianapolis: Indiana University Press, 1998.

Huxley, Aldous. *Brave New World*. New York: Perennial Classic/Harper & Row, 1969.

———. *The Doors of Perception*. New York: Harper and Row, 1963.

Independence Day. Directed by Roland Emmerich. Screenplay by Emmerich and Dean Devlin. 20th Century Fox/Centropolis Entertainment, 1996. DVD, 20th Century Fox, 2001.

Invasion of the Body Snatchers. Directed by Don Siegel. Screenplay by Daniel Mainwaring. Walter Wanger Productions Inc., 1956. DVD, Republic, 1998.

I, Robot. Directed by Alex Proyas. Screenplay by Jeff Vintar and Akiva Goldsman. 20th Century Fox/Canlaws Productions, 2004. DVD, 20th Century Fox Home Entertainment, 2004.

Island, The. Directed by Michael Bay. Screenplay by Caspian Tredwell-Owen, Alex Kurtzman, and Roberto Orci. Dreamworks SKG/Warner Bros./Parkes/MacDonald Productions, 2005.

James, William. *The Varieties of Religious Experience: A Study in Human Nature*. New York: Modern Library, 1994.

Jensen, Jan Lars. *Shiva 3000*. New York: Harcourt Brace & Co., 1999.

Jonas, Hans. *The Gnostic Religion: The Message of the Alien God and the Beginnings of Christianity.* 2nd ed. Boston: Beacon Press, 1963.

Julian of Norwich. *Showings*. Ed. and trans. Edmund Colledge and James Walsh. Mahwah, NJ: Paulist Press, 1978.

Kanaly, Michael. *Thoughts of God*. New York: Ace Books, 1997.

Kant, Immanuel. *Fundamental Principles of the Metaphysics of Morals*. Trans. Thomas K. Abott. In *Basic Writings of Kant*, ed. Allen W. Wood. New York: Modern Library, 2001.

Karounos, Michael. "*Equilibrium*," review. *The Journal of Religion and Film* 7:2 (October 2003); http://www.unomaha.edu/jrf/Vol7No2/reviews/equilibrium.htm.

Kelly, James Patrick. "Saint Theresa of the Aliens." In *Sacred Visions*, ed. Andrew M. Greeley and Michael Cassutt, 123–47. New York: Tor/Tom Doherty Associates, 1991.

Kerr, Katharine. "Asylum." In *The Year's Best Science Fiction: Twelfth Annual Collection*, ed. Gardner Dozois, 549–80. New York: St. Martin's Press, 1995.

Ketterer, David. *New Worlds for Old: The Apocalyptic Imagination, Science Fiction, and American Literature*. Garden City, NY: Anchor Books/Doubleday, 1974.

Knight, Damon. "Shall the Dust Praise Thee?" In *Dangerous Visions*, ed. Harlan Ellison, 320–25. New York: Signet Books, 1967.

Kress, Nancy. "Computer Virus." In *The Year's Best Science Fiction: Nineteenth Annual Collection*, ed. Gardner Dozois, 106–40. New York: St. Martin's Griffin, 2002.

Kube-McDowell, Michael P. "A Green Hill Far Away." In *Perpetual Light*, ed. Alan Ryan, 235–71. New York: Warner Books, 1982.

Le Guin, Ursula K. *The Telling*. New York: Ace Books, 2001.

Leiber, Fritz. *Gather, Darkness!* New York: Pyramid Books, 1969.

Lem, Stanislaw. *The Invincible*. Trans. Wendayne Ackerman. Middlesex, England, and Baltimore, MD: Penguin Books, 1976.

———. *Memoirs of a Space Traveler*. Trans. Joel Stern and Maria Swiecicka-Ziemianek. New York: Helen and Kurt Wolff/Harcourt Brace Jovanovich, 1982.

———. *The Star Diaries*. Trans. Michael Kandel. New York: Avon, 1977.

L'Engle, Madeleine. *A Wind in the Door*. New York: Laurel Leaf/Dell, 1976.

———. *A Wrinkle in Time*. New York: Laurel Leaf/Dell, 1976.

Lethem, Jonathan. *Amnesia Moon*. New York: Tor/Tom Doherty Associates, 1996.

Lewis, C. S. *Out of the Silent Planet*. New York: Macmillan Paperbacks, 1965.

———. *Perelandra*. New York: Macmillan, 1965.

———. *That Hideous Strength*. New York: Macmillan Publishing Co., 1965.

Logan's Run. Directed by Michael Anderson. Screenplay by David Zelag Goodman. Metro-Goldwyn-Mayer, 1976. DVD, Warner Home Video, 2000.

Lovecraft, H. P. *At the Mountains of Madness and Other Tales of Terror*. New York: Ballantine Books, 1971.

Lowndes, Robert. *Believer's World*. New York: Avalon Books, 1961.

MacLeod, Ian R. "New Light on the Drake Equation." In *The Year's Best Science Fiction: Nineteenth Annual Collection*, ed. Gardner Dozois, 1–43. New York: St. Martin's Griffin, 2002.

Mad Max beyond Thunderdome. Directed by George Miller and George Ogilvie. Screenplay by Miller and Terry Hayes. Kennedy Miller Productions, 1985. DVD, Warner Home Video, 1997.

Mars Attacks! Directed by Tim Burton. Screenplay by Jonathan Gems. Warner Bros., 1996. DVD, Warner Home Video, 1997.

Matrix, The. Directed and screenplay by Larry and Andy Wachowski. Groucho II Film Partnership/Silver Pictures/Village Roadshow Pictures, 1999. DVD, Warner Home Video, 1999.

Matrix Reloaded, The. Directed and screenplay by Larry and Andy Wachowski. Warner Bros./Village Roadshow Pictures/Silver Pictures, 2003. DVD, Warner Home Video, 2003.

Matrix Revolutions, The. Directed and screenplay by Larry and Andy Wachowski. Warner Bros./Village Roadshow Pictures/Silver Pictures, 2003. DVD, Warner Home Video, 2004.

McDevitt, Jack. "Gus." In *Sacred Visions,* ed. Andrew M. Greeley and Michael Cassutt, 1–25. New York: Tor/Tom Doherty Associates, 1991.

McDonald, Ian. "Tendeléo's Story." In *The Year's Best Science Fiction: Eighteenth Annual Collection,* ed. Gardner Dozois, 558–609. New York: St. Martin's Griffin, 2001.

McNelly, Willis E., ed. *The Dune Encyclopedia.* New York: Berkley Books, 1984.

Meagher, Robert. *Augustine: On the Inner Life of the Mind.* Indianapolis/Cambridge: Hackett Publishing, 1998.

Metropolis. Directed by Fritz Lang. Script by Lang and Thea von Harbou. Universum Film A.G. (UFA), 1927. DVD, ufa Home Entertainment, 2003.

Millar, Mark, and Peter Gross. *Chosen* #1–3 (January–August 2004), Dark Horse Comics.

Miller, Walter M., Jr. *A Canticle for Leibowitz.* New York: Bantam Books, 1976.
———. *St. Leibowitz and the Wild Horse Woman.* New York: Bantam Books, 1997.

Minority Report. Directed by Steven Spielberg. Screenplay by Scott Frank and Jon Cohen. Dreamworks SKG/20th Century Fox, 2002. DVD, Dreamworks, 2002.

Mohs, Mayo, ed. *Other Worlds, Other Gods.* New York: Avon Books, 1971.

Moody, Rick. "The Albertine Notes." In *Year's Best SF 9,* ed. David G. Hartwell and Kathryn Cramer, 426–97. New York: Eos/HarperCollins, 2004.

Moorcock, Michael. *Behold the Man.* New York: Avon Books, 1970.

Moore, Alan, and David Lloyd. *V for Vendetta.* New York: DC Comics/Vertigo, 1989.

Moore, Alan, and John Totleben. "Olympus." *Miracleman* #16, December 1989, Eclipse Comics.

Moore, Brian. *Catholics.* New York: E. P. Dutton/Obelisk, 1986.

Niffenegger, Audrey. *The Time Traveler's Wife.* Orlando, FL: Harvest Books/Harcourt, 2004.

O'Donnell, K.M. "Chronicles of a Comer." In *Chronicles of a Comer and Other Religious Science Fiction Stories,* ed. Roger Elwood, 113–20. Atlanta, GA: John Knox Press, 1974.

Orwell, George. *1984*. New York: New American Library, 1961.

Pak, Greg, and Charlie Adlard. *Warlock* #1–4 (November 2004–February 2005), Marvel Comics.

Palumbo, Donald. "Adam Warlock: Marvel Comics' Cosmic Christ Figure." *Extrapolation* 24:1 (1983): 33–46.

Planet of the Apes. Directed by Franklin J. Schaffner. Screenplay by Michael Wilson and Rod Serling. 20th Century Fox/APJAC Productions, 1968. DVD, 20th Century Fox Home Entertainment, 2000.

Plato. *The Last Days of Socrates*. Trans. Hugh Tredennick and Harold Tarrant. London and New York: Penguin Books, 1993.

———. *The Republic*. Trans. Desmond Lee. Middlesex, England, and Baltimore, MD: Penguin Books, 1974.

Pohl, Frederik. *The Annals of the Heechee*. New York: Ballantine Books/Del Rey, 1987.

———. *The Far Shore of Time*. New York: Tor/Tom Doherty Associates, 1999.

———. *Heechee Rendezvous*. New York: Ballantine Books/Del Rey, 1984.

———. *The Other End of Time*. New York: Tor/Tom Doherty Associates, 1996.

Popkes, Steven. "The Ice." In *The Year's Best Science Fiction: Twenty-First Annual Collection,* ed. Gardner Dozois, 73–107. New York: St. Martin's Griffin, 2004.

Primer. Directed and screenplay by Shane Carruth. ThinkFilm Inc., 2004. DVD, New Line Home Video, 2005.

Pseudo-Dionysius. *The Complete Works*. Trans. Colm Luibheid. New York and Mahwah, NJ: Paulist Press, 1987.

Pullman, Philip. *The Amber Spyglass*. New York: Dell Yearling, 2003.

Quantum Leap. Episode 1, "Genesis." Directed by David Hemmings. Written by Donald P. Bellisario. Original broadcast March 26, 1989, NBC. DVD, *Quantum Leap: The Complete First Season*, Universal, 2004.

Reilly, Robert, ed. *The Transcendent Adventure: Studies of Religion in Science Fiction/Fantasy*. Westport, CT: Greenwood Press, 1985.

Rhodes, Richard. *The Making of the Atomic Bomb*. New York: Simon & Schuster, 1986.

Robinson, James M., ed. *The Nag Hammadi Library in English*. 3rd ed. San Francisco: HarperSanFrancisco, 1988.

Rogers, Katherin A. "Augustinian Evil in C. S. Lewis' *Perelandra*." In *The Transcendent Adventure: Studies of Religion in Science Fiction/Fantasy,* ed. Robert Reilly, 83–91. Westport, CT: Greenwood Press, 1985.

Rucker, Rudy. *Realware*. New York: Eos/HarperCollins, 2001.

———. *Software*. New York: Avon/Eos, 1987.

Russell, Bertrand. *Why I Am Not a Christian and Other Essays on Religion and Related Subjects*. New York: Clarion Books/Simon & Schuster, 1957.

Russell, Mary Doria. *The Sparrow*. New York: Fawcett Columbine/Ballantine, 1996.

Ryan, Alan, ed. *Perpetual Light*. New York: Warner Books, 1982.

Sagan, Carl. *Contact*. New York: Simon & Schuster, 1985.

Sanders, Winston P. "The Word to Space." In *Other Worlds, Other Gods*, ed. Mayo Mohs, 69–85. New York: Avon Books, 1971.

Sawyer, Robert J. *Calculating God*. New York: Tor/Tom Doherty Associates, 2000.

———. *Flashforward*. New York: Tor/Tom Doherty Associates, 1999.

———. *Hominids*. New York: Tor/Tom Doherty Associates, 2002.

———. *Hybrids*. New York: Tor/Tom Doherty Associates, 2003.

———. *Mindscan*. New York: Tor/Tom Doherty Associates, 2005.

———. *The Terminal Experiment*. New York: HarperPrism, 1995.

Serenity. Directed and screenplay by Joss Whedon. Universal Pictures/Mutant Enemy Inc./Barry Mendel Productions, 2005.

Sharlet, Jeff. "Soldiers of Christ: Inside America's Most Powerful Megachurch." *Harper's*, May 2005, 41–54.

Shelley, Mary Wollstonecraft. *Frankenstein*. New York: Dover Publications, 1994.

Short Circuit. Directed by John Badham. Screenplay by Brent Maddock and S. S. Wilson. PSO, 1986. DVD, Image Entertainment, 2000.

Signs. Directed and screenplay by M. Night Shyamalan. Blinding Edge Pictures/The Kennedy/Marshall Company/Touchstone Pictures, 2002. DVD, Touchstone, 2003.

Silverberg, Robert. "Basileus." In *The Collected Stories of Robert Silverberg*, vol. 1, *Secret Sharers*, 55–72. New York: Bantam Books, 1992.

———. "Born with the Dead." In *Born With the Dead: Three Novellas*, 1–85. New York: Berkley Books, 1979.

———. "The Feast of St. Dionysus." In *The Feast of St. Dionysus: Five Science Fiction Stories*, 1–60. New York: Berkley Books, 1979.

———. "Good News from the Vatican." In *The New Awareness: Religion through Science Fiction*, ed. Patricia Warrick and Martin Harry Greenberg, 158–73. New York: Delacorte Press, 1975.

———. "The Pope of the Chimps." In *Perpetual Light*, ed. Alan Ryan, 15–37. New York: Warner Books, 1982.

———. "Schwartz between the Galaxies." In *The Feast of St. Dionysus: Five Science Fiction Stories*, 61–83. New York: Berkley Books, 1979.

Simmons, Dan. *Hyperion*. New York: Bantam Books/Spectra, 1990.

Spinrad, Norman. *Deus X*. New York: Bantam Books, 1993.

Stanton, Steve. "On the Edge of Eternity." In *Divine Realms: Canadian Science Fiction and Fantasy*, ed. Susan MacGregor, 71–83. Winnipeg: Raventone/Turnstone Press, 1998.

Stapledon, Olaf. *Last and First Men and Last Men in London*. Middlesex, England, and Baltimore, MD: Penguin Books, 1972.

———. *Nebula Maker & Four Encounters, The*. New York: Dodd, Mead & Co., 1983.

———. *Star Maker, The*. Middlesex, England, and Baltimore, MD: Penguin Books, 1972.

Stargate. Directed Roland Emmerich. Screenplay by Emmerich and Dean Devlin. Carolco Pictures Inc./Centropolis Film Productions/Le Studio Canal+, 1994. DVD, Artisan Entertainment, 1999.

Stargate SG-1. Episode 179, "The Powers That Be." Directed by William Waring. Written by Martin Gero. Original broadcast Aug. 12, 2005, SciFi Channel.

Star Trek. Episode 31, "Who Mourns for Adonais?" Directed by Marc Daniels. Written by Gilbert A. Ralston. Original broadcast Sept. 22, 1967, NBC Television. DVD, *Star Trek: The Original Series, Volume 17.* Paramount, 2000.

Star Trek: Deep Space Nine. Episode 1, "Emissary." Directed by David Carson. Written by Michael Piller. Original broadcast Jan. 3, 1993 (Syndicated). DVD, *Star Trek: Deep Space Nine—Season 1*, Paramount, 2003.

————. Episode 61, "Destiny." Directed by Les Landau. Written by Martin A. Winer and David Samuel Cohen. Original broadcast Feb. 19, 1995 (Syndicated). DVD, *Star Trek: Deep Space Nine—Season 3*, Paramount, 2003.

————. Episode 168, " 'Til Death Do Us Part." Directed by Winrich Kolbe. Written by David Weddle and Bradley Thompson. Original broadcast Apr. 14, 1999 (Syndicated). DVD, *Star Trek: Deep Space Nine—Season 7*, Paramount, 2003.

————. Episode 169, "Strange Bedfellows." Directed by Rene Auberjonois. Written by Ronald D. Moore. Original broadcast April 21, 1999 (Syndicated). DVD, *Star Trek: Deep Space Nine—Season 7*, Paramount, 2003.

Star Trek: The Motion Picture. Directed by Robert Wise. Screenplay by Harold Livingston. Century Associates/Paramount Pictures, 1979. DVD, Paramount, 2001.

Star Trek: The Next Generation. Episode 35, "The Measure of a Man." Directed by Robert Scheerer. Written by Melinda M. Snodgrass. Original broadcast February 13, 1989 (Syndicated). DVD, *Star Trek: The Next Generation—The Complete Second Season*, Paramount Home Entertainment, 2002.

————. Episode 85, "Data's Day." Directed by Robert Wiemer. Written by Harold Apter and Ronald D. Moore. Original broadcast Jan. 7, 1991 (Syndicated). DVD, *Star Trek: The Next Generation—The Complete Fourth Season*, Paramount, 2002.

Star Trek II: The Wrath of Khan. Directed by Nicholas Meyer. Screenplay by Jack B. Sowards. Paramount Pictures, 1982. DVD, Paramount, 2003.

Star Trek III: The Search for Spock. Directed by Leonard Nimoy. Screenplay by Harve Bennett. Cinema Group Ventures/Paramount Pictures, 1984. DVD, Paramount, 2003.

Star Trek V: The Final Frontier. Directed by William Shatner. Screenplay by David Loughery. Paramount Pictures, 1989. DVD, Paramount, 2003.

Star Wars: Episode III—Revenge of the Sith. Directed and screenplay by George Lucas. Lucasfilm Ltd., 2005.

Star Wars: Episode IV—A New Hope. Directed and screenplay by George Lucas. Lucasfilm Ltd., 1977. DVD, *The Star Wars Trilogy*, 20th Century Fox Home Entertainment, 2004.

Star Wars: Episode V—The Empire Strikes Back. Directed by Irvin Kershner. Produced by George Lucas. Screenplay by Leigh Brackett and Lawrence Kasdan. Lucasfilm Ltd., 1980. DVD, *The Star Wars Trilogy*, 20th Century Fox Home Entertainment, 2004.

Star Wars: Episode VI—Return of the Jedi. Directed by Richard Marquand. Screenplay by Lawrence Kasdan and George Lucas. Lucasfilm Ltd., 1983. DVD, *The Star Wars Trilogy*, 20th Century Fox Home Entertainment, 2004.

Stephenson, Neal. *Snow Crash.* New York: Bantam Spectra, 1993.

Stewart, Ian, and Jack Cohen. *Heaven.* New York: Warner Books/Aspect, 2004.

———. *Wheelers.* New York: Warner Books/Aspect, 2000.

Stone, Bryan P. "Religious Faith and Science in *Contact.*" *Journal of Religion and Film* 2:2, October 1998, http://www.unomaha.edu/jrf/stonear2.htm.

Straczynski, J. Michael, and Gary Frank, et al. *Supreme Power: Contact.* New York: Marvel Comics, 2004.

Sturgeon, Theodore. "Dazed." In *The New Awareness: Religion through Science Fiction,* ed. Patricia Warrick and Martin Harry Greenberg, 261–97. New York: Delacorte Press, 1975.

———. "The Microcosmic God." In *The Microcosmic God: The Complete Stories of Theodore Sturgeon,* vol. 2, ed. Paul Williams. Berkeley, CA: North Atlantic Books, 1992.

Superman. Directed by Richard Donner. Screenplay by Mario Puzo, David Newman, Leslie Newman, and Robert Benton. Alexander Salkind/Dovemead Films/Film Export A.G./International Film Production, 1978. DVD, Warner Home Video, 2001.

Suvin, Darko. *Metamorphoses of Science Fiction: On the Poetics and History of a Literary Genre.* New Haven, CT, and London: Yale University Press, 1979.

Teilhard de Chardin, Pierre. *Christianity and Evolution.* Trans. René Hague. New York: Helen and Kurt Wolff/Harcourt Brace Jovanovich, 1969.

———. *The Phenomenon of Man.* Trans. Bernard Wall. New York: Harper Torchbooks/Harper & Row, 1965.

Teller, Astro. *Exegesis.* New York: Vintage Contemporaries, 1997.

Tepper, Sheri S. *Grass.* New York: Bantam Spectra, 1990.

Terminator 2: Judgment Day. Directed by James Cameron, Screenplay by Cameron and William Wisher Jr. Carolco Pictures Inc./Le Studio Canal+/Lightstorm Entertainment/Pacific Western, 1991. DVD, Artisan Entertainment, 2000.

Tevis, Walter. *The Man Who Fell to Earth.* New York: Laurel/Dell, 1989.

Thomas Aquinas. *Summa Theologica.* Trans. The Fathers of the English Dominican Province. *Christian Classics Ethereal Library.* Ed. Harry Plantinga. Calvin College, http://www.ccel.org/a/aquinas/summa/home.html.

THX-1138. Directed by George Lucas. Screenplay by Lucas and Walter Murch. Zoetrope Studios/Warner Bros., 1971. DVD, *THX 1138: The George Lucas Director's Cut,* Warner Home Video, 2004.

Turing, A. M. "Computing Machinery and Intelligence." *Mind* 49 (1950):

433–60. Online: *Cogprints: Cognitive Science Eprint Archive*. University of Southampton, England, http://cogprints.org/499/00/turing.html.

Twelve Monkeys. Directed by Terry Gilliam. Screenplay by David and Janet Peoples. Atlas Entertainment/Classico/Universal Pictures, 1995. DVD, Universal, 1998.

Twilight Zone, The. Episode 127, "The Old Man in the Cave." Directed Alan Crosland Jr. Written by Rod Serling. Original broadcast Nov. 8, 1963, CBS. DVD, *The Twilight Zone Volume 17*, Image Entertainment, 2000.

2001: A Space Odyssey. Directed by Stanley Kubrick. Screenplay by Kubrick and Arthur C. Clarke. Metro-Goldwyn-Mayer/Polaris, 1968. DVD, MGM Home Entertainment, 1998.

V for Vendetta. Directed by James McTeigue. Screenplay by Andy and Larry Wachowski. Warner Brothers/Silver Pictures, 2006.

Varley, John. "In Fading Suns and Dying Moons." In *Year's Best SF 9*, ed. David G. Hartwell and Kathryn Cramer, 177–96. New York: Eos/HarperCollins, 2004.

Vonnegut, Kurt, Jr. *The Sirens of Titan*. New York: Laurel/Dell, 1988.

War of the Worlds. Directed by Steven Spielberg. Screenplay by Josh Friedman and David Koepp. Paramount Pictures/Dreamworks SKG/Amblin Entertainment, 2005.

War of the Worlds, The. Directed by Byron Haskin. Screenplay by Barré Lyndon. Paramount Pictures, 1953.

Warrick, Patricia, and Martin Harry Greenberg, eds. *The New Awareness: Religion through Science Fiction*. New York: Delacorte Press, 1975.

Watson, Ian. *God's World*. New York: Carroll & Graf, 1990.

Wells, H. G. *The Island of Doctor Moreau*. In *The Complete Science Fiction Treasury of H. G. Wells*, 69–157. New York: Avanel Books, 1978.

———. *The Time Machine*. In *The Complete Science Fiction Treasury of H. G. Wells*, 3–66. New York: Avanel Books, 1978.

———. *The War of the Worlds*. In *The Complete Science Fiction Treasury of H. G. Wells*, 265–388. New York: Avanel Books, 1978.

Whitehead, Alfred North. *Process and Reality: An Essay in Cosmology*. New York: Free Press, 1978.

Williamson, Jack. "Afterlife." In *Year's Best SF 8*, ed. David G. Hartwell and Kathryn Cramer, 418–34. New York: Eos/HarperCollins, 2003.

———. *Terraforming Earth*. New York: Tor/Tom Doherty Associates, 2001.

Wilson, Douglas. "Recovering Cultural Soul." *Credenda Agenda* 7:6 (1995), http://www.credenda.org/issues/7-6repairingtheruins.php.

Zahn, Timothy. *Angelmass*. New York: Tor/Tom Doherty Associates, 2001.

Zebrowski, George. *Heathen God*. In *Creations: The Quest for Origins in Story and Science*, ed. Isaac Asimov, Martin H. Greenberg, and George Zebrowski, 126–34. New York: Crown, 1983.

Zelazny, Roger. *Lord of Light*. New York: Avon Books, 1967.

Index